Using Narrative in Social Research

Qualitative and Quantitative Approaches

Jane Elliott

SAGE

Los Angeles | London | New Delhi
Singapore | Washington DC

First published 2005

Reprinted 2009, 2011

SAGE Publications Ltd
1 Oliver's Yard
55 City Road
London EC1Y 1SP

SAGE Publications Inc.
2455 Teller Road
Thousand Oaks, California 91320

SAGE Publications India Pvt Ltd
B 1/I 1 Mohan Cooperative Industrial Area
Mathura Road
New Delhi 110 044

SAGE Publications Asia-Pacific Pte Ltd
33 Pekin Street #02-01
Far East Square
Singapore 048763

British Library Cataloguing in Publication data

A catalogue record for this book is available from the British Library

ISBN 978-1-4129-0040-9 (hbk)
ISBN 978-1-4129-0041-6 (pbk)

Library of Congress Control Number 2004099497

Typeset by C&M Digitals (P) Ltd, Chennai, India
Printed in Great Britain by CPI Antony Rowe, Chippenham, Wiltshire
Printed on paper from sustainable resources

Summary of contents

Contents

Acknowledgements

First I would like to thank Brendan Burchell and the late Cathie Marsh, who introduced me to the joys and complexities of quantitative data analysis as an undergraduate, and without whom I would never have become interested in methodology in the social sciences. I would also very much like to thank Angela Dale, Richard Davies, Damon Berridge, and Rob Crouchley for all that they have taught me about event history analysis and the modelling of longitudinal data. Mike Savage's comments on some early versions of chapters in this book were also extremely valuable. Finally, I would like to thank Jon Lawrence whose detailed and critical reading of some of the later chapter drafts has been most helpful and supportive.

Narrative and new developments in the social sciences

Introduction

This book is different from the majority of books on methodology in two respects. First, it does not focus exclusively on either quantitative or qualitative approaches to research, but instead aims to discuss recent developments in social research methods across the quantitative/qualitative divide. Second, while it aims to give practical guidance on the techniques for carrying out research, and therefore focuses on methods, it also explores current theoretical, methodological, and epistemological debates that (should) underlie the practice of research.

As the title indicates, the theme unifying the book is the use of narrative in social research. While the influence of narrative on *qualitative* research over the past twenty years is readily apparent from the contents pages of leading journals, the suggestion that *quantitative* techniques, such as the multivariate analysis of survey data, can also be understood as having elements of narrative is rather more unconventional. However, as will be discussed in the chapters that follow, the growing availability of longitudinal data, coupled with an appreciation of their value for understanding social processes, means that statistical models increasingly have a temporal or chronological dimension that gives them a certain narrative quality. In addition, debates about causality raise questions about how we should best interpret the results of multivariate models and once again the use of narrative as a sensitizing concept can be helpful here. Finally, recent work on the nature of the self, which destabilizes the concept of the individual as having a fixed, immutable, identity, has led to theoretical interest in the idea that people might be thought of as having what has been called a 'narrative identity'. While this body of writing has had an impact on the way that some researchers approach the collection and analysis of *qualitative* data, there is as yet very little acknowledgement of the implications of this for research based on the analysis of *quantitative* data. A more ambitious aim of this book is therefore to begin a consideration of the implications of views about ontology for the way that the results of quantitative research should be interpreted and written up and for how qualitative and quantitative techniques might be combined.

One of the dilemmas inherent in writing a book such as this is that while the aim is to bridge the gap between qualitative and quantitative research, and to suggest that there are as many differences within the two approaches as there are between them, the distinction is such a well-established one that it is difficult not to perpetuate rather than disrupt the dichotomy. For example, the first part of this book consists of two chapters on the collection and analysis of qualitative data followed by two chapters on the collection and analysis of quantitative data. The structure here therefore seems to mirror, rather than question, the conventional understanding that there are two distinct approaches to investigating the social world. In practical terms, however, this division can be helpful. It is straightforward to distinguish between (a) research that uses a standardized set of questions with a large sample of individuals and which therefore generates data that can be coded and expressed in numerical form, i.e. quantitative research, and (b) research that adopts a less structured set of questions, allows the respondent to set the agenda within the parameters of the topic under investigation, and generates rich textual or observational data, i.e. qualitative research. The method of collecting data and the type of data that are collected are closely linked, and the quantitative/qualitative distinction is a useful shorthand for describing these two rather different approaches. However, the distinction becomes blurred once the issue of analysis is introduced. As will be discussed in Chapters 3 and 5, it is possible to analyse qualitative data using quantitative techniques that result in numeric or statistical summaries and it is conversely possible to use detailed survey data to build up case histories of individuals and to present these in a narrative form. In practice, of course, relatively few researchers use quantitative approaches for the analysis of qualitative data, and it is even more rare for quantitative data to be analysed using a more qualitative case-based approach. It is much more usual to see quantitative evidence analysed and summarized using statistics while qualitative evidence is commonly interpreted and presented as text or rich description. It is for this reason that the distinction between qualitative and quantitative approaches to research has become so firmly established, with the majority of researchers seeing themselves as belonging to one or other group. The aim of this book is therefore not to be so radical as to suggest that the practical distinction between qualitative and quantitative approaches is redundant, but rather to examine in more detail what the foundations of this distinction really are. Although introductory undergraduate texts tend to equate quantitative methods with a scientific or 'positivist' approach and qualitative methods with an interpretative or hermeneutic approach, it is more complicated than this. As books on the philosophy of the social sciences make clear, for a time positivism became almost synonymous with survey research. However, the social survey is in fact a practical device developed for pragmatic reasons and therefore 'has no necessary identification with the ideals, aspirations or requirements of positivism' (Hughes and Sharrock, 1997).

At a more practical level, some authors have suggested that while quantitative methods present a relatively static understanding of society, qualitative methods allow for a focus on process. In addition, qualitative research is frequently described as providing more comprehensive or fine-grained information than quantitative research. However, as will be discussed more fully in Chapters 4 and 5, the growing availability of quantitative longitudinal datasets means that it is increasingly possible to address questions about social process and social change using quantitative methods. When data are collected every few years using a structured face-to-face interview lasting ninety minutes or more, and respondents are followed from birth to middle age (e.g. in the National Study of Health and Development), the level of detail contained in longitudinal quantitative studies rivals that of many qualitative projects.

The aim of this chapter is to provide the foundations for the rest of the book. It therefore starts by providing a discussion of the concept of narrative with particular attention to the elements of narrative that have made it a recurring theme within qualitative approaches to research over the past two decades. Issues about causality and temporality are briefly introduced here but will be developed further in the chapters which follow. The next section of this chapter will provide a basic discussion of some of the key elements of narrative and will highlight the widespread use of narrative across a wide range of substantive fields. The final section of this introductory chapter will then provide an overview of the organization of the rest of the book.

Definitions of narrative

What is narrative? What are its defining features and which of its attributes explain its appeal to social scientists? Why, in short, should we be interested in narrative? There is obviously a long *literary* tradition of studying the art of narrative, which focuses on conventions of literary style, and the development and use of different genres as well as examining the creativity of individual narrators. However, as will be demonstrated below, in recent years there has been a great deal of interest in the concept of narrative and its application across the human and social sciences (Abbott, 1990; 1992a; Finnegan, 1992; Hinchman and Hinchman, 1997; Mishler, 1995; Riessman, 1993; Somers, 1994). There is therefore a growing literature on the possible definitions of narrative, as well as on the controversies and analytic approaches that attach to them (Riessman, 1993).

To begin by summarizing the defining elements of narrative, which will be elaborated below, a narrative can be understood to organize a sequence of events into a whole so that the significance of each event can be understood through its relation to that whole. In this way a narrative conveys the meaning of events. A useful definition of narrative is thus offered by Hinchman and Hinchman who propose that:

> Narratives (stories) in the human sciences should be defined provisionally as discourses with a clear sequential order that connect events in a meaningful way for a definite audience and thus offer insights about the world and/or people's experiences of it. (1997: xvi)

This definition provides a helpful framework for the current discussion because it stresses three key features of narratives. First, that they are *chronological* (they are representations of sequences of events), second, that they are *meaningful*, and third, that they are inherently *social* in that they are produced for a specific audience. As will be demonstrated below, it is these key features that underpin the importance of narrative within sociology. First, there is a growing recognition among sociologists of the importance of the temporal dimension for understanding the interrelation between individual lives and social contexts. The paradigmatic example of this is the growing body of work around the concept of the 'Life Course', instigated by Glen Elder in the United States in the mid-1970s (Elder, 1974; Giele and Elder, 1998). In Britain the past twenty years have seen an increased appreciation and availability of sources of longitudinal data such as the British Household Panel Study, the Youth Cohort Studies, and the British Birth Cohort Studies. These have been referred to by the Economic and Social Research Council as the 'jewels in the crown' of British social science research resources. The development of statistical modelling techniques such as quantitative event history analysis makes it increasingly possible to exploit the chronological nature of these longitudinal data. Some authors have argued that event history modelling should increasingly become part of the standard repertoire of any sociologist prepared to countenance using quantitative techniques (Hutchison, 1988). This will be discussed in detail in Chapter 5. Sociologists, and social scientists more broadly, are therefore increasingly attending to the temporal qualities of social life (Adam, 1990; 1995). Second, there is a long humanist tradition within sociology which stresses the importance of attempting to understand the meaning of behaviour and experiences from the perspective of the individuals involved. In this context narrative can perhaps be understood as a device which facilitates empathy since it provides a form of communication in which an individual can externalize his or her feelings and indicate which elements of those experiences are most significant. Third, sociological research is clearly carried out within a social context. In the past two decades, there has been a growing awareness of the role of the interviewer in helping to construct, and not just to collect, biographical information from interviewees (Hollway and Jefferson, 2000; Holstein and Gubrium, 1995; Maynard, 1994; Stanley and Wise, 1983; 1993). The ways in which an interest in narrative has influenced interviewing practices will be discussed in more detail in Chapter 2. Attention to the narrative qualities of research material therefore serves as an important reminder that this material cannot be understood without acknowledgement of the audience or audiences for whom it has been produced.

It is these three facets of narrative, namely its temporal, meaningful, and social elements, that will structure the first half of this chapter. Although for the purposes of discussion, it is helpful to treat these elements separately, it is also important to be aware that they are perhaps not strictly separable. In particular, the meaning of events within a narrative derives both from their temporal ordering and from the social context in which the narrative is recounted. This will be discussed in more detail later in this chapter. Before examining what is meant by narrative in more detail, however, it is useful to highlight the growing interest that has been shown in narrative by researchers interested in a wide range of different substantive fields across the social sciences.

Narrative and social research

The explicit interest in narrative in the social sciences can perhaps be traced back to the early 1980s. In 1981, Daniel Bertaux's edited collection *Biography and Society* began with a manifesto for the importance of attention to stories in sociology. In his introductory chapter, 'From the life history approach to the transformation of sociological practice', Bertaux pointed out that while there is a great deal of lay interest in reading history, there is much less enthusiasm among the public for works of sociology. He attributed this to the dry presentational style of much sociological work and suggested that more attention should be given to individual stories both as evidence in sociology and as a means of presenting insights about the social world. On the other side of the Atlantic, in the United States, Elliot Mishler's book *Research Interviewing: Context and Narrative*, published in 1986 emphasized the need to listen to individuals' stories in the context of qualitative interviewing and cautioned researchers to take care not to suppress such stories. This has become a much cited book, and has clearly been influential in shaping the practice of interviewing for many qualitative researchers.

If the beginnings of an interest in narrative can be traced back to the 1980s, this trend really gathered momentum in the early 1990s. The journal *Narrative and Life History* (now published as *Narrative Inquiry*) was launched in the United States in 1991, and a series of edited collections on *The Narrative Study of Lives* (Josselson and Lieblich, 1993) was started in 1993 and has been published regularly ever since. The publication, in 1993, of Riessman's short text on narrative analysis, in the long-running Sage series on qualitative research methods, can also be seen as a milestone in establishing narrative as part of the methodological toolkit for qualitative researchers.

Over the past two decades, the awareness of the importance of narrative among qualitative researchers has spread through a wide range of different substantive areas. For example, in the sociology of health there has been a focus on lay perspectives on disease and patients' own experiences of ill health. In particular for those suffering from chronic disease, the idea of an 'illness career' has been a useful analytic tool and this can be readily expressed in the form of a narrative. Researchers such as Kleinman (1988), Charmaz (1991), Kelly and Dickinson (1997), and Williams (1997) have therefore written about the impact of chronic ill health on individuals' sense of identity, while Faircloth (1999) and Crossley (1999) have used narrative in the context of researching specific conditions such as AIDS and epilepsy. Narrative has also surfaced in the literature on health behaviour and health education, e.g. in the work of Williamson (1989), Moffat and Johnson (2001), and Workman (2001).

Another major discipline that has begun to use narrative as a methodological tool is criminology. The importance of examining individual lives holistically in order to understand more about patterns of reoffending and desistance from crime can be seem most clearly in the work of Sampson and Laub (1993), who adopt a life course approach and have followed up the longitudinal study of delinquent young men begun by Glueck and Glueck in 1930. Work that discusses narrative more explicitly in this field includes a qualitative study on the fear of crime carried out by Hollway and Jefferson (2000).

In the sociology of the family and relationships, Riessman's book *Divorce Talk*, published in 1990, stands out as one of the key texts that helped promote an interest in the use of narrative. The approach she used to collect and analyse the material she collected will be discussed in more detail in Chapters 2 and 3. In Britain, Day-Sclater (1998a; 1998b) has also used a narrative approach to analyse biographical interview material about individuals' experiences of divorce. In the related area of sexuality, Plummer's 1995 book *Telling Sexual Stories* makes use of narrative as an analytic device to understand changing attitudes to sexuality in modern society. In contrast to the work of Riessman and Day-Sclater, however, Plummer's focus is less on the experiences of individuals and more on narratives within a broader societal context.

The sociology of education, too, includes examples of researchers who have made a great deal of use of narrative in their research. For example, in Britain, Cortazzi (1991) has used narrative in his research on the experiences of primary school teachers and Smith (1996) emphasizes that she was interested in listening to women's stories in interviews about their experiences of returning to education as mature students in order to understand more about the support or barriers presented by their husbands and partners. In North America too, those in the field of education have found the use of narrative very fruitful in their research (Clandinin and Connelly, 2000; Connelly and Clandinin, 1999).

There is not space here to give a thorough or comprehensive review of the ways that narrative has been used by social scientists, but the aim has been to highlight the broad range of subject areas that are amenable to a narrative approach. Some of the common themes that run through research that pays attention to narrative in respondents' accounts are:

1   An interest in people's lived experiences and an appreciation of the temporal nature of that experience.
2   A desire to empower research participants and allow them to contribute to determining what are the most salient themes in an area of research.
3   An interest in process and change over time.
4   An interest in the self and representations of the self.
5   An awareness that the researcher him- or herself is also a narrator.

As will be seen from the multitude of further examples employed throughout the book, there is virtually no area within social research where narrative has not been discussed. All of the examples provided above fall within the broad field of sociology and the emphasis throughout the book will be on the use of narrative in sociology. However, much of the material presented here will also be of use and interest to other social scientists including geographers, anthropologists, historians, and psychologists. It is important to stress that narrative crosses the usual disciplinary boundaries and has been taken up as a useful analytic tool by researchers with very diverse backgrounds.

Understanding narrative form

Having established a basic definition of narrative and demonstrated its widespread use in the social sciences, particularly by qualitative researchers, over the past two decades, it is now necessary to provide a slightly more detailed discussion of some of the definitional elements of narrative. In particular, as was highlighted by Hinchman and Hinchman's characterization of narrative above, the temporal, meaningful, and social aspects of narrative will be explored.

Temporality and causality within narrative

Perhaps the simplest definition of narrative, and one that has been traced back to Aristotle in his *Poetics*, is that a narrative is a story with a beginning, a middle, and an end (Chatman, 1978; Leitch, 1986; Martin, 1986). Temporality is certainly widely accepted as a key feature of narrative form. In a frequently cited and influential paper, Labov and Waletzky (1967)[1] stated that narrative provides a 'method of recapitulating past experiences by matching a verbal sequence of clauses to the sequence of events that actually occurred' (p. 12). It is this placing of events in a sequence which is therefore considered by many to be the defining feature of narrative. The term narrative is sometimes used more loosely by social scientists to refer to any extended prose; however, within this book, it is the more restricted definition of narrative as *chronology* that will be used.

Intimately linked with the temporal qualities of narrative is the notion of plot. An important feature of narrative is that rearranging the narrative clauses, or the events within a narrative, typically results in a change of meaning (Franzosi, 1998a; Labov, 1972). Stories rely on the presumption that time has a uni-linear direction moving from past to present to future. The plot within a narrative therefore relates events to each other by linking a prior choice or happening to a subsequent event (Polkinghorne, 1995). A story also normally involves a change in situations. Events in a story usually disrupt an initial state of equilibrium or represent a change in fortunes for the main characters. A plot has therefore been described by some analysts as being formed from a combination of temporal succession and causality. A frequently cited example here is E.M. Forster's argument that 'The king died and then the queen died' is merely a 'chronicle', whereas 'The king died and then the queen died of grief' is a plot because it includes an explicit *causal* link between the two events in the sequence (Forster, 1963 [1927]). However, as Chatman has argued, even without an explicit causal link being made between the events in a narrative, readers will tend to read causality into a sequence of events recounted as a narrative. Events are 'linked to each other as cause to effect, effects in turn causing other effects, until the final effect. And even if two events seem not obviously interrelated, we infer that they may be, on some larger principle that we will discover later' (Chatman, 1978: 46).

The idea that causality is a central element adding to the coherence of a narrative is an important one, particularly since, as will be discussed in more detail in Chapter 6, narrative accounts and causal explanations have often been treated as opposing sides of a dichotomy (Abbott, 1992a; Bruner, 1986; Polkinghorne, 1988; Somers and Gibson, 1994). It is important to establish, therefore, that although causality has not been universally recognized as a necessary feature of narrative (in the way that temporality has been), nevertheless a narrative account does not preclude a causal understanding of the links between events (Rimmon-Kenan, 1983). In addition, it is useful to stress that an audience will routinely assume causal links between the events in a narrative even if these are not made explicit. If it is reported that event A was followed by event B it is a short step to assuming that, in the context of a narrative account, event B occurred *because of* event A. However, to argue that there are frequently causal links between the elements of a narrative is not to say that a narrative and a causal explanation are equivalent. The problem occurs because of the multiple ways in which the word 'cause' is used. The imputation of a causal link between two specific events in a narrative is clearly not the same as proposing a causal *law* such that the first event is both necessary and sufficient for the second event across a wide range of different contexts (Ricoeur, 1984). In other words, while a causal explanation suggests that a particular event will *invariably* be followed by a necessary outcome, a narrative provides an account of how one event followed another *under a specific set of circumstances*. However, to argue that this distinction implies an *opposition* between narrative and causality is mistaken. For example, consider the simple narrative sentence, 'Her fingers were numb with cold, she dropped the half-finished bottle of gin and it smashed on the pavement.' While this provides an account of a specific incident, our understanding of this minimal narrative is aided by our awareness of more universal causal laws such as the effects of cold on the body and the effect of gravity. This issue of the mutual dependence of narrative and causality will be returned to in Chapter 6 and discussed in the context of debates about the meaning of causality within the social sciences.

Evaluation and the meaning of narrative

As the discussion above has underlined, a key defining feature of narrative is its temporal dimension. It is the importance of the *chronology* of events within a narrative that distinguishes it from a description. However, as authors as diverse as the socio-linguist Polanyi (1985) and the historian White (1987) have emphasized, a successful narrative is more than just a sequence or chronicle of events. Indeed, Labov and Waletzky (1967, republished 1997) suggested that although a minimal narrative is composed of a sequence of actions such a narrative is 'abnormal: it may be considered as empty or pointless narrative' (Labov and Waletzky, 1997: 13). They described fully formed narratives as having six separate elements: the abstract (a summary of the subject of the narrative); the orientation (time, place, situation, participants); the complicating action (what actually happened); the evaluation (the meaning and significance of the action); the resolution (what finally happened); and lastly the coda, which returns the perspective to the present. Labov and Waletzky (1997) argued that these structures are typically used by the teller to construct a story out of past experiences, and to make sense of those experiences both for him- or herself and for the audience. Although not all narratives necessarily include all of these six elements, at a minimum a narrative must include the complicating action, i.e. a temporal component, while it is the evaluation that has been highlighted as crucial for establishing the point or the meaning of the story.

A number of authors have argued that the evaluation is *socially* the most important component of the narrative (Linde, 1993; Polanyi, 1985). In a conversational setting, for example, the narrator must guard against the 'so what?' response to a story. This is accomplished by providing an adequate evaluation of the events that have been recounted (Polanyi, 1985). It is the evaluation that conveys to an audience how they are to understand the *meaning* of the events that constitute the narrative, and simultaneously indicates what type of response is required. The evaluation should not therefore be understood as simply provided by the narrator; rather the achievement of agreement on the evaluation of a narrative is the product of a process of negotiation. While the speaker can be understood as responsible for producing a narrative with an acceptable evaluation, the addressee or audience must collaborate by demonstrating that the evaluation has been understood.

Labov and Waletzky (1997) have suggested that the evaluation is typically placed between the complicating action and the resolution, and in this position creates an element of tension and suspense in a well-formed narrative, as the audience wait to hear 'what happened next'. However, subsequent writers have underlined that the structural analysis of narrative provided by Labov and Waletzky is in many respects too rigid. The evaluation may in some cases be explicit, and may be located prior to the resolution, but the expression of the evaluation within a narrative need not take this form. A narrator may communicate evaluative elements more implicitly. As Tannen (1980) has argued, not only do narratives make explicit evaluations of actions and characters but judgements can be communicated in more subtle ways as well. She suggested that lexical choice (i.e. the use of specific words) within the other components of the narrative is a clear example of this type of implicit evaluation. In addition, it could be argued that the very telling of a narrative represents an evaluative act. It suggests that certain events and decisions are reportable by virtue of their significance or their unusual or unexpected qualities. Obvious examples here would be stories about the death of a parent, or the birth of a child. Within modern culture, these events are understood to have an emotional significance for the individual that makes them worthy of recounting. Alternatively many conversational stories are centred upon a coincidence, which while relatively trivial is seen as sufficiently unexpected to make it interesting to relate.

It is because the evaluation within a narrative provides an insight into how the narrator has chosen to interpret the events recounted that the evaluative elements of narratives can be of particular interest for sociologists. In particular there is a link here between an interest in these evaluative elements of narratives and a commitment to a humanist sociology which prioritizes 'understanding' or *Verstehen*. The inherently social nature of evaluation also takes us back to Plummer's suggestion in his book *Documents of Life* (Plummer, 1983) that individual stories and personal documents can potentially take us beyond the individual to an appreciation of that individual in society. This clearly leads to questions about how we might use the idea of narrative, and the work of socio-linguists such as Labov and Waletzky, Linde, and Tannen, to inform the techniques we use in the analysis of this type of material. These questions about how an explicit engagement with narrative might influence our methods of analysis will be explored in Chapter 3.

Narrative, audiences, and social contexts

The word narrative derives from the Indo-European root 'gna' which means both 'to know' and 'to tell' (Hinchman and Hinchman, 1997). As White puts it, 'Narrative might well be considered a solution to a problem of general human concern, namely, the problem of how to translate knowing into *telling*' (White, 1987: 1, my emphasis). Many authors with an interest in narrative have highlighted the importance of the context of this telling and the role of the listener in the construction of narratives (Bernstein, 1997; Gubrium and Holstein, 1998; Holmes, 1997; Mishler, 1986). Oral narratives presuppose an audience, or as Plummer puts it, 'stories can be seen as *joint actions*' (Plummer, 1995: 20). As was discussed above, the evaluative aspects of a narrative in particular can perhaps be understood as dependent on the agreement of the audience.

At the most basic level, an individual will need the 'conversational space' to tell a story to another person. The narrator needs at minimum the co-operation of a conversational partner. In friendly conversation, participants routinely take turns at talking. Conversation analysts have, of course, extensively studied the social negotiation of this turn taking in different contexts. However, when someone begins to tell a story this turn taking is disrupted, or suspended, for a time and the other conversational participants give the story-teller privileged access to the floor (Coates, 1996; Sacks, 1992). The listeners therefore immediately become active co-participants in the recounting of a narrative. In addition, any speaker in an interaction needs to decide how best to communicate their message, and in making this decision will attempt to take into account what the listener can reasonably be expected to know (Brown, 1995). For example, the choices that the speaker makes about how much detail to include in a narrative will carry a certain amount of risk with them. If the speaker provides too much detail the listener may become bored or will focus on aspects of the narrative that are not salient. Alternatively, if not enough detail is provided the listener may misunderstand what the speaker is trying to communicate.

Listeners can be expected to participate in the telling of a narrative through non-verbal cues, short responses or back channel utterances such as 'right', or 'hmm', and by asking additional questions or making statements (Mishler, 1986). There is also evidence that the role of the listener should be understood as culturally variable (Holmes, 1997). In an analysis of narratives told by men and women in New Zealand, Holmes found that Pakeha listeners provided more explicit verbal encouragement during a narration and were also more likely to ask questions than Maori listeners (Holmes, 1997). She also found gender differences in the listeners' behaviour so that women were more likely than men to use strategies that explicitly expressed support for the narrator.

Of course the teller of a narrative will be influenced not only by the immediate listener, the person who is directly being addressed, but also by those who might overhear the conversation – on a train, at a party, or in a crowded pub, for example. In addition, within certain contexts the narrator may be influenced by imagined or possible future audiences (Bernstein, 1997). This is perhaps particularly likely to be true of tape-recorded research interviews. The very fact that the conversation is being recorded suggests that it will at least be listened to at some future time and may also be transcribed and parts of it translated into a written text.

Temporality and the meaning of narratives

So far this chapter has emphasized three key features of a narrative, namely that it has a temporal dimension, it is meaningful, and it is inherently social in that stories are produced for specific audiences. However, these three facets cannot be understood as wholly independent or as straightforwardly separable. For example, the meaning of a narrative will depend on the social context in which it is produced. As was discussed above, the evaluative elements of a narrative will require collaboration between the narrator and the audience. The evaluation emphasizes the point of the story and as such legitimates the act of narration as a social act. In particular, however, it is also important to stress the link between the temporal and meaningful dimensions of narratives. First, as was suggested above, the sequencing of events can lead to a particular reading of their meaning in relation to each other. If we are told that one event followed another this raises an expectation of causality in our minds, namely that the subsequent event was caused by the previous event. This is not to say that those events will invariably be linked in all situations, but rather that in a particular context (specified by the orientation of the narrative) later events can be read as dependent upon earlier ones. Second, the temporal dimension of a narrative can be understood as fundamental to establishing the meaning of events due to the way that narratives impose beginnings, middles, and ends on what might more accurately be understood as continuous streams of happenings. As several authors have emphasized, narrative depends not only on sequence or temporality but also on narrative closure (Chatman, 1978; Leitch, 1986; Ricoeur, 1984). Endings are critical for narratives because it is the ending that determines the meaning of the actions and events within the narrative. In other words, 'The audience wants to know not only what happens next but

11

what this is all leading to, what it all means' (Leitch, 1986). Narratives impose meaning on events and experiences therefore, not only when they provide an explicit evaluation of those events and experiences, but also by the very act of structuring them into a story with a beginning, a middle, and an end. This is the problem that Bearman et al. refer to as 'casing':

> Casing is a prerequisite for meaning, for only when we can provide a begin-ning and an end to a sequence of interrelated events can we understand the meaning of an event within the sequence and, by extension, the mean-ing of an event sequence as a whole. That narrative and meaning are the product of casing is hardly a new idea for historians. For social scientists, this insight has come harder. (1999: 503)

As Bearman et al. argue, the problem of analysing narrative accounts of historical occurrences (rather than focusing on fictional narratives) is that the meaning of an event is contingent on subsequent events. An historical narrative can never properly achieve closure therefore, since there is always the possibility that future events will change our interpretation of the meaning of events in the past.

The ability of narrative to render events meaningful, even without providing an explicit evaluation of those events, but simply by imposing beginnings and ends on what might otherwise be thought of as continuous sequences, has implications for the way that sociologists use data with a temporal dimension. As will be argued in more detail in Chapter 9, in relation to both qualitative and quantitative research, an appreciation of narrative structures should make us more reflexive about our own research practice, once we recognize the power of those structures to organize our understandings, interpretations, and representations of people's lives.

First-order and second-order narratives: the importance of narrative for sociologists

Having discussed the key features which can be understood as providing the defin-ing qualities of narratives in general, a conceptual distinction can usefully be made between 'first-order narratives' and 'second-order narratives' (Carr, 1997) or what might alternatively be termed 'ontological narratives' and 'representational narra-tives' (Somers and Gibson, 1994). First-order narratives can be defined as the stories that individuals tell about themselves and their own experiences. First-order narratives occur spontaneously in everyday life during the course of normal inter-action. They would include the stories produced by a family around the dinner table in the evening, each member of the family recounting the significant events that had occurred during the day – at work or school perhaps. First-order narra-tives would also include personal testimonies produced in more formal settings. For example, in the context of a job interview or a self-help group, an individual may be expected to provide a coherent account of key biographical events. The special significance of these first-order narratives, as we shall see in Chapter 7, is that they can be understood as in some senses constitutive of individual identities. This is why Somers and Gibson describe them as 'ontological narratives' (1994).

Distinct from these individual or personal first–order narratives, second–order narratives are the accounts we may construct as researchers to make sense of the social world, and of other people's experiences. These narratives are therefore methods of presenting social and historical knowledge. In addition, these second–order narratives do not necessarily focus on individuals. For example, Abbott's account of the formation of a profession might be defined as a second–order narrative (Abbott, 1988). However, within this book I am primarily concerned with the representation of individual lives in both qualitative and quantitative approaches to research. The second–order narratives I discuss in subsequent chapters will therefore mainly be concerned with individuals as the unit of analysis and might therefore be understood as a particular type of second–order narrative, namely a 'collective story' (Richardson, 1990). Richardson suggests that:

> The collective story displays an individual's story by narrativizing the experiences of the social category to which the individual belongs, rather than by telling the particular individual's story. ... Although the narrative is about a category of people, the individual response to the well-told collective story is 'That's my story. I am not alone.' (1990: 25–6)

While an interest in first–order narratives may perhaps be thought of as a preference for a certain type of qualitative evidence at the level of *method,* an interest in second–order narratives requires a decisive shift to the level of *methodology* or even epistemology. As will be discussed further in subsequent chapters, much of the information about the social world that is available to sociologists is likely to be in narrative form. It is important, therefore, as we incorporate this information into our analyses, to consider how and why it has been produced. An awareness of the narrative structures that are commonly used within a culture can be helpful to inform an analysis that goes beyond the ostensible content of an account; this will be discussed further in Chapter 3. In addition, once we start to become aware of, and pay closer analytic attention to, the narrative structures within empirical data, it becomes difficult to ignore them in our own work. Social science writing also depends on narrative structures and narrative devices. Researchers make selections, have opinions about what is significant and what is trivial, decide what to include and what to exclude, and determine the boundaries, or beginnings and endings, of their accounts.

Organization of the book

The book can broadly be divided into two parts. Following this introductory chapter, in Chapters 2 to 5, the focus is at the level of methods, in other words practical techniques for the collection and analysis of data. These chapters introduce recent developments in both quantitative and qualitative research by discussing examples of empirical research from a wide range of sociological subject areas. These include the sociology of health and illness, criminology, the sociology of the family, the sociology of organizations, and the sociology of employment. The aim, however, is not to provide detailed instructions on how to conduct particular qualitative or quantitative analyses, but rather to provide broad guidelines and a conceptual account with suggestions for further reading. Although the chapters are organized in terms of two chapters on qualitative methods followed by two chapters on quantitative methods, the aim is to demonstrate that there is no single qualitative or quantitative approach to data collection and analysis and indeed that there are some innovative types of analysis based on an interest in narrative that start to blur the distinction between qualitative and quantitative methods.

Chapters 6 to 10 draw on the material in the first part of the book to move the discussion to the level of methodology, epistemology, and ontology. Two debates in particular will be explored which are of central importance to the philosophy of the social sciences. These are, first, the insights into causal mechanisms in the social world that can be provided by different approaches to research and, second, the ontological status of the subject or individual respondent in research. While these are arguably issues of practical relevance for anyone engaged with empirical research, much of the existing theoretical literature on these topics is rather abstract and abstruse. The aim here therefore is to give a more practically focused discussion with examples from existing research. The second half of the book will also provide a discussion of the politics and ethics of research as well as exploring notions of reflexivity in relation to quantitative as well as qualitative research. Once again these issues will be discussed specifically in relation to the material on narrative methods introduced in the first five chapters. Chapter 10 considers some of the possibilities for combining qualitative and quantitative research. Rather than arguing that they are necessarily complementary, or that they can be integrated unproblematically, this final chapter will suggest that it is the very tensions between the two approaches that make it important that they are both used in understanding aspects of social change.

One of the challenges of writing a book on methods and methodology that aims to engage with current debates relating to both qualitative and quantitative approaches is that the majority of readers will be more comfortable with either qualitative or quantitative methods. Some terms and concepts are therefore likely to be unfamiliar to different groups of readers. An explanation of the more technical vocabulary will therefore be found within the text. However, it is acknowledged that many readers will dip into specific sections of the book and for this reason a glossary is provided which aims to cover those terms that are most likely to be unfamiliar.

Following the introductory discussion of the key features of narrative in this chapter, the next chapter will focus more specifically on the way that narrative has informed recent developments in interviewing practice in social research. In particular it will outline the methodological literature that emphasizes the importance of allowing individuals to tell stories in the context of qualitative research interviews. As I will argue in more detail below, the relevance of a sociology informed by narrative hinges on the fact that while a narrative is inherently social, both in its practice or performance and in the cultural resources it relies upon to be intelligible, it is simultaneously the unique and creative production of an individual actor. These dual facets of narrative also have important implications for using narrative to inform analysis and this will be discussed in Chapter 3. The themes that have been sketched here will therefore be elaborated in more detail in the chapters that follow. This is only the beginning of the story.

Summary

This chapter has introduced the concept of narrative in the context of social research. Three key features of narrative have been stressed. First, that it has a temporal or chronological dimension in that it provides a representation of a series of events or experiences rather than describing a state of affairs. Second, that it communicates the meaning of events or experiences through the use of evaluative statements and through the temporal configuration of events. Third, that there is an important social dimension to narrative: narratives are ubiquitous in society and are a popular form of communication. Narratives are usually told in a specific social context for a particular purpose. These defining elements of narrative will provide the foundations of the chapters that follow, which provide an exploration of how narrative can be understood to have informed some of the recent methodological advances in the social sciences.

It has also been suggested that although in many circumstances the *practical* distinction between qualitative and quantitative research is a useful one, some of the boundaries between the two approaches become less clear once we appreciate the rich detailed information that is increasingly being collected in the context of quantitative longitudinal studies such as the British Cohort Studies, the German Social and Economic Panel, or the Panel Study of Income Dynamics in the United States.

Further reading

Bertaux, D. (1981) 'From the life-history approach to the transformation of sociological practice', in D. Bertaux (ed.), *Biography and Society.* Beverly Hills, CA: Sage. pp. 29–46.

Franzosi, R. (1998) 'Narrative analysis – or why (and how) sociologists should be interested in narrative', *Annual Review of Sociology*, 24: 517–54.

Hinchman, L.P. and Hinchman, S.K. (1997) 'Introduction', in L.P. Hinchman and S.K. Hinchman (eds), *Memory, Identity, Community: The Idea of Narrative in the Human Sciences.* New York: State University of New York. pp. xiii–xxxii.

Maines, D. (1993) 'Narrative's moment and sociology's phenomena: toward a narrative sociology', *The Sociological Quarterly*, 34: 17–38.

Exercise

1 Ask a friend to tell you a brief story about something interesting or frustrating that has happened to him or her over the past three months. Write down the main points and compare the structure of your friend's narrative with the typical structure identified by Labov and Waletzky and discussed above.

Note

1 A discussion of the impact of this article formed the basis of a whole volume of the *Journal of Narrative and Life History* (Volume 7, 1997). The original Labov and Waletzky paper from 1967 was reprinted as the first paper in this 1997 volume and the page numbers provided will refer to this later edition.

2

Listening to people's stories: the use of narrative in qualitative interviews

Approximately fifty years ago, in 1956, Benney and Hughes stated that 'Sociology has become the science of the interview ... by and large the sociologist in North America, and in a slightly less degree in other countries has become an interviewer. The interview is his tool; his work bears the mark of it' (Benney and Hughes, 1956: 137). In this editorial preface to a special volume of the *American Journal of Sociology*, dedicated to sociology and the interview, Benney and Hughes argued that interviews had become not only the *means* which sociologists used to find out about the world, but also the *object of enquiry*. They suggested that sociology could appropriately be understood as the science of the interview in the deep sense that sociology was concerned with social interaction and that the interview, as a form of social interaction, was therefore 'not merely a tool of sociology but a part of its very subject matter' (Benney and Hughes, 1956: 138). This notion that the interview is not just a means for collecting data, but itself a site for the *production* of data and can become a focus for enquiry in its own right, has become central to epistemological and methodological discussions about interviewing over the past twenty years. It is these recent debates on qualitative method and more specifically those that focus on the role of narrative in qualitative interviews that form the central theme of this chapter.

As was discussed in Chapter 1, over the past twenty years there has been a dramatic increase in interest in narrative among those adopting qualitative approaches to research. In particular, it has been suggested that allowing respondents to provide narrative accounts of their lives and experiences can help to redress some of the power differentials inherent in the research enterprise and can also provide good evidence about the everyday lives of research subjects and the meanings they attach to their experiences. The emphasis in this chapter is therefore on the role of narrative in shaping new approaches to qualitative research interviewing over the past two decades. Rather than trying to provide instructions for conducting a specific type of qualitative interview, the focus is on the theoretical and epistemological foundations of interview practices within qualitative approaches to research. Where this chapter will provide a more practical discussion, however, is in relation to the interview encounter itself: the interaction between the interviewer and interviewee and methods for eliciting narratives. It is here perhaps that the theoretical and epistemological underpinnings of research practice are most evident or most explicitly realized.

The use of narratives in qualitative interviews: realist and constructivist approaches to research

It is well established that interviews are central to much research in the social sciences, and the distinctions made between in-depth, semi-structured, and standardized survey interviews have become commonplace (Arksey and Knight, 1999; Brenner, 1985; Seidman, 1998; Weiss, 1994). However, over the past two decades, qualitative research has arguably become more methodologically self-conscious and there has been a proliferation of discussions about the variations in approaches to in-depth interviews. This means that rather than simply contrasting the methodological foundations of in-depth interviews and structured survey interviews, it is important to recognize that there are also distinctions to be drawn within the group of researchers who advocate the use of in-depth interviews. As Gubrium and Holstein have argued, 'Qualitative research is a diverse enterprise. Perhaps because it is typically counterposed with the monolith of quantitative sociology, qualitative method is often portrayed in broad strokes that blur differences' (Gubrium and Holstein, 1997: 5). Before embarking on a detailed exploration of the use of narrative within in-depth interviews, it is therefore helpful to bring the major differences *within* the qualitative research enterprise into sharper focus. This will make it easier to see how an emphasis on the methodological importance of narrative fits within existing debates about qualitative methods and qualitative research questions.

Gubrium and Holstein provide a clear exposition of the major differences within the qualitative research paradigm in their book *The New Language of Qualitative Method* (Gubrium and Holstein, 1997). In particular, they contrast the naturalist approach which 'seeks rich descriptions of people as they exist and unfold in their natural habitats' with the constructivist or ethnomethodological approach which focuses on 'how a sense of social order is created through talk and interaction'.[1] This notion that there is a distinction between qualitative researchers who understand interviews as a resource and those who see the interview itself as a topic for enquiry has been echoed by a number of other authors (Hammersley, 2003; Harris, 2003; Seale, 1998). Both the naturalist approach and the constructivist approach are concerned primarily with individuals' everyday lives and experiences. However, while the naturalist view is that the social world is in some sense 'out there', an external reality available to be observed and described by the researcher, the constructivist view is that the social world is constantly 'in the making' and therefore the emphasis is on understanding the *production* of that social world.

Although both the constructivist and naturalist approach to interviewing may appear similar, the constructivist approach requires a much greater sensitivity to the interpretive procedures through which meanings are achieved within the interaction between interviewer and interviewee (Harris, 2003).

Within the naturalist approach, the central research questions are therefore *what* questions: 'what experiences have people had?', 'what is happening?', 'what are people doing?', 'what does it mean to them?' We might therefore expect those adopting this approach to be most interested in the complicating action and the evaluation elements of narrative, i.e. to be interested in the temporal and meaningful aspects of the narrative form. In contrast, the constructivist approach prioritizes *how* questions: the research focus is on identifying meaning making *practices* and on understanding the ways in which people participate in the construction of their lives (Gubrium and Holstein, 1997). In other words, constructivists, such as ethnomethodologists, are interested in the ways that social activities are locally organized and conducted. They seek to answer the questions 'what does a social activity consist of and how is that activity recognizably produced?' (Hester and Francis, 1994: 678). For constructivists an interest in narrative would therefore stem from the fact that it is a social accomplishment, needing the collaboration of an audience.

In discussing the 'naturalist impulse' Gubrium and Holstein (1997) focus mainly on older studies conducted in the 1950s and 1960s, and contrast the classic studies of researchers such as Whyte and Liebow with a more recent ethnomethodological and constructivist focus on interviews as a site for the *creation* of meaning. However, this is not to deny that there are still researchers who are clearly operating within the naturalist or realist paradigm. Texts on the use of qualitative interviewing in social research routinely begin from the premise that semi-structured and in-depth interviews provide the ideal method for discovering more about individuals' lives and intimate experiences. For example, under the introductory heading 'Why we interview', Weiss writes:

> Interviewing can inform us about the nature of social life. We can learn about the work of occupations and how people fashion careers, about cultures and the values they sponsor, and about the challenges people confront as they live their lives. We can learn also, through interviewing about people's interior experiences. … We can learn the meanings to them of their relationships, their families their work, and their selves. We can learn about all the experiences, from joy through grief, that together constitute the human condition. (1994: 1)

In a similar vein, Arksey and Knight state that 'Qualitative interviewing is a way of uncovering and exploring the meanings that underpin people's lives' (1999: 32). These texts on how to conduct qualitative research interviewing therefore clearly belong within the naturalist approach.

Many research studies also still adopt a naturalist or realist perspective on the evidence collected. For example, in Kleinman's book *The Illness Narratives* (1988) he explicitly states that his interest lies in 'how chronic illness is lived and responded to by real people' (Kleinman, 1988: xii). In addition, in a more recent study on the meanings of marriage for young people living in the Netherlands, Korteweg describes how she interviewed a small sample of heterosexual women and men in their twenties. She writes:

> Talking to them gave me insight into the extent to which the idea of marriage still had power in their lives. I was particularly curious about how people used the idea of marriage in the development of their relationships and asked them to tell me about the histories of their relational lives, listening for mentions of marriage. I evaluated the different, sometimes contradictory, sets of meanings people associated with marriage without trying to arbitrate among them. (Korteweg, 2001: 510–11)

In this recent study the focus is therefore clearly on the *content* of the interview, on *what* is said rather than on *how* it is said. The research can therefore be understood as following a naturalist approach. Indeed, with its roots stretching back into the Chicago school, the naturalist approach might still be thought of as constituting the mainstream approach to qualitative research.

There are some who view the naturalist and ethnographic approaches to qualitative interviews as in competition, or as mutually exclusive, so that researchers are expected *either* to treat interviews as a resource for collecting detailed information from respondents (the naturalist or 'realist' approach) *or* to focus on the interview interaction itself as a topic for investigation (the ethnomethodological or constructivist approach) (Seale, 1998). For example, Potter and Mulkay argue that the accounts provided in interviews can *only* be understood in relation to the specifics of the interaction between the interviewer and interviewee, and that these accounts cannot therefore be treated as an unproblematic window onto the social world (Potter and Mulkay, 1985). However, many treat interviews as both a topic and a resource (Seale, 1998). As will be discussed below, and returned to in subsequent chapters, many researchers advocate a reflexive approach to research in which the role of the interviewer, relevant aspects of his or her identity, and the details of the interaction between researched and researcher are understood as constituting an important part of the research evidence. In other words, the interactional form of the interview is seen as having an important relation to the content of the accounts provided by the interviewee. As such the form of the interview is a topic for inclusion in the research agenda. It is analysed in conjunction with the content of the interview, but does not replace the substantive content of the interview as the primary research focus. For example, as the following quotation demonstrates, Hollway and Jefferson are primarily interested in the content of the interviews they conducted on the fear of crime, but their extended reflexive discussion of the nature of the interview interaction demonstrates that they were also sensitive to the way that meaning was constructed as part of the interview interaction:

> The focus of our analysis is the people who tell us stories about their lives:
> the stories themselves are a means to understand our subjects better. While

stories are obviously not providing a transparent account through which we learn truths, story-telling stays closer to actual life events than methods that elicit explanations. (Hollway and Jefferson, 2000: 32)

This slightly extended introduction to the theoretical and methodological under-pinnings of different approaches to qualitative research is necessary because it pro-vides a background to the variety of motivations behind the recent interest in narrative within qualitative research and particularly within in-depth interviewing. As will be discussed in more detail below and in Chapter 3, while some who advocate attention to narrative are primarily interested in the content of the stories provided by interviewees, and can therefore be aligned with the naturalist approach to qualitative research, others focus their attention on the research subject as an artful narrator and are interested in the interpretive effort required to con-struct coherent life stories. This clearly fits more closely with the constructionist approach.

Narratives in qualitative interviews

A good starting point for understanding the link between in-depth interviewing and narratives is Mishler's *Research Interviewing: Context and narrative* (1986). In this frequently cited book, Mishler argues that paying attention to the stories that respondents tell potentially leads to a radical re-examination of the standard prac-tices adopted in qualitative interview research. He emphasizes the need to under-stand that the discourse of the interview is jointly constructed by the interviewer and the interviewee and, at the same time, draws attention to the ubiquity of narratives in unstructured interviews. Although telling stories is common in every-day conversation (Gee, 1986; Polanyi, 1985), Mishler argues that many forms of research interview suppress stories either by 'training' the interviewee to limit answers to short statements, or by interrupting narratives when they do occur. This is perhaps clearest in the case of structured interviews where the respondent is encouraged to give succinct answers to relatively closed questions. However, even in the context of semi-structured and in-depth interviewing Mishler suggests that there has been a tendency to suppress stories or to treat them as problematic in the analysis phase of research.

   Although Mishler makes it clear that variations across interviews and between interviewers should not be understood as errors or technical problems but as data for analysis, he does not go so far as to suggest that the whole focus of the research should shift towards an ethnomethodological interest in the practical accomplish-ment of the interview interaction. Rather he retains an interest in using in-depth interviews as a means for collecting data about individuals' lives, experiences, and perceptions while advocating that the role of the interviewer in producing the data should be taken seriously (Mishler, 1999).

   Almost a decade later, many of Mishler's arguments were echoed and developed by Holstein and Gubrium in *The Active Interview* (1995). They also focus on the quality of the interaction between the interviewer and the interviewee as central to qualitative in-depth interviewing. They stress that conventional approaches to interviewing treat respondents as epistemologically passive and as mere vessels of answers. In contrast, and in line with Mishler, they suggest that the aim of an interview should be to stimulate the interviewee's interpretive capacities and that the role of the interviewer should be to 'activate narrative production' by 'indicating – even suggesting – narrative positions, resources, orientations, and precedents' (Holstein and Gubrium, 1995: 39). The interview therefore becomes a site for the production of data and an opportunity to explore the meaning of the research topic for the respondent.

Reliability and validity

There is a growing body of work on the issues of reliability and validity in qualitative research and also, more specifically, in relation to research which focuses on individuals' narratives in interviews (Kvale, 1989). While reliability is generally defined as the replicability or stability of research findings, validity refers to the ability of research to reflect an external reality or to measure the concepts of interest. As Kerlinger succinctly expresses it, 'The commonest definition of validity is epitomized by the question "are we measuring what we think we are measuring?"' (1973: 456). In addition, a distinction is usually made between internal and external validity, where internal validity refers to the ability to produce results that are not simply an artefact of the research design, and external validity is a measure of how far the findings relating to a particular sample can be generalized to apply to a broader population. These terms originate in quantitative research methods such as surveys and experiments, which are frequently characterized as belonging within the positivist paradigm. There are some authors who argue therefore that these criteria for good research are less appropriate for evaluating qualitative research with a naturalist or hermeneutic emphasis (Becker, 1996). In particular the concept of 'measuring' sits uneasily with much in-depth interviewing, where it is more usual for the researcher to be aiming to provide a detailed description of individuals' experiences and the meanings made of those experiences. The notion of measurement clearly has connotations of quantification and comparison, which is rare in qualitative research.

However, even if the focus is shifted from measurement to description, the researcher must still confront the question of whether the accounts produced in a qualitative interview study are 'accurate' or 'valid' representations of reality. The scope or specificity of the description is another important issue to address. In qualitative studies it is common to interview a small, relatively homogeneous sample of individuals living in a specific geographic area. This immediately raises questions about the extent to which descriptions based on those interviews can be extended to cover a wider population. It is clear therefore that all researchers must pay attention to the stability, trustworthiness, and scope of their findings even if the terms 'reliability' and 'internal and external validity' are seen as problematic in relation to qualitative or naturalistic enquiry.

Internal validity

Among those with an interest in the use of narratives in research there are two rather different views on the relationship between the use of narrative interviews and the internal validity of the information obtained. As was discussed above, some researchers have advocated the use of narrative interviews because they empower the respondent to set the agenda and prevent respondents' experiences from becoming fragmented (Graham, 1984; Mishler, 1986). Both of these considerations imply that interviews that attend to individuals' narratives would produce data that are *more* accurate, truthful, or trustworthy than structured interviews that ask each respondent a standardized set of questions.

However, others who are explicitly interested in the use of narratives in interviews stress that narratives are never simply reports of experiences, rather they make sense of and therefore inevitably distort those experiences. While for some this is itself almost an advantage of narrative-based research, as the focus of interest is on individuals' subjective interpretations and the meanings they make of their lives, others are more concerned that narrative obscures a clear description of life as it is lived. This will be discussed with examples in more detail below.

For some authors, internal validity is therefore thought to be improved by the use of narrative because participants are empowered to provide more concrete and specific details about the topics discussed and to use their own vocabulary and conceptual framework to describe life experiences. For example, in a chapter on the experiences of mature women students, Susan Smith demonstrates that the use of in-depth interviews and a focus on women's narratives gave a radically different and, to her mind, more accurate, view of the support they received from their husbands and partners compared with earlier quantitative work on the same topic. In her conclusions she writes:

> By enabling women to tell their own stories and creating a context in which they felt comfortable exploring their feelings and experiences I was able to learn more about those aspects of their lives which crucially affect their chances of success when they return to study. (Smith, 1996: 71)

Smith suggests that by asking for women's stories about how *they* met their husbands or partners and then for the details about how their husbands felt about the returning to education as mature students, it was possible to 'unpack' the notion of the support they received with their studies. She argues that the women's 'private accounts revealed the reality of the preconditions of their husbands'/partners' support' (Smith, 1996: 67). Cox (2003) takes a similar approach to the issue of internal validity in in-depth interviews. In a discussion of her interview study of individuals who had decided to have a genetic test for Huntingdon's disease, she writes:

> [P]articipants were encouraged to talk about what they felt was most important and to frame this in whatever ways seemed most appropriate to them. This enhanced validity by allowing participants to pattern the timing, sequence and context of topics discussed. (Cox, 2003: 260)

In common with Smith, Cox argues that the qualitative and narrative approach she adopts to interviewing results in more accurate or 'valid' evidence.

However, other researchers emphasize that narratives do not transparently reflect experience, rather they give meaning to it (Ferber, 2000). In order to provide the details of life experiences in the form of a story, individuals are forced to reflect on those experiences, to select the salient aspects, and to order them into a coherent whole. It is this process of reflection and 'making sense' out of experience that makes telling stories a meaning making activity. For some this evaluative or 'meaningful' dimension of narratives is understood as an important advantage for the qualitative researcher. For example, drawing on the work of Polanyi (1985), Chase (1995a) argues that there is a major distinction between a 'report' and a 'narrative' in that stories are told to make a point, and it is the narrator who assumes responsibility for making the point of the telling clear. She argues that by shifting the narrative responsibility to the interviewee, researchers can gain a better understanding of the perspective and life world of their research subjects.

A further important issue in determining the validity of narrative interview evidence is the question of whether narratives are produced specifically for the researcher in a qualitative interview or whether the narratives told in interviews are closely related to those which occur spontaneously in conversation and other aspects of daily life. Some authors have explicitly argued for attention to narratives in interviews because they are ubiquitous in everyday life. As Cox succinctly phrases it, 'Stories are in life as well as about life' (Cox, 2003: 259). In addition, Linde has argued that, 'in the case of the life story, interview data can be used because the life story, as a major means of self presentation, occurs naturally in a wide variety of different contexts (including interviews) and is therefore quite robust' (1993: 61). She suggests that the fact that the social science interview is not the only kind of interaction in which individuals would expect to give an account of their life means that it is difficult to make a sharp distinction between the interview and 'real life'. This would lead to greater confidence in the validity of interview studies. However, depending on the nature of the research and the topics covered in the research interview, it is not necessarily the case that narratives similar to those recounted in interviews will have been told by the interviewee before. In particular, although it is common to tell brief anecdotes in everyday life, it is rare that anyone is given the opportunity to provide an extended account of their life experiences of the type elicited in a research interview.

This in turn implies that the meanings and understandings that individuals attach to their experiences are not necessarily pre-formed and available for collection, rather the task of making sense of experiences will be an intrinsic part of the research process. As was discussed above, this is the main tenet of Holstein and Gubrium's approach to qualitative interviewing described in their book *The Active Interview*. They argue that while the traditional approach to qualitative research viewed interviews as 'a pipeline for transmitting knowledge', the interview is better understood as a site for the production of knowledge. In other words, as Halford et al. have written, 'In-depth interviews do not allow any privileged or unmediated access to people's thoughts and feelings, but rather produce specific accounts designed to meet the particular situation' (1997: 60). Halford et al. describe how in their research on the careers of men and women in banking, nursing, and local organizations, many respondents used the research interview as an opportunity to 'let off steam' in what they perceived to be a 'safe' and confidential environment. Although this provided interviews that were full of incidents and anecdotes, Halford et al. question the validity of some of this material in that it may not reflect the respondents' feelings and attitudes as they would be expressed outside the research interview.

One way of resolving this issue about whether narrative approaches produce more 'valid' evidence is to understand that the validity of evidence in qualitative interviews is crucially dependent on the type of research question that is being asked (Kvale, 1989, 1996). In other words, in order to decide whether an interviewee is telling us 'the truth' we need to consider what questions or topic are being addressed in the research, and what type of truths or insights we are hoping to gain from an interview. To illustrate this point, Kvale uses a short extract from Shakespeare's *Hamlet* in which the Prince Hamlet is questioning or 'interviewing' Polonius, a courtier in a medieval court:

Hamlet:	Do you see yonder cloud that's almost in shape of a camel?
Polonius:	By the mass, and 'tis like a camel indeed.
Hamlet:	Methinks it is like a weasel.
Polonius:	It is back'd like a weasel.
Hamlet:	Or like a whale?
Polonius:	Very like a whale.
Hamlet [aside]:	They fool me to the top of my bent.
	(Act III, Scene 2)

As Kvale demonstrates by use of this example, if Hamlet is really interested in finding out which animal Polonius thinks the cloud represents, this is a very poor method of interviewing and the leading questions are likely to produce distorted responses. However, if the research question is not the shape of the cloud but rather the form or nature of Polonius's personality then the interview provides a great deal of valid information on this topic. Hamlet's final aside summarizes his own interpretation of the exchange that has just taken place, and clearly in the context of the play, it is Polonius's untrustworthiness that is the subject of Hamlet's investigation.

A further, telling, example of this same point is provided by Portelli's oral history work on the murder by the police of a young steel worker, Luigi Trastulli (Portelli, 1991). In his analysis of the narrative accounts of workers in an industrial town in the north of Italy, Portelli demonstrated that the individual narratives produced by his respondents contained many factual errors. In particular, while some gave the correct date of the murder as 1949, others reported that it had happened in 1953 in the same year as a mass strike. The variation in the date given for the murder could be interpreted as evidence that the accounts were not valid, i.e. they did not provide a trustworthy account of the past. However, an alternative approach is to recognize that these accounts may not provide the best data about *the date* of the murder (which can be ascertained from other sources in any case). Portelli argued that many people reported the murder as taking place in 1953 because they understood the mass strikes that took place in that year to represent the workers' revenge for the death of Trastulli. Portelli suggests that the people interviewed found it too painful to believe that a worker had died for no reason and that his death had not been avenged. By interpreting the accounts in this way, Portelli vividly demonstrates that they can provide important insights into the importance attached to dignity and pride in the lives of these workers. As he writes: 'Oral sources … are not always reliable in point of fact. Rather than being a weakness, this is however, their strength: errors, inventions and myths lead us through and beyond facts to their meanings' (Portelli, 1991: 2).

The centrality of the research question in determining the validity of the evidence produced in narrative interviews clearly resonates with the point made above about the differences in research questions asked by naturalists and constructivists. If the focus is on providing a realist description of the social world and of individuals' experiences then it must be acknowledged that narratives in qualitative interviews are unlikely to provide an unproblematic window on to what happened. A narrative will not capture a simple record of the past in the way that we hope that a video camera might. However, if the research focus is more on the meanings attached to individuals' experiences and/or on the way that those experiences are communicated to others then narratives provide an ideal medium for researching and understanding individuals' lives in social context.

External validity

In comparisons with discussions of internal validity, much less has been written about the external validity of qualitative studies or the implications of the use of narrative for the generalizability of qualitative evidence. For some researchers there is simply a trade-off between depth and breadth, i.e. researchers must make a decision about whether to prioritize detailed descriptions and contextualized data or whether to aim for breadth in the form of large samples of cases which yield more generalizable findings. For those adopting this perspective, the particular strength of the qualitative approach has been that it allows the researcher to 'create a deeper and richer picture of what is going on in particular settings' (Goodwin and Horowitz, 2002: 44). Many would therefore argue that it is mistaken for qualitative researchers to try to produce law-like statements that are expected to hold true across a wide range of historical and cultural contexts.[2] However, it would clearly be pointless to do research if findings were considered to be completely ungeneralizable. Qualitative research therefore often adopts what we might call a 'common-sense' view of generalizability such that the reader is left to make up his or her own mind as to how far the evidence collected in a specific study can be transferred to offer information about the same topic in similar settings. For example, Cox (2003) describes a study in which she interviewed sixteen individuals, living in both urban and rural British Columbia, who had decided to request predictive testing for Huntingdon's disease. Although she does discuss the fact that her sample is restricted to those who had made the decision to request the test, and does not cover those deciding *not* to request the test, she does not give any further discussion about the generalizability of her findings. However, implicit in the description of the sample is the idea that by including those from both urban and rural areas the results are more widely generalizable than if they had focused only on those in a very specific geographical location. It is, however, left to the reader to decide whether the description she provides of the decision-making process could also apply to individuals living elsewhere in Canada, across North America, or to all individuals at risk of Huntingdon's disease in countries where genetic testing is available.

Other writers have also stressed the problems of generalizing on the basis of qualitative research (Denzin, 1983; Ward-Schofield, 1993; Williams, 1998). As Williams (1998) has argued, qualitative researchers who prioritize the interpretation of the actions and meanings of agents are caught in a dilemma. If they argue that the variability between individuals and situations makes generalization impossible then 'research can suggest nothing beyond itself'. However, if it is accepted that at least some generalization is possible, then it is not clear on what basis these generalizations can be made (Williams, 1998: 9). As Williams writes:

> In empirical research the conclusion that the intentional nature of individual consciousness produces far too much variability for generalizations to be made from one interaction to another has never really embarrassed interpretivists, whose attitude is somewhat akin to that of the Victorian middle classes toward sex: they do it, they know it goes on, but they never admit to either. Almost every classic interpretivist study, while acknowledging the subjectivity of the researcher and the uniqueness of the repertoire of interactions studied, nevertheless wishes to persuade us that there is something to be learned from that situation that has a wider currency. (1998: 8)

It is important to be aware, however, that different questions about the external validity of qualitative interview evidence arise if the focus of research is not on respondents' *individual* beliefs, attitudes, and subjective understanding of their experiences but rather, to use a term coined by Charles Taylor, on the 'intersubjective' meanings that constitute a community. Taylor makes a persuasive argument that the social or 'human' sciences should concern themselves not simply with the interior life of individuals but with those aspects of human experience that are socially constructed; that is, those social practices that are not reducible to the individual subjective experiences of the people that make up a society or community (Taylor, 1987). It is these social practices that he terms 'intersubjective meanings'. Using as an example the concept of negotiation he writes:

> The actors may have all sorts of beliefs and attitudes which may be rightly thought of as their individual beliefs and attitudes, even if others share them; they may subscribe to certain policy goals or certain forms of theory about the policy, or feel resentment about certain things and so on. They bring these

with them into negotiations, and strive to satisfy them. But what they do not bring into the negotiations is the set of ideas and norms constitutive of negotiations themselves. These must be the common property of the society before there can be any question of anyone entering into negotiation or not. Hence they are not subjective meanings, the property of one or some individuals, but rather intersubjective meanings which are constitutive of the social matrix in which individuals find themselves and act. (Taylor, 1987: 57–8)

It is beyond the scope of Taylor's article to discuss the practical implications of the need to focus on intersubjective meanings. His emphasis is on theory rather than techniques or methods of research. However, within the burgeoning methodological literature on narrative in qualitative research there are several authors whose discussion of the use of narrative resonates with the arguments made by Taylor. For example, in the following extract, Chase is clearly arguing that narratives do not simply provide evidence about individuals, but provide a means to understand more about the broader culture shared by a community of individuals:

Life stories themselves embody what we need to study: the relation between this instanciation (this particular life story) and the social world the narrator shares with others; the ways in which culture marks shapes and/or constrains this narrative; and the ways in which this narrator makes use of cultural resources and struggles with cultural constraints. (1995a: 20)

If narratives become the focus of research not simply because they provide an insight into individuals' experiences and the meanings they make of them, but because their form tells us something about the cultural framework within which individuals make sense of their lives, then the close analysis of narratives produced by a relatively small sample of individuals may produce evidence that is considered to provide an understanding of the intersubjective meanings shared by the whole of a community. The external validity or generalizability of this evidence will therefore depend on a demonstration of how widely those intersubjective meanings are shared or in other words what delineates the boundaries of the community or culture that is being studied. This difficult issue is one that has, as yet, received very little discussion in the literature on qualitative research.

Eliciting stories in interviews

Asking the right questions

Having established *why* social scientists might be interested in hearing people's narratives in the context of research interviews, it is appropriate to turn to a consideration of *how* researchers might best elicit narratives from interviewees. Authors such as Graham (1984), Mishler (1986), and Riessman (1990) have each emphasized that interviewees are likely spontaneously to provide narratives in the context of interviews about their experiences, unless the structure of the interview itself or the questioning style of the interviewer suppresses such stories. Most people like telling stories and with a little encouragement will provide narrative accounts of their experiences in research interviews. For example, Mishler explicitly links the notion of obtaining narratives in interviews to the aim of empowering respondents as he succinctly explains:

> Various attempts to restructure the interviewer–interviewee relationship, so as to empower respondents, are designed to encourage them to find and speak in their own 'voices.' It is not surprising that when the interview situation is opened up in this way, when the balance of power is shifted, respondents are likely to tell 'stories.' In sum, interviewing practices that empower respondents also produce narrative accounts. (1986: 118–19)

However, in contrast to this view that narratives will emerge naturally during in-depth interviews (if only researchers are prepared to hear them), some authors have described situations in which they failed to obtain narratives from respondents even though this was the primary aim of the interview. This raises questions about the most effective ways of encouraging respondents to provide detailed storied accounts of their experiences in interviews.

Qualitative researchers are in general agreement that questions in interviews should be framed using everyday rather than sociological language. Chase (1995a) provides a telling account of how the failure to adhere to this principle prevented respondents from providing the narratives about their work experiences that she was hoping for. She explains that in a research project on women's experiences in the white- and male-dominated profession of public school superintendents in the United States she and her co-researcher Colleen Bell wanted to hear about the concrete experiences of women school superintendents. In the early interviews they included a series of questions specifically about what it is like to be a woman in a male-dominated profession and, in the spirit of developing an egalitarian relationship with these women professionals, these questions were introduced with a few statements about the sociological thinking behind them. Chase describes how eventually they realized that they needed to drop these 'sociological questions', and the discussion of their sociological interests, in favour of asking much more straightforward and simple questions. For example, a brief request for an individual's work history proved to be effective in encouraging the respondents to tell stories about their professional lives. Chase explains that the problem with sociological questions is that 'they invite reports. They do not invite the other to take responsibility for the import of her response because the weight of the question lies in the sociological ideas' (1995a: 8). From her own experiences of interviewing, Chase therefore concludes that we are most likely to succeed in eliciting narratives from our research subjects when we ask simple questions that clearly relate to their life experiences.

Hollway and Jefferson (2000) also describe their unsuccessful attempts to get interviewees to give narrative responses in their pilot interviews for a study on the fear of crime. They suggest that although their questions were open ended and

29

framed in everyday language they were still too focused on the interests of the researcher and were not broad enough to allow respondents to provide the detailed narrative accounts they were hoping to elicit. As they write:

> Our opening question to Ann, 'What's the crime you most fear?' is open but in a narrow way, which may account for its failure to elicit much from her. In linking fear with crime it reveals what sort of fear interests the interviewer, but in so doing, it may work to suppress the meaning of fear to Ann, which may have no apparent connection to crime. To learn about the meaning of fear to Ann a more open question such as 'What do you most fear?' would be necessary. The presumption of the biographical method is that it is only in this way, by tracking Ann's fears through her meaning frames, that we are likely to discover the 'real' meaning of fear of crime to her – how it relates to her life. (Hollway and Jefferson, 2000: 34)

Following careful analysis of the transcripts of pilot interviews, Hollway and Jefferson revised their interview guide to make the questions more open. The seven main questions that structured their first interviews with respondents are presented in Box 2.1. It can be seen that each of these questions asks the interviewee to talk directly about his or her experiences. Hollway and Jefferson (2000) comment that, although it did frequently elicit stories, in retrospect the first question was probably 'insufficiently narrativised'. They argue that the best questions for narrative interviews invite the interviewee to talk about specific times and situations, rather than asking about the respondent's life over a long period of time (Hollway and Jefferson, 2000).

Box 2.1   Questions developed by Hollway and Jefferson to elicit narratives in their first interview

1 Can you tell me about how crime has impacted on your life since you've been living here?
2 Can you tell me about unsafe situations in your life since you have been living here?
3 Can you think of something that you've read, seen or heard about recently that makes you fearful? Anything [not necessarily about crime].
4 Can you tell me about risky situations in your life since you have been living here?
5 Can you tell me about times in your life recently when you have been anxious?
6 Can you tell me about earlier times in your life when you have been anxious?
7 Can you tell me what it was like moving to this area?

In addition to asking appropriate questions, the interviewer who wants to encourage the production of narratives during an interview must clearly also be a good listener. Thompson argues that, in oral history interviewing, the interviewer should 'Wherever possible avoid interrupting a story. If you stop a story because you think it is irrelevant, you will cut off not just that one but a whole series of subsequent offers of information which will be relevant' (1978: 172). This is consonant with Elliot Mishler's suggestion that a process takes place at the beginning of a research interview that might be thought of as the interviewer training the interviewee to give appropriate responses. It is widely recognized in the social sciences that the subjects of research are eager to comply with the wishes of the researcher and to provide the type of responses that the researcher is looking for. If the researcher implicitly communicates that narrative responses are not what is wanted, by interrupting the interviewee's stories for example, this in some senses 'trains' the respondent to provide a different type of information.

Collecting life histories – the use of a life history grid

If the primary aim of carrying out qualitative biographical interviews is to obtain individuals' own accounts of their lives, it is clearly important not to impose a rigid structure on the interview by asking a standardized set of questions. However, it is also important to be aware that some individuals might find it very difficult to respond if simply asked to produce an account of their life. This is a particular problem if the focus of the research is on the broad life course or on experiences (such as education and training or employment) that may span a great many years. As was mentioned above, respondents are likely to find it easier to talk about specific times and situations rather than being asked about a very wide time frame. One approach is therefore to make use of a pre-prepared life history grid at the beginning of the interview. The life history grid can have a number of different formats. The 'Balan' type of grid, discussed by Tagg (1985), has a row for each year, and the respondent's age is entered in the left hand column. The remaining columns are used to record major events under a number of different headings such as education history, work history, housing history, and family history. Clearly these categories will vary somewhat depending on the exact focus of the research. For example, research on those with a chronic illness might include a column for events related to health, and research in criminology may have a column for arrests and incarcerations. Completing the grid will ideally be a joint task undertaken by the interviewer and interviewee at the beginning of the interview. By moving backwards and forwards between the different areas of the respondent's life, the memory is stimulated. For example, individuals may have no difficulty remembering the year when their first child was born but may not remember the date when they returned to college as a mature student. However, if they remember that this occurred the year after their child was born the life history grid helps to locate this educational event. Once the grid is completed, the respondents can be asked to use it to help guide them as they recount the story of their life, starting from

31

whatever point is most appropriate for them as individuals or for the purposes of the research.[3]

The length of narrative interviews

The emphasis within in-depth interviews on allowing the respondents to set the agenda and on listening to, rather than suppressing, their stories also raises practical questions about the appropriate length for these types of interviews. For example, Riessman discusses how a research project that was originally conceived as using a structured interview to examine the differences between the post-separation adaptation of men and women was modified to allow interviewees more of an opportunity to talk and to tell the story of how their marriage had ended (Riessman, 1990). She explains that in the pilot phase of the study, the structured interviews typically took under two hours to complete, but in the research itself, when interviewees were allowed to tell their stories, many of the interviews lasted for up to six hours. Several authors suggest that ninety minutes is the optimum length for a qualitative research interview (Hermanowicz, 2002; Seidman, 1998). If the quantity of material to be covered in an interview is judged to need more than two hours then the most practical solution is to conduct a second and even a third interview. Regardless of decisions about the exact length of the interview, what is important is to make the timing clear to the interviewee from the start. In my own research with graduate women in their forties (Elliott, 2001), I suggested to interviewees that the interview would probably last for approximately an hour and a half, but might go on for as long as two hours. This appeared to be helpful to interviewees as it gave them a sense of how much detail to provide. Interviews of this length yield transcripts of approximately twenty to thirty pages of text (or approximately 15,000 to 20,000 words). In terms of the task of analysis this clearly provides a wealth of material to examine.

Repeated interviews

A further practical consideration when using the method of biographical interviews is whether to rely on a single interview or whether to conduct a series of interviews with each respondent, and practice among researchers is very variable in this respect. Seidman (1998) makes a persuasive case for conducting a series of three interviews with each respondent. He suggests that the first interview should focus on the life history of the respondent, who should be asked to provide an account of his or her past life leading up to the topic or event of interest. The second interview should then focus on the concrete aspects of the respondent's present experiences, and Seidman advocates encouraging the respondent to tell stories as a way of eliciting detailed information. In the final interview, the researcher can then move on to encourage the respondent to reflect on his or her understandings of those experiences. Seidman argues that this three-interview structure also helps with establishing the internal validity of the findings as the researcher can check that the respondent is consistent across the three separate interviews.

Hollway and Jefferson also give a helpful account of the process surrounding the use of two interviews in their research on the fear of crime in a British city (Hollway and Jefferson, 2000). Between the first and the second interview, a week later, the researchers together listened carefully to the recording of the first interview and discussed the material covered. The comments and analysis of the researcher who had not carried out the initial interview were valuable in that they provided a slightly more detached perspective on the interview. The notes taken during this process would then lead to the construction of further narrative questions to ask in the second interview. The use of two interviews also enabled the researchers to build up a trusting relationship with the interviewees and to demonstrate that they were interested in hearing about their experiences. Hollway and Jefferson argue that it enabled the interviewee to build up confidence that stories were what the researchers wanted. Because the narrative approach to interviewing differs from individuals' usual expectation that researchers ask lots of closed questions, it can take time to build up a respondent's confidence that telling stories about his or her experiences is valid within the interview context (Hollway and Jefferson, 2000: 44).

Recording narrative interviews

Given the focus in in-depth narrative interviews on the interaction between the interviewer and interviewee and on the form of the narratives provided rather than simply on the content, it is clearly very useful to be able to tape-record the interview. This also allows the interviewer to give full attention to the interviewee rather than needing to pause to take notes. For interviews lasting ninety minutes or more it would be impractical to try and remember the interviewee's responses and make detailed notes at the end of the interview. Recording is therefore now generally thought to be good practice in all qualitative interviewing (Hermanowicz, 2002). Without tape-recording all kinds of data are lost: the narrative itself, pauses, intonation, laughter. In particular if the interview is understood as a site for the production of meanings and the role of the interviewer is to be analysed alongside the accounts provided by the interviewee, it is important to capture the details of the interaction. Clearly, once an interview is tape-recorded the next set of questions involves how to transcribe the recording in order to preserve an appropriate amount of information about what was said as well as about the interaction itself. This will be discussed towards the end of the next chapter, which examines how an interest in narrative might shape the *analysis* of qualitative interview material.

Summary

This chapter has focused on the use of narrative in qualitative interviews. It has explored the questions of why researchers might be interested in listening to individuals' narratives and has also focused on examples of research using narrative interviews to show how storied accounts of individuals' experiences can be elicited. While some authors have suggested that narratives are produced spontaneously during interviews and that if the interviewer is willing to listen to respondents' stories they will be forthcoming, others such as Chase (1995a) and Hollway and Jefferson (2000) have demonstrated that even when an interview schedule is designed to encourage respondents to tell stories, grounded in their own experiences, the results can be disappointing. The need to ask open-ended questions in everyday language that address the interests of the interviewee rather than the sociological interests of the researcher has been emphasized. An important theme in this chapter has been that although the qualitative approach to research is made to seem like a coherent paradigm when it is contrasted with a quantitative approach, qualitative enquiry is in reality relatively diverse. The naturalist and constructivist approaches to qualitative research have been contrasted, but it has been suggested that narratives are relevant both to those researchers who are interested in producing rich descriptive accounts of individuals' lives and to those who focus more on the way in which individuals make sense of their experiences in the context of a research interview. In the next chapter this distinction between an interest in the content and the form of narratives will be extended in the context of exploring different approaches to the *analysis* of qualitative material.

Introductory books on qualitative interviewing

Arksey, H. and Knight, P. (1999) *Interviewing for Social Scientists*. London: Sage.

Chase, S.E. (2003) 'Learning to listen: narrative principles in a qualitative research methods course', in R. Josselson, A. Lieblich, and D.P. McAdams (eds), *Up Close and Personal: The Teaching and Learning of Narrative Research*. Washington, DC: American Psychological Association. pp. 79–100.

Kvale, S. (1996) *InterViews: an introduction to qualitative research interviewing*. Thousand Oaks, CA: Sage.

Seidman, I. (1998) *Interviewing as Qualitative Research*. New York: Teacher's College Press.

Weiss, R.S. (1994) *Learning from Strangers*. New York: Free Press.

Readings for discussion

Cox, S.M. (2003) 'Stories in decisions: how at-risk individuals decide to request predictive testing for Huntingdon's Disease', *Qualitative Sociology*, 26: 257–80.

1 *How central is narrative to Cox's approach to the collection and analysis of qualitative evidence?*

2   *Why did Cox sometimes find it difficult to elicit the story of how the interviewee
    had arrived at the decision to be tested for Huntingdon's disease?*
3   *Should Cox's findings be generalized beyond the sample she interviewed? How
    might you improve the generalizability of her findings?*

Harris, S.R. (2003) 'Studying equality/inequality: naturalist and constructionist approaches to equality in marriage', *Journal of Contemporary Ethnography*, 32: 200–32.

1   *What kinds of questions is Harris attempting to ask about equality in marriage and
    how do these differ from the research questions other qualitative (and quantitative)
    researchers might want to ask?*
2   *How does Harris describe constructivist interviewing as compared with naturalist
    approaches to interviewing?*
3   *How important is narrative within Harris's constructivist approach to the collection
    and analysis of qualitative evidence?*

Notes

1   Gubrium and Holstein describe four different approaches to, or 'languages of', qualitative research: naturalism, ethnomethodology, emotionalism, and post-modernism. However, for the purposes of the current discussion the distinction between naturalism and ethnomethodology is perhaps the most telling. Emotionalism can perhaps be understood as a variant on naturalism but one that is more concerned with the interior subjective life of the respondent. Post-modernism arguably has more implications for how research is reported, i.e. the crisis of representation, than on the interview process itself, and although it will be discussed in the following chapters it is bracketed in the current discussion.

2   Indeed, even among researchers who work firmly within a quantitative paradigm, there is an increasing awareness that research results are context specific and that scope statements are needed to specify more clearly the limitations of the applicability of any theory derived from empirical research (Walker and Cohen, 1985). The implications of taking a narrative approach for issues of external validity in quantitative research will be discussed in more detail in Chapter 5.

3   These types of grids have also been used in large-scale quantitative surveys, such as the National Child Development Study, to help respondents remember the dates of events before completing a life history questionnaire. This will be returned to in Chapter 4.

Interpreting people's stories: narrative approaches to the analysis of qualitative data

As was highlighted in the previous chapter, the last two decades have witnessed an explosion of interest in narrative evidence in the social sciences. In part this can be traced to the growing dissatisfaction with rigidly structured research interviews, which can artificially fragment individuals' experiences. In addition there has been a great deal of theoretical interest in the notion of the narrative construction of identity, a move away from the modernist understanding of 'self' as an enduring, immutable essence, and a growing interest in the way that identity is shaped in interaction and through discourse (this theme will be returned to in Chapter 7). Despite this growing interest in narrative within sociology and the social sciences more generally, there is as yet no single analytic approach that can provide *the* definition for narrative analysis. A number of researchers have suggested ways in which an interest in narrative might inform the analysis of textual material, such as the transcript of a research interview or a newspaper article. However, there is no standard approach or list of procedures that is generally recognized as representing the narrative method of analysis. Indeed, in Mishler's words, there is a 'state of near anarchy in the field' (1995: 88).

The current diversity of approaches can, in part, be traced to the different features of narratives that are seen as being of primary importance by researchers. As was discussed in Chapter 1, narratives can be defined as 'discourses with a clear sequential order that connect events in a meaningful way for a definite audience' (Hinchman and Hinchman, 1997). This definition helpfully encapsulates three central features of narratives and, depending on the nature of their research questions, social scientists may focus on any one of these three different aspects of narrative accounts. First, some advocates of the use of narrative stress the temporal nature of social life as providing a rationale for a narratively informed methodology (Abbott, 1990; 1992a; 1992b; 1998; Graham, 1984; Smith, 1994). Second, others, who might be placed more centrally within a hermeneutic tradition, focus on the *evaluative* or *subjective* dimension of narratives and their ubiquity within everyday social interaction to justify a call for greater sociological attention to narratives (Cohan, 1997; Riessman, 1989). Finally a third group can be identified whose interest lies in the social processes surrounding the production and consumption of stories (Gubrium and Holstein, 1998; Linde, 1993; Ochs and Taylor, 1995; Plummer, 1995). However, it would be an oversimplification to suggest that an interest in one of these three facets of narrative translates in any straightforward way into a specific technique for the analysis of narrative material.

In particular, if we focus on research lying broadly within the hermeneutic or interpretive tradition, which emphasizes the evaluative dimension of narrative evidence, the idea that narrative analysis might represent a set of procedures becomes problematic. Interpretive analysis demands that we understand how the subjects of our research make sense of events and experiences and require dense, detailed, and contextualized description. One implication of this is that the type of understanding required on the part of the researcher is 'imaginative reconstruction' or 'empathy'. This is a subjective exercise that cannot be readily represented by an algorithm or method. In the words of Outhwaite, 'understanding is not a matter of trained, methodical, unprejudiced technique, but an encounter…a confrontation with something radically different from ourselves' (1985). That said, the researcher who wants to produce a convincing interpretation of qualitative evidence, one which improves on the understanding that could be arrived at by a lay person, needs some basic tools (heuristic devices) that enable him or her to go beyond the ostensible or most obvious content.

This chapter will therefore provide a discussion of the techniques and methods that have been developed for the analysis of qualitative material as a result of the growing recognition of the importance of narrative. In particular it will be demonstrated how researchers in the social sciences have borrowed ideas about narrative structure from literary studies and socio-linguistics to inform their analytic approaches. The focus here will primarily be on introducing some of the different methods that have been used to analyse narratives within qualitative (i.e. 'in-depth' or 'semi-structured') research interviews, although discussion of the analysis of other textual narrative materials, such as newspaper accounts, will also be included. The variety of approaches and heuristic devices outlined in this chapter, including methods that would generally be considered quantitative techniques, reinforces the point that there is no *single* narrative method, but rather a multitude of different ways in which researchers can engage with the narrative properties of their data.

A framework for classifying methods of narrative analysis

In order to make sense of the multitude of different techniques and approaches that can be included under the broad umbrella of 'narrative analysis', it is helpful to apply a classification or typology. In addition this can help to elucidate some of the methodological and epistemological differences that lie at the root of the various techniques described. In response to the burst of empirical work that has focused on the use of narrative, a number of authors have attempted to provide a classification of the wide variety of analytic methods that focus on the narrative properties of much qualitative data in the social sciences. Two rather different frameworks are described here.

Mishler's framework for understanding the different approaches to narrative analysis (Mishler, 1995) is based on what are commonly understood as the three different functions of language, namely meaning, structure, and interactional context (or in more technical linguistic terms: semantics, syntax, and pragmatics (Halliday, 1973)). First, researchers may be primarily interested in the actual events and experiences that are recounted in a narrative, i.e. they focus on *the content* of the narrative. To elaborate further, the content of a narrative can be thought of as having two functions: one is to describe past events, i.e. to produce a chronological account for the listener or reader, and the second is the evaluative function, making clear the meaning of those events and experiences in the lives of the participants (Labov and Waletzky, 1967; republished 1997). Second, researchers may be more interested in *the structure* or form of the narrative, i.e. the way in which the story is put together. Third, the interest may lie in *the performance* of narratives – the interactional and institutional contexts in which narratives are produced, recounted, and consumed.

A rather different typology is provided by Lieblich et al. (1998). They suggest that the wide variation in approaches to narrative research can be described using two dimensions. First, analyses can be characterized by whether they examine the *content* or the *form* of narratives. Whereas some readings focus on the explicit content of an account, i.e. what happened and why, other readings pay less attention to the content and concentrate on the structure of the plot, its coherence or complexity, the style or genre of the narrative, and the choice of metaphors and other images that are invoked. Second, while some researchers attempt an *holistic* analysis which seeks to preserve a narrative in its entirety and understand it as a complete entity, other analyses can be described as *categorical* analyses in that short sections of the text are extracted, classified, and placed into categories for analysis. Whereas holistic approaches attempt to understand sections of the text in the context of other parts of the narrative, categorical approaches do not attempt to preserve the integrity of the whole account. As Lieblich et al. argue, and as will be demonstrated below, these categorical approaches resemble traditional content analysis and are more amenable to quantitative or statistical methods of analysis.

It can therefore be seen that, in contrast to the typology provided by Mishler, Lieblich et al. do not include a discussion of approaches to narrative analysis which focus on the social context or functions of narratives. However, they do helpfully introduce the distinction between holistic and categorical analysis – a distinction that will be explored more fully below. As with all typologies these two rather different frameworks both represent something of an oversimplification. There are, of course, researchers who are interested in more than one of the three aspects or functions of narrative outlined above. For instance, it is unlikely that any researcher in the social sciences would examine the form or social function of a narrative without also paying attention to its content.

Having sketched these typologies, the next section will elaborate on the variety of approaches to narrative analysis that are generated by focusing on these different properties of narratives. Rather than discussing techniques for analysis in an abstract or formalized manner the aim is to introduce specific pieces of research that have adopted different approaches to analysis in order to exemplify the range of techniques that are available to researchers interested in narrative evidence. Using Mishler's framework, outlined above, there will be a particular emphasis on describing analytic techniques which enable the researcher to examine the form of narratives. It is in this area that there has arguably been the most fruitful adoption of techniques from socio-linguistics and related disciplines.

Narrative approaches: a focus on content

Perhaps the best examples of narrative analysis which focus primarily on content are provided by some of the most well-known sociological research from the Chicago tradition. Texts such as Thomas and Znaniecki's *The Polish Peasant* (1958 [1918]) and Shaw's studies of the life histories of delinquents such as *The Natural History of a Delinquent Career*, *The Jack-Roller*, and *Brothers in Crime* (1931; 1966; Shaw and McKay, 1938) demonstrate the sociological insights that can be gained from detailed examination of the content of a single, whole narrative. The emphasis in this type of analysis is on understanding an individual narrative, usually a biographical narrative, in its entirety. In other words, this would correspond to Lieblich et al.'s notion of holistic analysis. However, as will be shown below, this focus on the individual life does not preclude a sociological interest in social structures, norms, and constraints. As Plummer has persuasively argued, studying an individual biography does not bring with it the isolated individual, but rather an awareness of the individual *in society* (1983). For a sociologist, the aim of analysing an individual biography is therefore to use it to develop an understanding of social groups, classes, and cultures and the structural relationships between them.

In the first chapter of *The Jack-Roller*, Shaw helpfully provides a methodological discussion identifying the advantages of focusing on a delinquent boy's 'own story'. He stresses that it 'reveals useful information on 1) the point of view of the delinquent; 2) the social and cultural situation to which the delinquent is responsive and 3) the sequence of past experiences and situations in the life of the delinquent'. Shaw highlights the importance of understanding personal values, feelings, and attitudes through a delinquent's own account of his experiences. Shaw emphasizes that it is *not* necessary to assume that the delinquent will provide an objective or totally truthful account, but rather that it is preferable to obtain a story that reflects the interpretations and values of the individual. As was discussed in the previous chapter, therefore, the validity of a life history depends on the research question being addressed. According to Shaw, the social and cultural world in which the delinquent lives can also be accessed through his own account of his life, and more importantly, perhaps, the impact of these cultural factors on the young delinquent can also be found there. Indeed, one of Shaw's major empirical contributions is to show how delinquent behaviour has its origins in the social setting rather than the pathology of an individual. Finally, Shaw emphasizes the value of examining the sequence of past experiences in the life of the individual that can lead to delinquency. In other words, Shaw is clearly interested in both the evaluative and the referential functions of the life story provided by the young delinquent. Shaw's work provides a good example of research that focuses solely on the content of narrative because he makes no comment on the form of the life history, i.e. how it is structured. Although Shaw briefly describes how as researchers they encouraged Stanley (the delinquent) to write about his life in the kind of detail that was required, there is no reflection on how the conditions in which the life history was produced might have influenced the account. Indeed there is a sense in which Shaw does not provide any analysis of the material he presents, rather the life story is allowed to speak for itself.

A more recent example of the use of narrative life histories with a focus on the *content* of those life histories is provided by the work of Bertaux and Bertaux-Wiame (1981) in their research on the bakers' trade in France. In contrast to Shaw they profess to be less interested in the evaluative aspects of the biographical materials that they collect and more interested in the chronology of individuals' lives. They themselves write: 'We always tried to have bakers and bakers' wives focus upon what they had done in life (practices) *rather than what they thought about it*' (Bertaux and Bertaux-Wiame, 1981: 181, my italics). Interestingly, Bertaux and Bertaux-Wiame are quite explicit about the fact that they do not subject the biographies they collect to any formal analytic techniques. Rather they argue that in order to discover what was relevant for their research it was important to move from one life story to another checking that each new account confirmed the main features of the previous accounts. In other words, by identifying the common elements in the trajectories of the different bakers that they interviewed they develop what might be thought of as a collective story[1] which represents the common experiences and elucidates the structural features underpinning each individual's experiences. The closest that Bertaux and Bertaux-Wiame come to suggesting a technique or procedure in the analysis of their data can be found in their description of 'saturation'. This is arguably a procedure more connected with sampling than analysis. They argue that in order to be able to discern what is of broader sociological interest rather than what is just particular to an individual life, it is necessary to collect information from as diverse a range of cases as possible until each new life story appears to confirm the main elements of the previous stories. For example, they state that in examining the lives of bakery workers it took fifteen interviews before they began to perceive the common elements and a further fifteen interviews to confirm these.

Although the sample size used in the Bertaux and Bertaux-Wiame study of the bakers' trade did not necessitate a formal quantitative approach to the analysis of the data, there is clearly no reason why quantitative techniques and computer software packages should not be used to help uncover patterns in the content of narratives. Perhaps one of the most sophisticated examples of this approach can be seen in the work of Franzosi (1994; 1998b; 2003). Rather than analysing the narratives that are produced in interviews, Franzosi has focused on narratives in newspaper articles.

One of the main substantive research areas where he has applied his technique has been in the study of labour unrest in different sectors of the Italian economy. He argues that in contrast to official strike data which are based only on the *number* of strikes that have occurred in a particular time frame, newspaper accounts, which are generally in the form of narratives about what happened, provide richer and much more detailed information about the *characteristics* of strikes. The challenge is then to find a systematic approach to analysing these narratives in order to discover the patterns and regularities within the data. Franzosi demonstrates how the subject, action, object structure within narrative clauses (e.g. the policemen stopped the protesters) can be used as a framework for setting up a series of datasets derived from the narratives within newspaper articles. He then uses these datasets to examine issues such as the number of actors involved in each dispute, the actors most commonly involved in the dispute, and whether particular types of actors (e.g. local or central government officials) have a role as the subject or object in the narrative accounts. Using this method, Franzosi uses cross-tabulations and frequency tables to compare the characteristics of labour unrest in the service and industrial sectors of the economy (Franzosi, 1994; 1998b; 2003).

Franzosi uses this approach to analyse approximately 1000 different labour disputes; this contrasts with the study of the bakers' trade carried out by Bertaux and Bertaux-Wiame, which examined around a hundred narratives. Although, on first reading, Franzosi's method may seem to be technically more sophisticated, it can be argued that methodologically the approaches are very similar. In both cases the research focuses on the content of narratives and on actions and events rather than on the meaning that the narrator makes of those events. Franzosi does not focus on *the way* in which newspapers represent the labour disputes that he is interested in, rather he treats them as convenient sources of detailed information. As was emphasized above, Bertaux and Bertaux-Wiame also explicitly state that they are interested in the career patterns of the bakers they interviewed rather than in those bakers' feelings about, or perceptions of, their careers. Franzosi's work is also of particular interest because it demonstrates the permeability of the boundary between qualitative and quantitative research. As he writes in the introduction to his recent book: 'This is a book on ways of going from words to numbers, of using qualitative data for quantitative purposes' (Franzosi, 2003: 23).

These then are just three examples of researchers who have focused primarily on the *content* of their narrative evidence. They have been chosen, in part, to demonstrate that a narrative approach to research can be used with very different sample sizes and also to show that in this field the usual distinction made between qualitative and quantitative research is not always a particularly telling one. In addition, using Lieblich et al.'s framework, described above, it can be seen that whereas Franzosi's approach to analysis might be described as categorical, the life history approach taken by researchers within the Chicago school, and the approach to understanding bakers' careers used by Bertaux and Bertaux-Wiame, is better characterized as an holistic approach to analysis.

What unites these pieces of work is not so much the precise analytic methods or techniques they use, but rather their orientation to narrative as providing a relatively accurate description of events or experiences through time. In each case therefore the analysis focuses on what the substantive elements of the accounts tell us about the social world.

Analyses focusing on the form or structure of narratives

Over the past decade or so, the analysis of narratives in the social sciences has shifted away from an exclusive interest in their content. Analyses focus as much on the ways in which story-tellers, and the conditions of story-telling, shape what is conveyed as on what the content of those stories tells us about people's lives. As will be demonstrated below, researchers who are interested in examining the form or structure of narratives draw upon a wealth of material, available from within the fields of socio-linguistics and literary studies, to develop methods and procedures to help in the analysis of their data. Indeed, one of the interesting challenges here is to borrow from other disciplines while retaining a sociological focus to the research.

Labov and Waletzky's structural model of narrative

Perhaps the most obvious starting point for any analysis of narrative data that is interested in the *form* of those narratives is the often-cited structural model of narratives proposed by the American socio-linguists Labov and Waletzky in the late 1960s. As Riessman (1993) has argued, by beginning with the structure or form of the narrative, researchers can avoid reading simply for content. Coffey and Atkinson (1996) also advocate Labov and Waletzky's framework as a basis for the sociological examination of individual narratives. They argue that it is helpful because it provides an analytic perspective both on how the narrative is structured and on the functions of different elements within the story.

As was discussed in Chapter 1, Labov and Waletzky (1967) argued that narratives have formal structural properties and that the patterns which recur in narratives can be identified and used to analyse each element of the account. They described fully formed narratives as having six separate elements: these were outlined in Chapter 1 but are reproduced in Box 3.1.

Box 3.1   Labov and Waletzky's structural model of narrative form

Abstract	Summary of the subject matter
Orientation	Information about the setting: time, place, situation, participants
Complicating action	What actually happened, what happened next
Evaluation	What the events mean to the narrator
Resolution	How it all ended
Coda	Returns the perspective to the present

Although the most minimal narrative might be though of as comprising only the complicating action, which provides the basic chronological structure, the evaluative element is arguably what transforms a simple chronicle of events into a fully formed narrative. As is indicated in the summary above, the evaluation demonstrates what meaning events have for the narrator and makes the point or purpose of the story clear to the audience. It is because the evaluative dimension of a narrative provides an insight into how the narrator has chosen to interpret the events recounted that these evaluative elements can be of particular interest for sociologists in the hermeneutic tradition. Indeed, in his work on primary school teachers, Cortazzi calls his model of narrative analysis, which is based on the Labov and Waletzky structure, 'the evaluation model of narrative analysis' (1991). There is an important link between an interest in these evaluative elements of narratives and a commitment to a humanist sociology which prioritizes 'understanding' or *Verstehen*. As was discussed above, an hermeneutic approach to the social sciences emphasizes the importance of empathizing with the subjects of research and developing a detailed understanding and appreciation of how they make sense of the social world. Identifying and then examining the evaluative elements within individuals' stories therefore provides a practical tool to help with this process of empathy.

In the following example from my own research, a relatively short narrative section from a biographical interview with a British graduate woman in her forties is presented (Box 3.2). The interviewee is giving an account of the period in her life when her mother was seriously ill and died. This is presented using a method of transcription based on James Gee's work on the units of discourse, which will be discussed in detail below.

Box 3.2   Extract from a biographical interview with a British graduate woman

1	I: You said she'd had the cancer?
2A	R: Well, she died of cancer.
3A	This period all was really quite hellish,
4Ca	because they (i.e. health professionals) told us at one point that she had nine months to live,
5Ca	and um... then they told us they'd made a mistake,
6Ca	she was completely clear of cancer,
7Ca	she didn't have any cancer.
8Ca	And then in 1991, 9th February,
9Ca	they told her she had one month to live,
10R/Ca	and she died exactly a month after that.

(Continued)

> **Box 3.2** *(Continued)*
>
> 11E So it was toing and froing,
> 12E it was four o'clock in the morning phone calls,
> 13E it was a lot of crying
> 14E and leaping down to Wolverhampton
> 15E and staying at the hospice
> 16E and it was – it was horrible.
> 17E It was just awful really.
>
> 18R And then that wasn't even the worst of it.
> 19R The worst of it was living without her.
> 20C You know, the huge gap that's left in your life
> 21C when somebody dies.
>
> **Key: A = abstract; O = orientation; Ca = Complicating action;
> E = evaluation; R = resolution; C = coda**

Using Labov and Waletzky's structural model of narrative, it can be seen that in response to the interviewer's question the interviewee provides an abstract for the narrative in lines 2 and 3. It is not easy to identify any orientation here, but it could be argued that the orientation has already been established by earlier parts of the interview. The complicating action is provided by lines 4 to 9, and line 10 may provisionally be understood to provide the resolution to the narrative, i.e. the death of the interviewee's mother. The evaluative statements in lines 11 to 17 therefore initially appear to disrupt Labov and Waletzky's model, which suggests that the evaluation usually creates narrative tension by appearing just before the resolution. However, it could be argued that the resolution to this story is not actually the death of the interviewee's mother in line 10 but rather the acute sense of loss expressed in line 19, 'the worst of it was living without her.' Lines 20 and 21 then round off the narrative and return the perspective to the present. This can be understood as the coda of the narrative and the change in perspective can be seen both from the use of the colloquialism 'you know', which refers to the inter-viewer, and also from the phrase 'when somebody dies', which shifts the focus from the specific loss of the interviewee's mother to a more universal statement about bereavement in general.

At first sight, lines 11 to 17 of this narrative might be argued to be part of the com-plicating action, rather than being evaluative elements as I have suggested above. Indeed students who have examined this narrative in the context of workshops on qualitative analysis have sometimes suggested that lines 11 to 17 must be part of the complicating action because they continue the theme of 'what happened' at the time when the interviewee's mother was ill. However, the counter-argument would be that whereas in lines 4 to 10 the order of what happened is crucial to the sense of the story, lines 11 to 17 could occur in any order without substantially affecting the meaning of what is said. In other words, there is a much stronger sense of chronology in lines 4 to 10 than in lines 11 to 17. In addition, it is interesting to note the change in tense from the simple past in lines 4 to 10, i.e. 'they told', 'she died', to the rather ungrammatical use of the past continuous in lines 11 to 17, e.g. 'it was a lot of crying and leaping down'.

A rather shorter example of a narrative, taken from Cortazzi's study of primary school teachers (Cortazzi, 1991), is reproduced below in Box 3.3. Once again, the elements of the narrative structure are marked using Labov and Waletzky's framework.

Box 3.3   Teachers narrative extract from Cortazzi (1991: 18 and 92)

A	I've got quite a nice bunch at the moment
A	They have got a very nice sense of humour
O	But one...I think it was one day last term
Ca	I put a row of fossils out, animal fossils
Ca	And I put '120 million years old'
Ca	And as one of the kids walked by
R	He started [singing] 'Happy Birthday to you'
E	That's the sort of sense of humour they have got
E	It just sort of kills me. It kills me.

Key: A = abstract; O = orientation; Ca = Complicating action; E = evaluation; R = resolution; C = coda

---

Cortazzi uses this as an example of a humorous narrative underlining the emphasis given by teachers to the frequency of funny incidents that occur in primary teaching. He describes how the resolution was 'performed' as the narrator imitated the child's 'Happy Birthday' song by singing it, and suggests that the evaluation demonstrates the pleasure that the teacher derives from the children's humour. It is interesting to note that this is a very simple short narrative, and, although Cortazzi chooses the example to demonstrate how he applies Labov and Waletzky's framework, it does not fully conform to their model. First, the orientation is relatively undeveloped, the time referent is vague, and the place and context are not made explicit (presumably because in the context of the interview it is clear that the teacher is talking about the classroom and relations between teachers and pupils). Second, the complicating action is very simple; arguably it is barely a narrative as there is no extended chain of events, simply an action by the teacher (displaying some fossils) and a reaction on the part of one of the children. A final deviation from Labov and Waletzky's model is that the evaluation occurs at the end of the narrative rather than prior to the resolution.

Given the frequency with which Labov and Waletzky's work is cited and discussed by those with an interest in narrative, it is interesting that there are relatively few empirical studies that actually adopt their complete structural framework as a guide for analysis.[2] Mishler (1997) has suggested that one of the reasons for the initial popularity of their approach is that it provided for social scientists, who were keen to escape positivism and focus on the interpretation of qualitative material, a kind of 'positivism with a human face' (Mishler, 1997: 72). However, he stresses that there are a number of limitations to simply applying their original structural model to the analysis of interview material. First, within life history interviews respondents rarely provide strictly chronological accounts. Second, a great deal of the material in interviews has a story-like form but does not strictly consist of a sequence of event clauses (Riessman, 1990), and, third, interviews often include a whole set of different narratives leading to problems identifying the boundaries between them.

Thinking back to the distinction that was made above between examining the narratives that occur within interviews and understanding a whole interview (particularly a life history or work history interview) as a narrative, it is clear that the structural model of narrative form described by Labov and Waletzky can be useful in analysing short sections of interviews in which narratives occur, but is arguably of less utility when examining an interview more holistically.

There are two main strategies that have been outlined in relation to a more holistic analysis of the form of narratives (Lieblich et al., 1998). The first involves categorizing narratives using a typology or genre borrowed from literature (such as epic, comedy, or tragedy). The second focuses on the direction of the plot, whether it is progressive, regressive, or follows a steady line. These are both discussed below.

Genre

The concept of 'genre' is a further analytic resource that can be borrowed from literary studies by sociologists with an interest in examining the form of narratives in their research. Genre can be broadly defined as a pattern of narrative and imagery. Genres can be understood as providing a framework that is culturally shared and can therefore be used to structure events and experiences so that they are meaningful and easily communicated. As Todorov puts it, '(genres) function as "horizons of expectation" for readers and as "models of writing" for authors' (1990 [1978]: 10). For those unfamiliar with the genres typically used in works of literature, Riessman (1991) helpfully suggests that the concept of genre can be understood in relation to films. For example, the way that heroes and villains are depicted in the classic Hollywood western is rather different from the way that they are depicted in a horror movie, a science fiction movie, or a documentary film. These can all be seen as different genres within film-making. Examples of important genres in literature include the romance, the comedy, the tragedy, and the satire. To this could be added further examples found in literature or film such as the Gothic novel, horror, the detective story, the melodrama, the parable, the fable, etc.

An awareness of these different genres can provide an additional analytic tool when analysing interview narratives or other types of narrative discourse. For example, in research on the portrayal of AIDS/HIV in health promotion literature, journalism, and film, Williamson (1989) suggests that many journalistic representations of the virus can be understood as fitting within the genre of Gothic horror. In particular, the frequent reference to AIDS as a 'killer disease' as opposed to a mortal, deadly, or fatal disease animates the disease as if it is a monster. Accompanying this, Williamson argues that the idea that the disease 'claims victims' provides a type of narrative closure and is suggestive that those who suffer from AIDS have been invisibly chosen in some predetermined way. Williamson suggests that both of these linguistic devices bring the discourse around AIDS close to the Gothic horror form with which many people are familiar. This is one way in which accounts about AIDS/HIV try to make sense of the disease and incorporate it into pre-existing meaning structures within society (Williamson, 1989).

In a very different piece of research, Murray (1989) examines narratives about individuals' decisions to enter a marathon race, and classifies them with reference to the genres of comedy and romance. Murray characterizes the comic genre as emphasizing the victory of youth and desire over age and death, defining success in terms of a restoration of sociability or the social order. Whereas, in contrast, the romantic genre emphasizes individual responsibility and the goal is the 'restoration of an honoured past through a series of events that involve a struggle – typically including a crucial test – between a hero and forces of evil' (Murray, 1989: 182). Murray contrasts two specific narratives to exemplify the differences between the 'romantic' and 'comic' forms which he found in the interview narratives. In his analysis the use of genre is helpful in that it allows him to see patterns and similarities across the interviews that might otherwise have all appeared to be just so many different individual stories. Classification of his interview narratives using genre helps him to theorize about two rather different meanings that an activity such as marathon running can have in the lives of individuals.

While authors such as Murray and Williamson have explicitly borrowed the terminology of literary genres, these are clearly not the only cultural resources which narrators use to frame their experiences. For example, Squire (1999) focuses on the links between narratives about HIV and the 'coming out' genre, which she defines as a twentieth-century, largely western autobiographical form that 'documents the recognition, conflict, and acceptance of gay identity' (1999: 113). Plummer (1995) also identifies the genre of 'coming out' stories and examines the differences and similarities in the form of these stories in comparison to what he terms 'rape stories' and 'sexual recovery stories'.

Focusing on the genre adopted in the telling of a narrative therefore represents a further device that the researcher can use to attempt to discern how the narrator wishes the events and experiences that are being recounted to be interpreted. Genres can also be understood as representing some of the cultural resources that are available to individuals as they try to make sense of their lives. Analysis of the genres used by individuals as they recount their life stories can therefore be seen as a technique for understanding the cultural frameworks available to individuals in specific historical and societal contexts.

The dynamics of plot development: progressive and regressive narratives

A second strategy for the holistic analysis of the form of life stories, which is closely linked to the use of genre in narrative analysis, is to focus on the development of the plot over time (Gergen and Gergen, 1983; Lieblich et al., 1998). Using Gergen and Gergen's original formulation, Lieblich et al. explain that whereas in a progressive narrative the focus of the story is on advancement, achievement, and success, in a regressive narrative there is a course of deterioration or decline, while in the stable narrative there is no evidence of either progression or decline. Using this framework, life stories can be conceptualized as a series of chapters, each of which can be characterized by the direction of the plot. Lieblich et al. also demonstrate how a life course graph can be constructed for each individual, which illustrates the patterns of ascent, decline, and stability in the narrative of their life. To do this they look in turn at the different phases of the life course, defined as childhood, adolescence, young adulthood, etc. This then provides a practical method by which the transcript of a biographical interview may be analysed.

Narrative coherence

A further defining feature of narrative, discussed in Chapter 1, which can also be used to inform techniques of narrative analysis, is the concept of narrative coherence. As authors such as White and Ricoeur have emphasized, a narrative is more than just a succession of chronological events. A narrative must add up to something; it is more than the sum of its parts. In Ricoeur's terms a narrative has a 'configurational' as well as an episodic dimension (1981). It is this configurational dimension which allows the narrative to be comprehended as a unified whole, and it is this that makes coherent narratives intuitively satisfying.

The psychologists Baerger and McAdams provide a practical definition of coherence for use with the analysis of life stories as follows:

> A life story is coherent to the extent that it:
> 1) Locates the narrative in a specific temporal, social and personal context... 2) displays the structural elements of an episode system... 3) conveys an evaluative or reportable point, or series of such points about the speaker in such a way as to give the story emotional significance; and 4) imparts information in an integrated manner, ultimately communicating the meaning of the experiences described within the context of the larger life story. (1999: 74–5)

The first three parts of this definition clearly correspond closely to the elements of fully formed narratives as defined by Labov and Waletzky, and it is the fourth prerequisite for coherence that perhaps relates most directly to Ricoeur's notion of the configurational aspect of narrative. Baerger and McAdams' research was primarily concerned with the relationship between narrative coherence in the life story and mental health. They applied their definition to measuring coherence in a sample of life stories, collected from fifty adults using in-depth interviews, and in addition they used well-validated self-rating scales to measure happiness, satisfaction with life, and depression. By using standard statistical techniques such as regression and correlation Baerger and McAdams demonstrated that, as they had predicted, life story coherence was significantly associated with psychological well-being. This then is a further example of research that demonstrates that an interest in narrative does not rule out the use of traditional quantitative statistical procedures.

A rather different approach to the analysis of coherence in life stories is taken by Linde (1993). She introduces the concept of the 'coherence system'. This is defined as 'a discursive practice that represents a system of beliefs and relations between beliefs; it provides the environment in which one statement may or may not be taken as the cause of another statement' (Linde, 1993: 163). Linde identifies a number of different coherence systems within her interview data. These include popular Freudian psychology, behaviourist psychology, astrology, feminism, and catholicism. Each of these coherence systems lies somewhere between the specialist or expert domain and the common sense which can be expected to be shared by all members of a particular culture. They could therefore be understood as popular versions of expert theories.

Linde argues that a coherence system provides extra resources for creating narrative linkages by allowing causal connections that would not be available using only common sense. For example, using popular Freudian psychology, personality difficulties in adult life can be related back to early childhood experiences. However, in the very act of making those causal connections the narrator invokes the coherence system and indicates the framework within which he or she is interpreting his or her life. This can therefore create a global coherence for the narrative as a whole.[3]

Linde (1993) argues that the discovery of these coherence systems in individual life stories has implications for further research. She suggests both that it would be useful to look at the range of coherence systems available to individuals within specific historical and cultural contexts and also that it would be informative to develop a better understanding of the link between expert forms of coherence systems and their popular offshoots.

Narrative analysis that focuses on both content and form

Although all the examples of research discussed in the previous section have adopted analytic techniques focused on the form of narratives, this is not to say that they have ignored their content. Rather an examination of the way a narrative has been put together is used in conjunction with looking at the content of narratives in order to understand what meaning is made of specific events and experiences. One very formalized approach which more explicitly examines the specific relation between the form and content of narratives in the context of bio-graphical interviews is the Biographic–Narrative–Interpretive Method (BNIM). This has been developed by a group of researchers at the University of East London, Centre for Biography and Social Policy (Chamberlayne and Rustin, 1999; Chamberlayne et al., 2000). A very detailed, practical account of this approach is provided by Wengraf (2001) and it will not therefore be discussed at length here. However, what is distinctive about the method is that it advocates producing a summary of the content of a biographical interview (i.e. the 'life lived') and a separate summary of the form of the biography as told in the interview, and then requires the analyst to examine the connection between these analytic docu-ments in order to produce a case history documenting theories about how the two are related. Some examples of the application of this approach can be found in Chamberlayne et al. (2000).

Narrative in its social context

As has been shown above, a focus on the content and the form of narrative research material provides a helpful entry point to a consideration of the types of narrative analysis that can be applied to qualitative data. However, there is an important aspect of narrative so far overlooked, namely the performative or social dimension. This is the third element of the framework proposed by Mishler (1995), discussed above. As Plummer has argued, a sociological approach to narrative 'does not stay at the level of textual analysis: it insists that story production and consumption is an empir-ical social process involving a stream of joint actions in local contexts themselves bound into wider negotiated social worlds' (1995: 24). As Plummer indicates, within this third area of narrative research, two rather different approaches can be identified. First, there are those who are most interested in the 'stream of joint actions in local contexts', i.e. researchers who focus on specific interactions between individuals as they narrate and attend to stories. This work borrows heavily from the analytic tools of socio-linguists and conversation analysts. The emphasis is on how individuals 'do narrative' in the micro-contexts of everyday life: in work organiza-tions (Boje, 1991), around the family dinner table (Ochs and Taylor, 1995), in gen-eral conversation (Polanyi, 1985), and in the playground (Goodwin, 1997). Second, there are sociologists whose focus is on how narratives are 'bound into wider nego-tiated social worlds'. Plummer himself fits best within this second approach. He uses the area of 'sexual stories', e.g. 'coming out' stories, rape stories, and 'recovery stories' about sexual issues more generally, to explore the social role that stories can play – the functions of such stories in the lives of individuals and within society more generally. In particular, he raises questions about how new types or 'genres' of stories emerge around a topic that was previously hidden from view. He argues that stories can be used to maintain the status quo, but can also have an emancipatory function transforming individual lives and the wider culture.

It is difficult to provide a separate summary of distinct analytic techniques used by researchers adopting either of these two approaches to the analysis of the social functions of narrative. In the first case the methods used are broadly congruent with the methods of other ethnomethodologists with an interest in the way that people accomplish verbal communication in everyday life (Drew and Herritage, 1992; Sacks, 1974). In some senses it can be argued that this is not a specifically narrative approach, it is simply that the focus of the study is the narrative rather than some other form of discourse.

In the second case the analytic focus is altogether different, in that what is being attempted is an analysis of society that focuses on the role of narratives and their contribution to the cultural fabric of society. In both cases researchers have tended to use concepts discussed in the previous section on the structure of narrative to inform their analysis. For example, Plummer uses the concept of genre to show the similarities between the rather different sexual stories that he discusses.

Preparing and transcribing data

In some respects it may seem strange that a section on organizing and transcribing narratives appears at the end of a chapter on the analysis of qualitative material rather than at the beginning. After all, the task of transcribing clearly comes at the beginning of the analytic process. However, it is important to recognize that the transcription process is more than a trivial, mechanical task and that decisions about how transcription should be carried out are intimately connected with the type of analysis that is intended. Indeed rather than understanding the transcription process as occurring prior to analysis it is more appropriate to understand it as part of the analytic process (Silverman, 1993; Wengraf, 2001). It is therefore helpful to have in mind some of the different approaches to the analysis of narrative material when considering what type of transcription should be undertaken.

It is now widely recognized that it is all but impossible to produce a transcription of a research interview, or any other type of conversation, which completely captures all of the meaning that was communicated in the encounter itself. Any transcription of speech must therefore be understood as a compromise. The more detail that is supplied in the transcription, the more clues are provided which may be important in interpretation. However, if a mass of detail is preserved the process of attending to it will slow up the reading of the text in a highly artificial manner (Brown, 1995). In most cases, the aim when transcribing in-depth interviews is to find a method for preserving some of the additional meaning that was conveyed by the speaker's use of intonation, pauses, rhythm, hesitation, and body language. Given the difficulty of producing a textual representation of *all* of these different factors, the researcher's particular analytical interests are likely to determine which speech practices are preserved and attended to in the transcription process (Chase, 1995b).

In order to demonstrate the range of possibilities for transcription, three contrasting examples will be outlined below which represent very different solutions to the dilemmas posed by the transcription process. First, the possibility of 'cleaning up' speech will be discussed; second, by way of contrast, the detailed transcription conventions used by conversation analysts will be briefly introduced. This type of transcription will not be discussed in detail, however, as it is covered very fully in several existing texts on research methods (Poland, 1995; Silverman, 1993; Wengraf, 2001). Finally a method of transcription based on James Gee's work on 'units of discourse' will be presented; this has been found to be particularly suited to the presentation of narratives in research.

Clean transcripts

Transcribing practices can be understood as ranging from those that attempt to record every detail of the verbal interaction to those that aim to preserve only the words which were spoken. At one extreme then, some researchers choose not to record any of the extra verbal material captured on the research tape such as pauses, intonation, etc., and in addition may remove repetition, false starts, and non-lexical utterances such as 'umms' and 'errs'. Providing a 'clean' or 'sanitized' transcript arguably focuses on the content of what was said. It makes the material easy to read, although it provides no extra information as to the manner in which it was communicated. A good illustration of this approach is provided by this quotation from Richardson's book *The New Other Woman*:

> When I met him I asked was he divorced or married. He lied. He kept lying. It was six months before I finally figured out that this guy was not even separated. For three and a half years he kept telling me he was working on the divorce. He was doing nothing. (1985: 137)

In this short extract, the combination of the short sentences 'He lied' and 'He kept lying' together with the phrase 'I finally figured out' brings the quotation to life and gives it the feel of spoken rather than written text. However, as anyone who has listened to a taped interview can testify, in reality people do not speak exactly like this. Richardson has clearly edited the transcript or at least tidied it up by adding appropriate punctuation, removing pauses and false starts, and editing out the messy features of everyday speech. Richardson does not explicitly discuss her approach to transcribing, although she includes many different quotations from her interviewees that serve to bring the book to life. She does, however, explain in the introduction that the book is intended for a general audience, as well as being of interest to an academic readership. This intention certainly makes sense of the manner in which she presents her data; cleaning the transcript up has certainly made it accessible to the lay reader.[4] In research which focuses solely on the content of narratives told within interviews this approach to transcription may well be appropriate in that it will capture the chronology of events that are being recounted and also some of the evaluative elements, whether these are explicit evaluative statements or embedded in the precise words chosen by the narrator. However, those who are interested in the function of narratives and how they are 'performed' by narrators in specific social contexts are more likely to adopt an approach to transcription which preserves greater information.

Detailed transcribing: conversation analysis

At the other end of the spectrum, when the focus is not solely on the content of the narrative but the way that a narrative is recounted is also salient, it is important to record the delivery of speech more faithfully. Formal notation systems for recording and preserving the way in which words were delivered have been developed by ethnomethodologists within the school of conversation analysis. In particular the transcription procedures established by Gail Jefferson are perhaps those most commonly used (see Atkinson and Heritage, 1984: ix–xvi). A simplified set of transcription symbols based on Jefferson's notation is provided by Silverman (1993) and this has been reproduced and further simplified by a number of other sociologists writing on transcription (e.g. Poland, 1995; Wengraf, 2001). Given that this rigorous method of transcription has been fully discussed elsewhere it would be redundant to reproduce the full set of transcription symbols or describe the technique at length. However, it is helpful to provide an example of this approach and in particular to link it to the study of narrative evidence. The example reproduced in Box 3.4 is taken from Ochs and Taylor's study of conversational narratives among two-parent middle-class American families with a 5-year-old child. Ochs and Taylor (1995) videotaped and audiotaped families having dinner. As can be seen in the box, this means that non-verbal communication (such as facial expressions etc.) is also captured and can be included in the transcript. Ochs and Taylor use the extract reproduced below to demonstrate the role of the mother in eliciting and introducing a narrative to be told by the young child to her father.

Box 3.4   An extract from a family conversation

Mom: ((to Jodie)) =oh:: You know what? You wanna tell Daddy what happened to you today?=

Dad: ((looking up and off)) =tell me everything that happened from the moment you went in – until:

            [

Jodie: I got a sho:t?

Dad: =EH ((gasping)) what? ((frowning))

Jodie: I got a sho::t

                [

Dad: *no*

Notation

oh::   colons are used to indicate prolongation of the prior sound; the number of colons indicates the extent to which the sound is prolonged

(Continued)

Box 3.4   (*Continued*)

EH   underscoring indicates stress on the word and capitalization indicates louder or shouted talk

[left square brackets indicate where one person's speech is interrupted by the next person's speech

(())   double parentheses enclose non-verbal and other descriptive information

=   equals signs link utterances by different speakers showing there is no pause between them

?   a question mark indicates rising intonation as a syllable or word ends

Source: Ochs and Taylor (1995: 101)

In the research carried out by Ochs and Taylor the focus was on the roles of mother, father, and children in the collaborative activity of recounting narratives around the dinner table. They analyse the videotaped interactions to show how mothers frequently act as the initiators of narratives that place the father in the role of audience or recipient and also allow the father to take up the role of evaluator of other people's actions and feelings. In this type of research, where the focus is on naturally occurring narratives (rather than those produced in an interview), it is clearly the social function of the narrative which is as important as its content or form. It is specifically in this type of research that this more detailed method of transcription is appropriate as the emphasis is on capturing as much as possible of the interaction between people.

Transcribing using Gee's units of discourse

An approach to transcription, which perhaps could be understood as lying somewhere between the two extremes outlined above, has been used by a number of researchers with an interest in the narrative elements of qualitative interviews. It is informed by the work of James Gee, a socio-linguist who has worked on the structure of oral language. Gee suggests that despite the variation in discursive styles between individuals of different ages and from different cultural backgrounds, the basic units of discourse that organize its structure are maintained. Using Gee's framework, the smallest unit of discourse is the 'line'. Each 'line' is made up of a short sequence of words comprising one 'idea unit'. The ends of lines are typically marked by the speaker with a short pause and a fall in the pitch of the voice. Within an oral performance these 'lines' are typically grouped together to form stanzas; these can be understood as similar to stanzas in poetry. The lines within a stanza will often display a parallel structure so that they match each other in terms of content or topic. Once again the breaks between stanzas are usually marked by a longer pause on the part of the speaker. Gee states that: 'Stanzas crucially look both ways: they organize the lines of the texts while at the same time they constitute the internal structure of the sections' (1986: 401). The larger unit or the section is what we might think of as an episode within a longer narrative. The beginning of a new section is often marked by a good number of hesitations and false starts.

By applying Gee's typology of the different units within a discourse it is possible to produce a transcript which preserves some of the rhythm and structure which characterizes speech. This is a practical alternative to inserting punctuation marks which indicate pauses dictated by grammatical rules. As Portelli (1991) has argued, conventional punctuation rarely coincides with the rhythms and pauses of speech and can therefore suppress the emotional style and content of the interview. As will be shown below, by identifying the lines, stanzas, and sections within an oral narrative it is possible to produce a written version of speech, which invokes the pauses and breaks within the discourse without using the very detailed, but potentially distracting, notation used in conversation analysis. The extract in Box 3.5 is taken from a biographical interview with a British graduate woman in her early forties from my research. She had explained earlier in the interview that she had been pregnant with twins but one of them was stillborn. The transcript was produced by listening carefully to the tape and attending to the pauses marking the end of lines and longer pauses marking the end of a stanza. It can also be seen that the repetitions and false starts have been preserved so that the spoken nature of the text is as clear as possible.

Box 3.5   Example of James Gee's unit of discourse approach applied to interview data

1.   Um, now I had Katherine in December 1996,
2.   and er so a lot of the last two years
3.   has been spent very much focused on
4.   I suppose two parallel things really.
5.   One, looking after Katherine, er, and
6.   the other one is,
7.   is finding a way of grieving at the same time,
8.   but separate from Katherine mostly.

9.   I'm not saying she's never seen me cry,
10.   but I didn't want her childhood
11.   to be ruined by my grief,
12.   um, and I didn't – also didn't want
13.   her to be totally shielded from that, because, after all,
14.   she's involved in that grief,
15.   because she lost a sister.

Source: Elliott (2001: 237)

However, one way in which the transcribed extract has been subtly cleaned up is that we only have a record of what *the interviewee* said. The interviewer has been edited out completely, even though we would expect that the tape also recorded a number of what are usually referred to as 'back channel utterances', i.e. where the interviewer uses words such as 'right' or utterances such as 'mmhhmm' to indicate that the interviewee should continue and is being listened to. It is noteworthy how common it is for researchers to edit the interviewer out of transcripts or more specifically out of the extracts of transcripts that are used in books, chapters, and journal articles.

As has been discussed above, the interest of the majority of social scientists who study narratives is not *purely* in talk as social action and therefore the very precise transcription conventions used within conversation analysis are not always appropriate. The style of transcription advocated by Gee has a practical analytic spin-off in that, by breaking the text into relatively small units, it focuses attention on the precise detail of what is said, lexical choices, use of metaphor, and repetition. When used in conjunction with Labov and Waletzky's structural models of the functional elements of narratives, it allows the researcher to look at each text fragment and decide whether it corresponds to one of the elements of narrative identified by Labov and Waletzky. In addition, the presentation of an interview transcript in this more poetic format is immediately suggestive of an analysis that attends to the use of particular words and metaphors and their contribution to the meaning of what is said. Giving extracts from an interview the form of a poem is also an important reminder that analysis of this type of material is always something of a subjective process and that more than one interpretation is possible. Examples of this type of transcription can be found in the work of Day-Sclater who has used it in her analysis of the narratives of couples going through the process of separation and divorce (Day-Sclater, 1998a; 1998b). Mishler also relies on Gee's model and uses relatively long extracts from his interviews with craft workers in his book *Storylines: Craft Artists' Narratives of Identity* (Mishler, 1999). Interestingly he modifies Gee's framework for transcribing by introducing some of the notation used in conversation analysis (as discussed above) and explicitly includes his utterances as the interviewer.

A major disadvantage of this style of transcription, however, is the amount of time it takes to listen to a tape and identify the beginning and end of lines and stanzas. Inevitably there will be sections of any interview that are less relevant or salient to the research question or where the content of what is being communicated is felt to be much more important than the way it is said. It is therefore unlikely that this technique of transcription would ever be used by a researcher to transcribe the whole of an interview. Rather it is generally more appropriate for use with short sections that the interviewer has already identified as being of specific interest and needing particular analytic attention.

Summary

At the beginning of this chapter it was emphasized that the explosion of interest in the concept of narrative over the past two decades has generated a diversity of analytic methods and techniques that can be applied to textual data. This chapter has therefore introduced a number of different ways in which an interest in narrative can inform the analysis of interviews and other textual research material. It has been argued that the work on narrative that has been carried out in the disciplines of socio-linguistics and literary studies provides a resource that can be tapped by researchers who wish to develop techniques and devices for looking at their research material in new ways. In particular, in recent years researchers have been attending to the form or structure of narratives rather than simply focusing on their content. However, it has also been argued that an interest in narrative and the use of textual evidence does not prevent the use of quantitative techniques. Whereas the term 'qualitative approach' is often used to imply both an interest in qualitative data and the rejection of statistical methods of analysis, it is clear from the work of researchers such as Franzosi, and Baerger and McAdams, that the use of statistics is perfectly compatible with certain types of analysis of qualitative material. Indeed, as will be demonstrated in Chapter 5, it is also possible to apply qualitative analytic techniques to the analysis of quantitative survey data (Singer et al., 1998).

In the final section of the chapter, three rather different approaches to transcription have been described. It has been emphasized that transcription is more than a simple or routine task and that it should be understood as an important part of the analytic process. The difficulty of producing a written text which is readable and which preserves the meaning communicated in the original interview or conversation has been stressed. As a possible practical solution to this problem a method of transcribing and presenting interview data based on James Gee's work on 'units of discourse' has been outlined. This has been used successfully by a number of researchers with an interest in narrative.

Further reading

Lieblich, A. et al. (1998) *Narrative Research: Reading, Analysis, and Interpretation.* Thousand Oaks, CA: Sage.

Linde, C. (1993) *Life Stories: The Creation of Coherence.* Oxford: Oxford University Press.

Plummer, K. (1995) *Telling Sexual Stories: Power, change, and social worlds.* London: Routledge.

Poland, B. (1995) 'Transcription quality as an aspect of rigor in qualitative research', *Qualitative Inquiry*, 1 (3): 290–310.

Silverman, D. (1993) *Interpreting Qualitative Data: Methods for Analysing Talk, Text and Interaction.* London: Sage.

Wengraf, T. (2001) *Qualitative Research Interviewing: Biographic Narrative and Semi-Structured Methods.* London: Sage.

Readings for discussion

Bertaux, D. and Bertaux-Wiame, I. (1981) 'Life stories and the bakers' trade', in D. Bertaux (ed.), *Biography and Society: The Life History Approach in the Social Sciences.* Beverley Hills, CA: Sage. pp.169–90.

Gubrium, J.F. and Holstein, J.A. (1998) 'Narrative practice and the coherence of personal stories', *The Sociological Quarterly*, 39 (1): 163–87.

Squire, C. (1999). '"Neighbours who might become friends": selves, genres and citizenship in narratives of HIV', *The Sociological Quarterly*, 40 (1): 109–37.

1   *Do Gubrium and Holstein demonstrate that 'narrative production in conversation is necessarily collaborative'? What are the different ways in which the 'audience' for a narrative shapes the way that it is told?*
2   *How helpful is Gubrium and Holstein's concept of 'analytic bracketing' for undertaking analysis which attends to both the content and form of narratives?*
3   *What are the main differences between the type of analysis of narratives carried out by Squire and Bertaux and Bertaux-Wiame?*
4   *What methods of transcription has Squire used in the interview extracts she presents? How effective are these for capturing the form and performance of the narratives she discusses?*

Notes

1   The concept of a 'collective story' originates in the work of Laurel Richardson and is not a term used by Bertaux and Bertaux-Wiame. However, it seems particularly appropriate here.
2   It seems to be the concept of the evaluation within the narrative, which is most frequently focused upon by those whose work is informed by Labov and Waletzky.
3   Agar and Hobbs suggest that there are three different kinds of coherence, which they label global coherence, local coherence, and themal coherence. For any segment of text within an account or a narrative, its *global coherence* can be defined as its relation to the speaker's overall goal or plan in speaking. Its *local coherence* can be defined as its relationship to neighbouring sections of text, and its *themal coherence* refers to its relation to other segments of text within the whole narrative which exemplify similar themes. It is therefore the themes, which can be found to figure again and again within accounts, that form the basis for themal coherence. As Agar and Hobbs write:

If global coherence gives us a top-down view of the production of extended talk, local coherence gives us a bottom-up view. The requirements of global coherence say, 'Given the overall goals I am trying to accomplish, what can I say next that will serve them?' Local coherence says, 'given what I just said, what can I say that is related to it?' For the most part, what is said next will satisfy both sets of requirements. (1982: 7)

4   An interesting discussion of the political implications of presenting quotations from interviews in this way is provided by Standing (1998).

Collecting quantitative narratives – a contradiction in terms?

In comparison with the explosion of interest, over the past decade, in the prevalence of narratives within *qualitative* data, there has been far less attention to the possibility of locating or producing narratives within the different types of *quantitative* data collected using survey methods. There is a growing awareness of the importance of the *temporal* dimension of social life, both in research focusing on the life course (Giele and Elder, 1998) and in the development of event history techniques for the analysis of longitudinal quantitative data (Allison, 1984; Dale and Davies, 1994; Yamaguchi, 1991). However, few authors make explicit links between their methodologies and the *narrative* characteristics of the data or the analyses that are produced (although exceptions such as Abbott and Singer will be discussed in Chapter 5). In contrast to the previous chapters, which focused on the collection and analysis of qualitative data, these next two chapters will therefore explore the narrative potential within the collection and analysis of more structured or *quantitative* longitudinal data about people's lives. In Chapters 6 and 7 this discussion will be extended to consider how longitudinal research can help in the understanding of causal relationships between variables, and also to explore the role of the individual in quantitative and qualitative analysis.

For some readers the notion that quantitative survey data bear any resemblance to the qualitative biographical data discussed in the previous two chapters may be surprising or even perplexing. However, by using the concept of narrative to think in more detail about the properties of qualitative and quantitative data, it will be possible to develop a better understanding of the precise nature of the similarities and differences between qualitative and quantitative evidence. Some authors have stressed the rich nature of qualitative data in comparison with less detailed quantitative data (e.g. Becker, 1996). In addition, qualitative data have been argued to take better account of contextual factors, largely ignored by quantitative studies (Watson, 1993). One aim of the next two chapters is to demonstrate that this conceptualization of the distinction between qualitative and quantitative evidence is somewhat oversimplistic. In particular, once the in-depth comprehensive nature of the data collected in many longitudinal studies is recognized, it is clear that some quantitative research may contain *more* detailed information about individuals than many qualitative studies.

Before turning to a consideration of the narrative properties of quantitative longitudinal data and the narrative potential of different approaches to analysis, it is helpful to start by providing a review of the different types of quantitative longitudinal data that are currently available in North America and Europe. The first section of this chapter will therefore have two principal aims: first, to discuss the main approaches used for the collection of longitudinal data; and second, to introduce some of the main longitudinal datasets currently available for analysis in North America, Britain, and the rest of Europe. In addition to the brief discussion of different longitudinal surveys included in this chapter, the Appendix provides further details of major datasets that are currently being used by sociologists and other social scientists with an interest in longitudinal data for examining individual change over time. The second section of the chapter looks in more detail at the collection and accuracy of event history data before discussing the extent to which these types of data can be understood to have narrative characteristics.

Research designs for collecting longitudinal data

Longitudinal data can broadly be understood as any information that tells us about what has happened to a set of research cases over a series of time points. The majority of longitudinal data take human subjects as the unit of analysis, and therefore longitudinal data commonly record change at an individual or 'micro' level (Ruspini, 2002). They can be contrasted with cross-sectional data, which record the circumstances of individuals (or other research units) at just one particular point in time. Longitudinal data are frequently collected using a longitudinal research design, i.e. the participants in a research study are contacted by researchers and asked to provide information about themselves and their circumstances on a number of different occasions. In educational and psychological research, in particular, participants may be tested at regular intervals in order to discover how their test scores change over time. This type of longitudinal design, where the same subjects are repeatedly interviewed or tested over a period of time, is known as a *prospective* or *panel study*. An example of this study design is the British Household Panel Survey (BHPS). This was started in 1991 with a sample of just over 5000 households containing approximately 10,000 individuals in total. Each year data are collected from the members of the households that constitute its sample. The prospective design of the BHPS means that information can be collected which would be difficult or impossible to collect retrospectively. For example, each year respondents are asked detailed questions about their pay and other sources of income. They are also questioned on more subjective topics such as job satisfaction, fear of crime, and perceptions of fairness with respect to the

61

domestic division of labour. Further information about the design of the BHPS can be found in the Appendix.

It is now well recognized that it is important to make a distinction between longitudinal data and longitudinal research designs (Featherman, 1980; Scott and Alwin, 1998; Taris, 2000). It is not necessary to use a longitudinal research design in order to collect longitudinal data as some types of longitudinal data can also be collected using a cross-sectional design. Indeed, the *retrospective* collection of longitudinal data is very common in social research and has become an established method for obtaining basic information about the dates of key events such as marriages, separations, and divorces and the birth of any children (i.e. event history data). Retrospective methods involve asking individuals to recall and record information about the past. Asking respondents about their past lives is clearly a very efficient way of collecting longitudinal data and obviates the need to re-contact the same group of individuals over a period of time. The fact that cross-sectional surveys can be used to collect retrospective data therefore demonstrates that longitudinal *data* should not be elided with longitudinal *research designs*. What can be additionally confusing, however, is that major surveys often combine a number of different data collection strategies so that they do not always fit neatly into the classification of prospective or retrospective designs. In particular, longitudinal event history data are frequently collected *retrospectively* as part of an ongoing *prospective* longitudinal study. For example, as was briefly discussed above, the BHPS is a prospective panel study. However, in addition to the detailed questions asked every year about current living conditions, attitudes, and beliefs, in the 1992 and 1993 waves of the BHPS, respondents were asked to provide information about their past employment experiences and their relationship histories. Thus the BHPS has combined both prospective and retrospective methods of collecting longitudinal data about individuals' lives.

A further type of prospective panel study is a linked panel: this uses census data or administrative data. This is the least intrusive type of longitudinal research study as individuals may well not be aware that they are members of the panel. Unique personal identifiers are used to link together data that were not initially collected as part of a longitudinal research study. For example a 1% subsample of records from the 1971 British Census have been linked to records for the same sample of individuals in 1981, 1991, and 2001. This is known as the Longitudinal Study of the British Census. A similar study linking the 1991 and 2001 Census records for 5% of the population of Scotland is currently being developed.

Table 4.1 provides a brief summary of a selection of research studies that have used different longitudinal panel designs. It is by no means an exhaustive list, but focuses on studies that are commonly used in Britain, North America, and Europe. It can be seen that among these studies, mainly used by sociologists and economists, data are typically collected every year or less frequently.

Many of the longitudinal studies in Table 4.1 are additionally described as 'cohort studies'. A cohort can be defined as an 'aggregate of individuals who experienced the

Table 4.1 *Examples of longitudinal panel studies in North America and Europe*

Study	Type	Country	Date started	Frequency of data collection	Main focus
Panel Study of Income Dynamics	Household	USA	1968	Annual	Income
National Longitudinal Study	Cohort	USA	1966	Annual	Employment
National Longitudinal Study of Youth	Cohort	USA	1971	Varies	Employment
Wisconsin Longitudinal Study	Cohort	USA	1957	Varies	Social mobility
Survey of Income and Program Participation	Household	USA	1984	Every 4 months	Income support
Study of American Families	Mothers and children	USA	1961	Varies	Attitudes and lifestyle
National Survey of Families and Households	Individuals	USA	1987	Varies	Relationships and family life
Longitudinal Study of Generations	Three-generation families	USA (Southern California)	1971	Varies, 1971, 1985, 1988, 1991, 1994, 1997, 2001	Intergenerational relationships and well-being
Oakland Growth Study	Individuals	Oakland, California	1931	Continuously from adolescence to 18, re-contacted 20 years later	Physical, physiological, personal–social development
National Longitudinal Study of Children and Youth	Cohort of children aged 0–11	Canada	1994	Every 2 years	Well-being and development of children into early adult life
National Survey of Health and Development	Cohort	Great Britain	1946	Varies but generally every 2 or 3 years	Health

(Continued)

Table 4.1 (*Continued*)

Study	Type	Country	Date started	Frequency of data collection	Main focus
National Child Development Survey	Cohort	Great Britain	1958	Varies, every 4 years since 2000	Child development but broader focus in later waves
British Cohort Study 1970	Cohort	Great Britain	1970	Varies, every 4 years since 2000	Child development but broader focus in later waves
Millennium Cohort Study	Cohort	Great Britain	2001	Varies, but every 2 to 3 years at early stages of children's development	Child health and development with a specific focus on the social conditions surrounding birth and early childhood
Longitudinal Study of the UK Census	Linked panel using census data	Great Britain/UK	1971	Links decennial census data	Demographic and employment topics included in the census
German Socio-economic Panel	Household study	West Germany and now includes the former GDR	1984	Annual	Broad focus on living conditions, social change, education, and employment
European Community Household Panel	Household study	European Community	1994	Annual	Living conditions, employment, income, health, and housing

Source: Adapted from Scott and Alwin in Giele and Elder (1998: 110, Table 5.2).

same event within the same time interval' (Ryder, 1965: 845). The term cohort derives from the name for a large group of soldiers in the Roman Army; it therefore indicates any large group of people moving forward together from a common starting point. The most obvious type of cohort is therefore the birth cohort, i.e. a sample of individuals born within a relatively short time period. For example, the National Child Development Study is an ongoing longitudinal study that follows all individuals born in Britain in a single week of 1958. However, cohorts need not necessarily be defined in terms of their date of birth. We might also choose to study samples of those who got married, or who became parents, or who were released from prison, in a particular month or year. In longitudinal cohort studies the focus is typically on the individual rather than on the whole household.

Catch-up studies

In Table 4.1 a distinction can also perhaps be made between studies that were originally designed as longitudinal studies and those which were initially planned as cross-sectional studies but have developed into longitudinal studies. Examples include the first two British Cohort Studies, conducted in 1946 and 1958. The focus of interest in both cases was initially on maternal health and perinatal mortality and they were planned as cross-sectional surveys. However, both of these studies have become a valuable source of longitudinal data. Studies that are based on locating and re-interviewing respondents who were initially surveyed years earlier have been called 'catch-up studies' (Dempster-McClain and Moen, 1998). The archiving of data at centres such as the Murray Research Center at Radcliffe College, the Institute of Social Research at the University of Michigan, and the ESRC data archive at the University of Essex, makes such catch-up studies more practically possible.

Dempster-McClain and Moen (1998) provide a useful description of their own experiences of attempting to re-contact and re-interview a sample of 427 married mothers who had initially been interviewed in 1956. The original sample of women were aged between 20 and 60 and lived in a medium-sized town in up-state New York. Dempster-McClain and Moen tried to re-contact these women in the mid-1980s as part of a project on women's roles and well-being. They describe how they managed to locate over 95% of the original sample using telephone directories, city directories, neighbourhood visits, obituary records, former employers, high school and college alumni records, and local informants. A total of 408 women were traced; 82 of these were deceased and of the remaining 326, 96% agreed to be interviewed. Based on their experiences, Dempster-McClain and Moen argue that given the costs of prospective research studies it is often cheaper and quicker to do catch-up studies than to launch a panel study and wait many years for the data. There are several other examples of major studies which have been archived and then the respondents, or their children, re-contacted many years later. While some studies that were originally cross-sectional have become longitudinal, others such as the Oakland and Berkeley Growth Studies, which started in the late 1920s, were initially designed as relatively short-term prospective studies and have become longitudinal studies covering virtually the whole of the life span.

The collection of event history data

The most common type of longitudinal data to be collected retrospectively is event history data, which are sometimes also referred to as 'life history data'. A quantitative life history or 'event history' can be simply defined as a longitudinal record of *when* particular events have occurred for an individual. In this context an event corresponds to any qualitative change occurring at a specific point in time. The birth of a child and the date of starting a job could both therefore be described as events within an individual's biography. Elder defines a life history as 'a lifetime chronology of events and activities that typically and variably combine data records on education, work life, family, and residence' (1992: 1122). Of course, almost any events could be recorded in an event history. However, because event history data are mostly collected retrospectively, there is a tendency to focus on culturally significant events whose dates are likely to be remembered easily by respondents. In many cases therefore an event marks a change in status – from unemployment to employment, or from being single to being married, for example.

During the 1980s and 1990s large-scale surveys increasingly included self-completion questionnaires or interview schedules designed to collect work and life history information. In 1980 the Women in Employment Survey collected life history data on over 5000 women aged 16 to 59. Then in 1986 the large-scale Social Change and Economic Life Initiative, funded by the ESRC, included the collection of some 6000 work histories. In 1981 and 1991 Sweep 4 and Sweep 5 of the 1958 cohort study, known as the National Child Development Survey, also collected life history data, while in 1992 and 1993 the BHPS incorporated retrospective life and work histories within its interview schedule. These life histories all involve recording the dates at which particular biographical events occurred. Of course there are also many other examples of event history data in addition to these British studies. For instance, the German Life History Study covers the whole life course of individuals (Mayer and Bruckner, 1989), and in the United States, the National Longitudinal Study has drawn samples of men and women from three different age cohorts and recorded their labour market experience over a lengthy period (National Longitudinal Surveys Handbook, 2003).

In order to give a better feel for the type of information that can potentially be collected using this event history approach, Figure 4.1 provides an example of the work history section of a self-completion questionnaire entitled 'Your Life Since 1974'. This was included in the 1991 sweep of the 1958 British Cohort Study, known as the National Child Development Survey (outlined in the Appendix). It can be seen that respondents are asked to record the dates at which they started and finished any jobs held, as well as being asked for some minimal information about each job. As will be discussed in the next section, although most individuals are able to complete work history and life history questionnaires, there are concerns about the accuracy of some of the data that are collected using this technique.

Problems with retrospective life history data

The accuracy of recall data

One widely recognized disadvantage with using a retrospective research design to collect information about individuals' lives is that people may not remember the past accurately enough to provide good-quality data. While some authors have argued that recall is not a major problem for collecting information about dates such as the beginning and end of jobs, periods in higher education or training, marriages, births, etc., other research suggests that individuals may have difficulty remembering dates accurately or may prefer not to remember unfavourable episodes or events in their lives. Experiences that are of low importance and of short duration are particularly difficult to obtain reliable information about using retrospective methods (Dex, 1995). A particular focus for research in this area has been on the recall of spells of unemployment. For example, Dex and McCulloch (1998) have compared unemployment rates for identical years and identical cohorts of individuals using life history data from wave 2 of the BHPS and the Family and Working Lives Survey (FWLS). They found that whereas men's reporting of episodes of unemployment was reasonably reliable, there were much greater inconsistencies for women. They suggest that the reliability of women's retrospective unemployment experiences may be sensitive to the definitions of unemployment and data collection categories used in the two different surveys. The unemployment rates obtained for women using the FWLS were often higher than those obtained using the BHPS. Dex and McCulloch argue that this may be because the BHPS provided a larger number of categories of non-employment than the FWLS. Women would seem to be less likely to define themselves as unemployed in Britain if there are alternative states of inactivity to choose from. Women therefore appeared to have more difficulties than men in defining themselves as unemployed.

Jacobs (2002) has also carried out a detailed evaluation of the accuracy of retrospective reporting of unemployment episodes. Comparing men and women's self-defined *current* labour force status in 1991 at wave 1 of the BHPS with their *remembered* labour force status in 1991, recorded in the wave 2 (1992) work histories, she found a high level of agreement for those reporting spells of employment but lower levels for those defining themselves as unemployed. Jacobs also confirmed Dex and McCulloch's findings that women's recall of episodes of unemployment is much less reliable than men's.

The techniques for helping respondents to remember accurately the dates of events of interest to the researcher can be similar to those used by some qualitative researchers and discussed in Chapter 2. For example, in the National Child Development Study, the first page of the self-completion questionnaire entitled 'Your Life since 1974' consisted of a calendar grid on which respondents were encouraged to note down all major events in their lives. It is by linking together experiences across different life domains that it becomes easier to remember exactly when specific events took place. For example, the majority of people find it easier to remember the dates of birth of their children than to remember the dates of moving house. Recalling that a house move took place just before a child's birthday can therefore help to determine exactly when the event took place. It would also be wrong to imply by the inclusion of this single example that event history data are routinely collected using self-completion questionnaires. Evidence shows that validity is improved when these types of data are collected in face-to-face interviews (Dex, 1991). The widespread use of computer-assisted personal interviewing also means that systematic checks can be built into the data collection process.

Jobs

7   Including any job you have now, how many paid jobs have you had in total since you left school? (See notes below).

Please write number in boxes below. If you have never had a paid job write in 00.

☐☐   (N507413)   13–14

Notes to help you count the number of jobs you have had

- Include any job, full-time or part-time, which you did for at least a month.

- If you changed the kind of work you did while working for an employer, count this as still the same job. Only a change of employer counts as a change of job.

- If you have worked in a Government Department, school or hospital, count as a change of job any change of Government Department, school or hospital.

- If you had a period of 'lemping', or free-lancing, or consultancy, or self-employed contract work, count the whole period as one job.

- Include work in sheltered workshops.

- Don't count work experience, sandwich jobs or holiday jobs while you were in full-time education.

- If you went on maternity leave or sick leave and went back to the same job, count the whole period as one job.

- Don't count time spent on a Government work or training scheme.

If you have _never_ had a paid job lasting at least a month please go to Q9 on page 16.

If you _have_ had a paid job for at least a month please answer Q8 below.

---

8   Please give details of each paid job you have done which lasted at least a month, by answering questions (a)–(f).
Please start with your first job and work forwards to your current or last job.
If you have had more than four jobs continue on pages 14 and 15.

**Jobs lasting
a month or more**

Job Number:	1	2	3	4
a) *Date job started:*	(N507415)	(N507425)	(N507435)	(N507445)
	15–16	25–26	35–36	45–46
MONTH (Jan = 01, Feb = 02 *etc*)	▢▢	▢▢	▢▢	▢▢
	17–18	27–28	37–38	47–48
YEAR 19–	▢▢	▢▢	▢▢	▢▢
	(N507417)	(N507427)	(N507437)	(N507447)

b) *Date job ended:*
   (If you are still doing this job,
   write in 00)

	1	2	3	4
	(N507419)	(N507429)	(N507439)	(N507449)
	19–20	29–30	39–40	49–50
MONTH (Jan = 01, Feb = 02 *etc*)	▢▢	▢▢	▢▢	▢▢
	21–22	31–32	41–42	51–52
YEAR 19–	▢▢	▢▢	▢▢	▢▢
	(N507421)	(N507431)	(N507441)	(N507451)

c) *Was job full-time or part-time?*

	1	2	3	4
	(N507423)	(N507433)	(N507443)	(N507453)
	23	33	43	53
Full-tlme	1	1	1	1
Part-tlme	2	2	2	2

Full-tlme = 30 hours/week or more
Part-time = less than 30 hours/week

d) *Were you an employee?*

	1	2	3	4
	(N507424)	(N507434)	(N507444)	(N507454)
	24	34	44	54
Employee	1	1	1	1
Self-employed	2	2	2	2
'Temping'	3	3	3	3

'Temping' = a series of jobs for one or more agencies

e) *What was your job title when you started this job?*
   (Please write in)

Job Number: 1 _____ TBA _____

Job Number: 2 _____ TBA _____

Job Number: 3 _____ TBA _____

Job Number: 4 _____ TBA _____

f) *What kind of work did you do most of the time?*
   (Please write in)

Job Number: 1 _____ TBA _____

Job Number: 2 _____ TBA _____

Job Number: 3 _____ TBA _____

Job Number: 4 _____ TBA _____

Figure 4.1 *Work history section of the self-completion questionnaire 'Your life since 1974' from Sweep 5 of the National Child Development Survey (1991)*

Retrospective data and sample selection bias

A further problem with the use of *retrospective* research to collect life history data is that, by definition, individuals can only be interviewed if they are 'survivors' (Gershuny et al., 1994). For example, if we wanted to conduct a study on how students integrate paid employment with the work involved in studying for a degree, one possible research design would be to interview students who had just finished their final year of study to obtain retrospective reports of their experiences. At the simplest level students might be asked for the details of any paid employment they had carried out while they were undergraduates, in terms of the start and end dates of any jobs and the number of hours worked. However, although this retrospective design would be an efficient means of generating longitudinal data, a major problem would be that it would exclude any students who enrolled for the degree but subsequently dropped out. This would be less of a problem if the reasons for exclusion from the sample were completely unrelated to the research topic. In this example, however, it can be seen that the results might well be biased if those students who were most disadvantaged financially and had the most demanding jobs were those who had failed to complete their studies. To avoid this problem a prospective design would be needed that would sample all those *enrolling* in a degree and then collect data from them at intervals throughout their time as undergraduates.

Sample attrition

The prospective collection of data from a cohort or panel of individuals is not without its methodological problems. The major issue for longitudinal studies is the problem of attrition. Each time individuals in a sample are re-contacted there is the risk that some sample members will refuse to continue to take part in the study, some will have moved and will not be easy to trace, and some may have emigrated or died. For example, the National Child Development Study (NCDS), which started in 1958, collected data on a cohort of just over 18,000 individuals at birth. However, in 2000 by age 42 this sample had reduced to just over 11,000. The prospective longitudinal nature of studies such as the NCDS means that quite a lot of information will have been collected in earlier sweeps about members of the sample that are not contacted or refuse participation in later sweeps. This makes it possible to weight the sample to make some allowance for possible distortion in results due to missing cases.

The narrative qualities of event history data

The retrospective and temporal nature of event history data is immediately suggestive of its narrative potential. Indeed Labov and Waletzky's definition that narrative provides a 'method of recapitulating past experiences by matching a verbal sequence of clauses to the sequence of events that actually occurred' (1997: 12) may almost directly be applied to the information encoded within a questionnaire collecting event history data, such as the one shown in Figure 4.1. In other words, by collecting these types of data social scientists are in some senses requesting that individuals provide a formalized or standardized narrative about various aspects of their life. However, what is clearly missing from these formalized narrative records is an *evaluation* of the events that are recorded. To this extent, each individual event history might be thought of as closer to a chronicle rather than fully realizing a narrative form (White, 1987). Each event history 'chronicle' is organized according to topic (work, children, partnerships, housing, etc.) and has as its central subject an individual member of the survey sample. Both of these facets give it a certain narrative coherence. However, unlike a fully formed narrative, a quantitative event history 'does not so much conclude as simply terminate; typically it lacks closure, that summing up of the meaning of a chain of events with which it deals that we normally expect from the well made story' (White, 1987: 16).[1] It would be tempting to suggest, therefore, that what distinguishes these event history records from fully formed narratives is their lack of a subjective element, the 'evaluation' which underlines what the events mean for the individual concerned. It might be thought that event histories provide an objective record of the underlying events in an individual's life, which have yet to be realized in narrative form. Are these quantitative event histories therefore properly understood as raw data without interpretation? There are clearly problems with this characterization. What is being collected in a structured event history questionnaire is not simply raw data about each individual's life, but rather a particular version of that life is being constructed.

By studying the self-completion questionnaires used to collect event history information in more detail (and the one shown in Figure 4.1 provides a good illustration) it can be seen that a number of different devices are used to shape the version of each life that is produced. For example, although respondents are instructed to record the dates marking the beginning and end of all the jobs they have held since leaving full-time education, they are simultaneously given a number of caveats regarding jobs that should *not* be recorded. First, all jobs lasting less than a month should be omitted, as should those held while in full-time education. If these instructions are adhered to, what will be produced is not necessarily identical with the chronology of job changes as experienced by the respondent. Similar types of instructions are provided for each section of the life history questionnaire so that in each case respondents are asked to provide a particular version of their life in line with the needs of the researchers who compiled the survey.[2]

This highlights the fact, flagged at the beginning of the chapter, that what distinguishes qualitative and quantitative evidence is not necessarily the level of *detail* included in the data. Indeed the structured interviews with respondents in longitudinal studies such as the British cohort studies frequently last for ninety minutes or more and these are often supplemented by self-completion questionnaires on values and attitudes. Over the lifetime of a study cohort members will be interviewed many times and therefore a great deal of extremely detailed information will be amassed. However, the data collected in these longitudinal quantitative studies are clearly different from those data obtained using qualitative methods in that the structured nature of the survey instrument does not allow respondents to speak about their lives from their own perspectives. An event history can record the date at which someone changes job or moves house but cannot reveal what the experience of that job change or house move *means* for the individual concerned.

Cohort studies, narrative, and the life course approach

Cohort studies, such as the National Child Development Study, the British Cohort Study 1970, and the Millennium Cohort Study in Britain, provide the opportunity to make explicit the social and cultural context that frames the experiences, behaviour, and decisions of cohort members. For example, in the case of the NCDS, it is important to understand the cohort's educational experiences in the context of profound changes in the organization of secondary education during the 1960s and 1970s, and the rapid expansion of higher education, which was already well underway by the time cohort members were leaving school in the mid-1970s. Only 6% of the sample attended independent or direct grant grammar schools, while the majority in state-maintained secondary schools experienced at first hand the expansion in comprehensive education and the decline of grammar schools and secondary moderns. Indeed, approximately 60% of those attending comprehensives had seen their schools change their designation while they were there. In addition, this cohort experienced the raising of the school leaving age from 15 to 16 in 1973. They were part of the first year group who were required to stay at school for an extra year (Bynner and Fogelman, 1993).

The use of data from a single cohort, coupled with an awareness of how the historical context may have helped shape the experiences of that generation of individuals, could be argued to lead to a more narrative understanding of the patterns of behaviour being investigated. One distinction that has been made between theories and narratives is that whereas theories might be understood as 'attempts to capture and elaborate some timeless, essential reality "behind" the world of human events', narratives 'undertake the more modest task of organizing and rendering meaningful the experiences of the narrator in that world' (Hinchman and Hinchman, 1997: xv). Drawing on this distinction, it could be argued that by analysing data collected from a single cohort, social scientists can avoid the implication that the insights and understandings they produce refer to a disembodied, a-temporal social reality. Instead any findings are clearly temporally and spatially situated. Comparisons between cohorts can also help to clarify how individuals of different ages may respond differently to particular sets of historical circumstances.

In the United States in particular, this emphasis on the importance of understanding individuals' lives and experiences as arising out of the intersection between individual agency and historical and cultural context has become articulated as the life course paradigm. A central objective of the life course approach is to understand individuals' lives through time and in particular to link historical context and social structure to the unfolding of people's lives. The term 'life course' 'refers to a sequence of socially defined events and roles that the individual enacts over time' (Giele and Elder, 1998: 22). It is conceptualized as a pathway or trajectory through the age–differentiated life span. The 'life course' is seen as distinct from the 'life cycle', which perhaps has more biological or developmental connotations. The explicit use of the 'life course perspective' is arguably much more common in the United States than in Europe or Britain.

Elder's study *The Children of the Great Depression* (1974) is frequently viewed as the first major example of the application of the life course approach. In this study, Elder focused on the differential effect of the 1930s' depression on specific cohorts of young people living in Berkeley and Oakland, California. Elder demonstrated that the age at which children had experienced economic deprivation, in their families during the depression era, was an important predictor of later outcomes in their lives. Children in the Berkeley study were eight years younger than children in the Oakland sample and it was these younger children whose lives were more disrupted by the depression. As a result of his research, Elder has identified four main factors that shape the life course: location in time and place, social ties to others, individual agency or control, and variations in the timing of key life events.

A further excellent example of the application of the life course approach is provided by Sampson and Laub in their research on criminal careers (1993; Laub and Sampson, 1998). The starting point for Sampson and Laub's research was the study of juvenile delinquency carried out by Sheldon and Eleanor Glueck in the 1940s. This prospective study of the formation and development of criminal careers involved 500 officially defined young male delinquents who had been recently sent to one of two correctional schools in Massachusetts. This group was matched with a corresponding sample of 500 non-delinquents drawn from state-funded schools in Boston. The average age of both groups was just over 14 years. The Gluecks followed up this original sample at age 25 years and again at age 32 years, with the data being collected between 1949 and 1965. The data were archived at the Murray Research Center in the early 1970s. Sampson and Laub recoded the Gluecks' data and used the original case records to construct a complete criminal history for each respondent in the study from the time of their first arrest until the final data collection at age 32. Quantitative analysis of this longitudinal event history data showed that both job stability and marital attachment in adult life had a positive effect on desistance from criminal activities independent of early childhood experiences. In other words, Sampson and Laub identified turning points such as getting a good, stable job and entering a satisfying marriage which appeared to protect individuals from further criminal activity. Sampson and Laub stress the importance of the historical context of their study. The men in the sample reached adulthood in the 1940s and 1950s and therefore had no contact with the wide variety of drugs, such as crack cocaine, available today. This historical period also represents a time when there were expanding employment opportunities and when early marriage rather than cohabitation was the norm. These factors all contribute to the life experiences and criminal careers of the men in the study.

Life course research therefore provides an example of a methodology that uses largely quantitative data, but might be thought to contribute to a more narrative understanding of the social world. In particular, the focus on using longitudinal data about the timing of salient events and experiences for individuals, coupled with an awareness of the importance of the historical and cultural contexts in which individuals are located, leads to research which shares several of the elements of narrative outlined in Chapter 1. However, in comparison with the qualitative approaches discussed in Chapters 2 and 3 it is the researcher's narrative that is more likely to be heard as a result of this type of research. When the collection of data is structured and standardized, respondents are likely to be asked to provide chronologies that describe their lives rather than being encouraged to produce the type of individual narratives discussed in Chapter 2.

Summary

In this chapter a number of different research designs for collecting longitudinal data, have been discussed. It has been emphasized that longitudinal data, and in particular event history data, are frequently collected using cross-sectional retrospective research designs. The time and resources needed to collect data using a prospective panel survey mean that cross-sectional studies and 'catch-up' studies are frequently used as alternative means of collecting longitudinal data. Although event history data, such as the dates of changes in employment status, are often collected retrospectively, it has been emphasized that there may well be problems with the validity of such data. In particular the difficulty of obtaining good-quality information on short spells of unemployment has been highlighted.

The question that has laid behind the material in this chapter is whether quantitative longitudinal data can be understood as having narrative properties. It has been suggested that although the data share the temporal or chronological dimension associated with narrative, they typically lack the evaluative element that distinguishes a narrative from a chronicle. The collection of event history data therefore does not allow *respondents* to provide fully formed narratives about their biographies and experiences. However, as will be discussed in more detail in Chapter 5 and Chapter 9, there is a sense in which *researchers* can be understood to construct narratives from this type of quantitative evidence.

Further reading

Dex, S. (1995) 'The reliability of recall data: a literature review', *Bulletin de Methodologie Sociologique*, 49: 58–80.

Gershuny, J., Rose, D., Scott, J., and Buck, N. (1994) 'Introducing household panels', in N. Buck, J. Gershuny, D. Rose, and J. Scott (eds), *Changing Households: The BHPS 1990–1992*. Colchester: ESRC Centre on Micro-Social Change.

Giele, J.Z. and Elder, G.H. (1998) *Methods of Life Course Research: Qualitative and Quantitative Approaches*. Thousand Oaks, CA: Sage. (Esp. Chapters 5, 6, and 7).

Exercises

1   Use the web to find out more about the research design of two of the studies summarized in Table 4.1. The Appendix also includes some helpful web addresses.
2   Using the self-completion questionnaire in Figure 4.1 as a model, design a self-completion questionnaire to collect event history data on any jobs held by undergraduate students since they started university.
3   Design a semi-structured interview schedule that could be used as part of a *qualitative* study on undergraduates' experiences of combining study with paid employment. What are the main differences between the type of information collected in this type of interview and the event history data collected in 2 above?

Notes

1   Of course White is not discussing event history data here, rather he compares historical annals, chronicles, and narratives. However, it is striking how his description of a historical chronicle matches the quantitative event history.
2   With any extensive survey such as the National Child Development Survey, or the British Household Panel Study, it is important to be aware that the team of social scientists charged with responsibility for compiling the questions will do so in the knowledge that the data collected should be comparable with those provided by other large datasets and also should be amenable for use by many other subsequent teams of researchers who will conduct secondary analysis of the data.

Statistical stories? The use of narrative in quantitative analysis

In comparison with the various approaches to the analysis of narratives within qualitative interview material discussed in Chapter 3, the analysis of quantitative event histories is arguably much more codified. There is already an extensive literature on the statistical analysis of these types of data (Allison, 1984; Cox, 1972; Lancaster, 1990; Yamaguchi, 1991), and while some of the approaches described have their roots in engineering and biomedical research, there are an increasing number of social scientists and applied social statisticians working on methods which are specifically applicable to sociological data (Dale and Davies, 1994; Tuma and Hannan, 1979; Yamaguchi, 1991). For the purposes of organizing the material presented in this chapter, a useful distinction can be made between traditional modelling strategies applied to event history data and more innovative approaches to analysis that aim to provide descriptions or classifications of samples of narratives (Abbott, 1992a). Although modelling is still the more common approach to analysing quantitative life histories, both approaches can be applied to the kind of event history data described in Chapter 4. In addition to examining these two groups of methods in some detail, this chapter will also discuss a technique proposed by Singer et al. (1998) that demonstrates the value of using quantitative survey data to construct narratives at the level of the individual. A common theme in the discussion of all these various methods of analysis will be their relation to the narrative form outlined in Chapter 1. For example, to what extent does each type of analysis capture the temporal nature of a sequence of events? To what extent does each approach to analysis incorporate an evaluative element? And how successful is each approach to analysis in making explicit the historical and social context?

A full discussion of the statistical theories and techniques underlying the methods discussed here is beyond the scope of this book, and is more appropriately provided elsewhere (see e.g. Allison, 1984; Blossfeld and Rohwer, 1995; Yamaguchi, 1991).

Instead, the aim is to provide an introduction to the longitudinal analysis of quantitative data that are accessible to those with a basic understanding of inferential statistics and multivariate modelling (e.g. ordinary least squares regression analysis and logistic regression). The emphasis in the discussion below will therefore be placed on the conceptual issues rather than the statistical theories associated with these methods and on the extent to which each type of analysis corresponds to a narratively informed approach to the data. This chapter therefore seeks to develop a clearer understanding of the potential and limitations of event history modelling, optimal matching analysis, and the construction of case histories, for analysing quantitative longitudinal data by applying ideas about the definition and properties of narratives explored in previous chapters.

Event history modelling

In many respects event history modelling resembles more widely understood regression techniques, such as ordinary least squares (OLS) regression and logistic regression (where the dependent variable is dichotomous). The emphasis is on determining the relative importance of a number of independent variables or 'covariates' for 'predicting' the outcome of a dependent variable. However, event history modelling differs from standard multiple regression in that the dependent variable is not a measurement of an individual attribute such as income or IQ, rather it is derived from the occurrence or non-occurrence of an event, which is *temporally* marked. This rather loose definition of the dependent variable is deliberate here because, as will be shown below, the exact specification of the dependent variable depends on the approach that is adopted. The types of data that are suitable for analysis using event history techniques can therefore be characterized as having a temporal dimension. For example, it includes the duration from redundancy to becoming re-employed, the duration from cohabitation to marriage, the duration until the birth of a first child, the duration from release from prison to rearrest. Figure 5.1 provides a diagrammatic representation of the form of these types of data. The fact that the *timing* of events is a central focus of event history analysis means that it is referred to as 'longitudinal analysis' as distinct from the 'cross-sectional analysis' represented by multiple regression. As was discussed in Chapter 4, however, the data suitable for this type of analysis are not necessarily collected longitudinally. Retrospective reports, relying on individuals' memories of the timing of events, are also frequently used.

A focus on understanding the timing of events leads to two problems which mean that event history data are not amenable to analysis using standard regression techniques but require a slightly different set of approaches. First is the problem of what duration value to assign to individuals or cases that have not experienced the event of interest by the time the data are collected – these cases are termed 'censored cases'. In Figure 5.1, cases 4 and 6 are examples of censored cases. For example, if the focus is on the length of cohabitation episodes (either until marriage

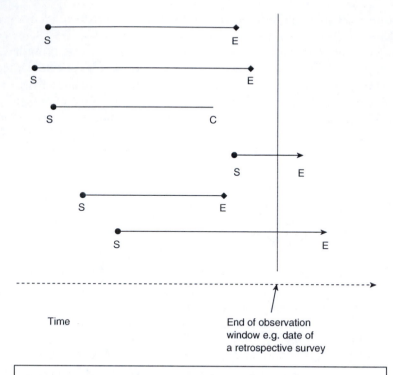

Time

End of observation
window e.g. date of
a retrospective survey

S: Start of episode, for example marked by entry into cohabitation.
E: Event of interest marking the end of a spell spent in a particular state, for example marriage would end a spell of cohabitation.
C: Event which censors a spell in a particular state before the event of interest occurs. For example a partner may die ending a spell of cohabitation without a transition to marriage.

Figure 5.1 *Diagrammatic representation of event history data*

or separation), what length of cohabitation should be assigned to individuals who are still cohabiting at the point when the data are collected? One solution might be to give the individuals a value equivalent to the duration over which they have been observed, i.e. if the period of observation is five years, then to assume that every member of the sample has married or separated by the end of this period. However, this is clearly problematic as it will result in a lower mean duration of cohabitation than if the sample had been observed over six or seven years. An alternative, particularly if the proportion of censored cases is small, might be to exclude all those who are still cohabiting from the analysis. However, once again this will lead to biased results as it is those cases with the longest durations, which would potentially push up the mean length of cohabitation, that will have been removed from the sample. This therefore is one of the key reasons that duration data are not suitable for analysis using multiple regression.

A second problem has less to do with the dependent variable than with the independent covariates. Once a sample is observed over several days, months, or years, rather than at a single point in time, there is the potential for the values of some of the independent covariates to change over time. The problem then arises as to how to incorporate these 'time-varying' covariates into the analysis. There is no satisfactory way of including time-varying covariates in standard regression models. The first problem of censored cases is a more common difficulty in modelling event history data, because in many research studies the explanatory variables are measured only once. However, as will be discussed in greater detail below, it is the ability of some event history techniques to incorporate variables that change value over time which gives the potential for models that are more narrative in nature.

These two problems have led to the development of a number of different modelling techniques specifically intended for the analysis of event history data. In essence, these techniques allow us to evaluate the relative importance of a number of different categorical and/or continuous variables, or 'covariates' for predicting the chance, or *hazard*, of an event occurring. The hazard is a key concept in event history analysis, and is sometimes also referred to as the hazard rate or hazard function. It can be interpreted as the probability that an event will occur at a particular point in time, given that the individual is at risk at that time. (The terms hazard and risk both originate from early applications of the methods in biomedical research when the models were constructed to predict the relative likelihoods of death for patients with different characteristics.)

The group of individuals who are at risk of the event occurring are usually referred to as the *risk set*. If the focus is on understanding the timing of a single event or transition it can be seen that this risk set will gradually diminish over time. For example, in an analysis of the age at which a cohort of women first become mothers, we would expect that at age 16 almost 100% of the sample would still be in some senses 'at risk' of having a first birth. However, by age 30, for example, a substantial proportion of these women will already have become mothers and therefore the risk set will have reduced to perhaps a quarter of the original sample. This reduction in the risk set over time has important implications for analyses that focus explicitly on the effects of duration, or 'time elapsed', on the hazard of an event occurring or in other words how the hazard rate changes over time. This is an issue that will be returned to and discussed, in relation to a specific example, in more detail below.

Different approaches to event history analysis

There are a number of different dimensions that can be used to distinguish different techniques of event history analysis (Allison, 1984, provides a good overview). Given the focus here on the narrative features of these different types of modelling, I will restrict the current discussion to a consideration of the conceptual differences between 'continuous time methods' and 'discrete time methods'. Although the statistical principles underlying the different approaches are similar, they lead to rather different conceptualizations of the data, both of which can be seen to have different implications for achieving analyses that can be understood to have *narrative* properties.

Techniques that assume that the time at which an event occurs has been measured exactly are known as 'continuous time methods', whereas if the unit of time that has been used is relatively large (years, or months perhaps) then 'discrete time' methods are more appropriate. Of course, in practice, time must always be measured in discrete units. It is therefore always possible to use discrete time methods. However, if these units are small so that it is unlikely that two events will be recorded as occurring at the same time, then it is possible to treat the data as though time has been measured on a continuous scale. As will be shown below, the approach adopted will partly depend on the specific analytic interests of the researcher.

Continuous time approaches to event history modelling

One of the most common continuous time approaches within the social sciences is to use the Cox proportional hazards models (Cox, 1972). This procedure is now available as part of one of the most popular and widely used statistical packages in the social sciences, namely SPSS (Norusis, 1994). The key feature of the Cox model is that it separates the hazard function into two separate factors, one of which only contains information about the coefficients attached to the covariates in the model; the other also incorporates information about how the hazard varies over time. Using the Cox model the formula for the hazard function can therefore be expressed as follows:

$$h(t) = h_0 t \, \exp[A(T)a] \qquad (1)$$

The method relies on the fact that the second factor in this equation can effectively be discarded and the first factor can then be estimated easily. In other words, emphasis is on how the covariates influence the hazard rather than on the shape of the hazard function itself.[1] The coefficients, which are estimated using this approach, have been shown to be unbiased as long as a significant proportion of events are not recorded as occurring at the same time. This is because the model, in effect, takes account only of the order in which events occur rather than the exact timing of events. This is why the technique is only appropriate when 'continuous' measures of time have been used.

The use of the Cox proportional hazards model is relatively common in criminological research on recidivism (Baumer, 1997; Finn and Muirhead-Steves, 2002; Gainey et al., 2000). In part this is because research on recidivism typically uses administrative data (rather than survey data) on the arrest histories of individuals and this provides relatively accurate dates for release from prison and subsequent arrests. The time between release from prison and a subsequent rearrest is typically measured to the nearest day, and the fact that precise dates are recorded makes the data suitable for analysis using a continuous time method. In addition, research on recidivism generally focuses on the factors that increase or decrease the likelihood that an individual will reoffend and be rearrested[2] and is less concerned with providing a detailed description of how the risk of offending and arrest changes over time. A Cox proportional hazards model that makes no assumptions about the form of the baseline hazard is therefore appropriate. An alternative approach to using an event history technique such as a Cox proportional hazards model would be simply to estimate models that predict whether or not an individual reoffends in a specified time period. However, the disadvantage of this is that it does not exploit the fact that data are frequently available about the timing of reoffence or rearrest.

The basic form of the Cox proportional hazards model was given above in equation (1). The dependent variable $h(t)$ is the hazard rate at time t. The model is called a 'proportional hazards' model because the difference between the hazard rates for the subgroups, defined by values of the independent variables, is assumed to be proportional over time. When using the COXREG procedure in the SPSS program the computer actually estimates a logistic form of the model given below in equation (2). As will be shown in the example discussed below, the baseline hazard h_0 is not reported (this can be understood as similar to the constant term in a standard OLS regression model). The emphasis is rather on how the hazard rate changes depending on different values of the independent variables.

$$\ln[h(t)] = \ln[h_0(t)] + A(t)a \tag{2}$$

A good example of the use of Cox proportional hazards models in research on recidivism is provided by research carried out by Gainey et al. (2000). They use event history techniques to examine the relationships between a number of independent variables, including time spent in jail and time spent on electronic monitoring, and recidivism among a sample of 276 offenders in Virginia in the United States between September 1986 and July 1993. Data were available on offenders for between five and twelve years after their release from electronic monitoring. A measure of recidivism was obtained through the National Crime Information Center. By subtracting the date of release from the date of first arrest a measure (in days) of time until rearrest was calculated. Clearly not all those in the sample had been rearrested, but the use of Cox proportional hazards models meant that these cases did not need to be excluded from the analysis. Almost half the criminals in the sample were traffic offenders (48%), approximately a third were felony offenders (35%), and the remainder were sentenced for misdemeanours (17%). Two dummy variables were created to represent those convicted of felonies or misdemeanours, while those who had committed traffic offences were treated as the reference category. The independent variables of sentence length, time served in jail, and time on electronic monitoring were all measured in days and can therefore be considered continuous (rather than categorical) variables. The number of prior convictions was included as a measure of criminal history and all of these four variables were logged to reduce the skewed nature of their distributions. As can be seen from Table 5.1, a number of demographic variables were also included in the model. These are relatively self-explanatory. The model for the hazard rate of rearrest, estimated using Cox proportional hazards models, is presented in Table 5.1.

The most important findings in the context of this study were that, whereas the length of time in jail did not have a significant impact on the hazard of rearrest,

Table 5.1 *Proportional hazards model of recidivism. Estimated effects of covariates on the timing of arrest using a Cox proportional hazards model*

	B	SE	Exp(B)
Felony offence	0.456	0.248	1.578
Misdemeanour offence	0.493	0.315	1.637
Number of prior convictions (logged)	0.696	0.120***	2.006
Days in jail (logged)	0.029	0.105	1.029
Days on EM (logged)	−0.316	0.161*	0.729
Sentence length (logged)	0.179	0.211	1.196
Female	−1.360	607*	0.257
Black	0.062	0.224	1.064
Age (logged)	−0.320	0.435	0.726
Employed	−0.192	0.401	0.825
Married	−1.119	0.257***	0.327
Number of persons in home	−0.006	0.067	0.994

$^*p < .05.^{**}p < .01.^{***}p < .001.$

Source: Adapted from Gainey et al. (2000: 744, Table 2).

the number of days on electronic monitoring *was* found to be significant. Those who spent longer on electronic monitoring were found to have a reduced risk of recidivism. Interpretation of the signs of the coefficients in the model is somewhat counter-intuitive. A *positive* coefficient, such as that associated with the number of prior convictions (0.696), implies that the variable has a positive effect on the hazard rate so that the time to rearrest is *shorter*. In this example then, those with more prior convictions are more likely to be rearrested and to be rearrested more quickly than those with fewer prior convictions. Conversely those who are female and those who are married have a lower hazard of rearrest. The exponents of the B coefficients are reported in the final column of Table 5.1. These values are useful because they show the effect of the independent variable on the hazard rate (as shown in equation (1) above) rather than the logistic form given in equation (2). This makes them more directly interpretable. For example, the recidivism rate for females is approximately one-quarter the recidivism rate for males (exp B = 0.257), and the recidivism rate for those who are married is approximately a third the rate for the unmarried (exp B = 0.327).

Continuous time event history analysis and narrative

The events and times that provide the analytic focus for this type of event history modelling introduce some temporal elements that begin to make the analysis more narrative in character. In this context, narrative might be understood as the waiting time until some event takes place, usually a transformative event such as birth or marriage, which involves a change in status for the individual concerned. In the example from Gainey et al.'s research, presented above, the model in some senses provides us with a story about who is most likely to reoffend following time in prison and focuses specifically on the role of electronic monitoring in that process. In addition to the chronological dimension introduced by the use of event history data, the model itself can be equated with a narrative because it selects the factors that are significant.

When event history modelling is applied to issues such as the time until re-employment following redundancy (Rosenthal, 1991), the duration until re-entry to the labour market for women looking after young children (Dex et al., 1998; Joshi and Hinde, 1993), there is an additional sense in which the classic narrative theme of a 'trouble' which must be overcome is embedded in these quantitative analyses. However, the fact that in continuous time models it is only a single transition that is predicted means that each narrative is constituted by only two events – a start and a finish (Abbott, 1992a). This reduces narrative to its simplest form and the concept of narrative as a sequence or chain of events is lost.

Discrete time approaches to event history analysis

Although numerous research projects have used the Cox model and it has been one of the most popular and widely applied approaches in the past, there are perhaps two main disadvantages to using this type of continuous time event history approach. First, it is relatively inflexible in terms of modelling duration dependence, i.e. for specifying exactly how the hazard may change over time, and second, it makes it difficult to incorporate time-varying covariates. For this reason, many researchers, with an explicit interest in how the probability of an event occurring changes over time, prefer to use the discrete time approach. This requires that the data are formatted somewhat differently from data analysed using continuous time methods. In simple terms a separate unit of analysis is created for each discrete time interval. Figure 5.2 provides an illustration of this type of 'discretized' data. In a discretized dataset each record therefore corresponds to a person/month or person/year (depending on the accuracy with which the dates of events have been collected). In Figure 5.2, for each person/year the dependent variable is coded with 1 if the person experienced the event in that year, otherwise it is coded 0. In this example, which looks at the timing of a first birth, it can be seen that the first woman (caseid 24) had her first baby when she was 26 years old and that the second woman (caseid 41) had not become a mother by age 33, at the time when the data were collected. Once the data have been reconfigured in this way the unit of analysis is transferred from being the individual case to being a person/year. These person/years are aggregated into a single sample and then logistic regression models can be estimated for the dichotomous dependent variable using maximum likelihood methods (Allison, 1984). In other words, by manipulating the data and changing the unit of analysis the event history data become amenable to analysis using a standard, and widely available, statistical technique.[3]

It can also be seen that once the data have been discretized in this way it is easy to include explanatory variables that vary over time because each year or month that an individual is at risk is treated as a separate observation. For example, it is straightforward to record the fact that whereas the first woman in Figure 5.2 lived

Case id	Age in years	Level of education	Partner present	Years with current partner	Birth of first child
024	18	2	0	0	0
024	19	2	0	0	0
024	20	2	0	0	0
024	21	2	0	0	0
024	22	2	1	0	0
024	23	2	1	1	0
024	24	2	1	2	0
024	25	2	1	3	0
024	26	2	1	4	1
041	18	6	0	0	0
041	19	6	1	0	0
041	20	6	1	1	0
041	21	6	1	2	0
041	22	6	1	3	0
041	23	6	0	4	0
041	24	6	0	0	0
041	25	6	0	0	0
041	26	6	1	0	0
041	27	6	1	1	0
041	28	6	1	2	0
041	29	6	1	3	0
041	30	6	1	4	0
041	31	6	0	5	0
041	32	6	0	0	0
041	33	6	0	0	0

Figure 5.2   *An example of 'discretized' data*

with a partner continuously from the age of 22, the second woman had episodes with and without a partner. It is also easy to include more than one measure of duration. In the example shown in Figure 5.2, age in years could be included as one duration variable in an event history model, while the length of time spent

Table 5.2 *Logistic regression model predicting the likelihood of marital separation and divorce over a six-year period between two waves of the National Survey of Families and Households*

Independent variables	Model 1		Model 2	
	B	Exp(B)	B	Exp(B)
Marital duration	−0.082*	0.921	−0.076*	0.927
Wife's age at marriage	−0.053*	0.949	−0.048*	0.953
Husband's age at marriage	−0.008	0.992	−0.007	0.993
Black	0.217	1.242	−0.073	0.930
Hispanic	−2.530	0.777	−0.133	0.876
Other race	−0.180	0.836	−0.003	0.997
Mixed race/ethnicity	0.278	1.321	0.226	1.253
Either spouse from single parent family	0.409*	1.506	0.312*	1.366
Either spouse in prior marriage	0.485*	1.623	0.469*	1.598
Husband works full time	−0.181	0.835	−0.165	0.848
Wife works full time	0.148	1.159	0.110	1.117
Wife works part time	0.132	1.141	0.162	1.176
Husband's education	−0.045	0.956	−0.024	0.976
Wife's education	−0.032	0.969	−0.038	0.962
Number of children	0.026	1.027	−0.017	1.017
Birth in interval	−1.225*	0.285	−1.187*	0.305
Wife's chances of divorce			0.570*	1.768
Husband's chances of divorce			0.271*	1.312
Model chi-square	**332.82**		**500.83**	
df	**16**		**18**	
p	**< .001**		**< .001**	

*$*p < .05$.

Source: From Heaton and Call (1995: 1089, Table 5)

living with the current partner could be included as a separate covariate. Discrete time methods are therefore thought to offer a preferable approach when the researcher wants to include several time–varying covariates or incorporate several different 'clocks' within the model.

An interesting and accessible example of a study that uses discrete time event history analysis is provided by Heaton and Call's research on the timing of divorce (1995). They analyse data from two waves of the longitudinal National Survey of Families and Households in the United States. The first survey was conducted in 1987/8 with a sample of over 13,000 people. Each individual was interviewed and data were also collected from the respondent's spouse or cohabiting partner. A follow–up survey was carried out approximately six years later in 1992–4. The discrete time model estimated by Heaton and Call is based on data from the 4587 individuals who were married at Wave 1 and also interviewed at Wave 2. Table 5.2 shows the results of two of the models estimated by Heaton and Call; the independent variable in each case is the probability of marital dissolution (expressed in terms of log odds). It can be seen that while the first model includes a number of demographic characteristics, the second model also incorporates each spouse's estimate that the marriage will end.

Focusing on the first model, it should first be noted that some of the independent variables in the model are constant over time. For example, wife's age at marriage, husband's age at marriage, and race will clearly stay constant over the six years of the study. However, other variables will change, e.g. marital duration will increase as the study progresses and the value for the variable 'birth in interval' will depend on whether a baby has been born to the couple in each year of the study. As was suggested above, a particular advantage of the discrete time approach is this ability to include these time-varying covariates within the model.

The results displayed for model 1 in Table 5.2 suggest that five independent variables were significantly associated with the risk of marital dissolution. Coefficients can be interpreted in a manner analogous to interpretation of the Cox proportional hazards model above, so that a positive coefficient implies that an increase in the covariate is associated with an increase in the hazard of marital dissolution. For example, marital duration appears to have a negative effect on the hazard of divorce/separation so that the longer a couple are married the less likely they are to split up.[4] Marital stability also increases with the increase of wife's age at marriage (i.e. older brides are at lower risk of subsequent divorce or separation), although interestingly the same association is not present for husband's age at marriage. Coming from a single parent family and being previously married both increase the risk of marital dissolution, whereas the birth of a child in any given year substantially reduces the risk of dissolution in that year. Finally model 2 shows that each spouse's estimate that the marriage will end has a strong association with dissolution. However, the higher coefficient for the wife's estimate is interesting as it suggests that women are better than their husbands at predicting the end of a marriage.

The magnitude of the associations can be interpreted in a similar fashion to interpretation of the results of the Cox proportional hazards model discussed above. For example, in model 2, having a baby in any particular year would appear to reduce the chances of marital dissolution to less than a third (30.5%) of the probability of marital dissolution if no baby was born. The model chi-square, which is reported at the bottom of the table, measures the improvement in predictability achieved by including the whole set of independent variables. This can also be used to judge whether a more complex model (i.e. one with more variables included) fits the data significantly better than a simpler (more parsimonious) model. For example, the improvement in the model chi-square for model 2 compared with model 1 above is 168.1 with an associated two degrees of freedom. This is highly significant, indicating that we are justified in including the spouses' estimates that the marriage will end as independent variables in the model.

Individual heterogeneity

One problem with the analysis carried out by Heaton and Call, which they do not discuss, is that their finding of a decline in the hazard of divorce over time, i.e. with increased marital duration, may well be an artefact of their approach to the analysis. A major limitation with the simple approach to the analysis of discretized longitudinal data briefly outlined above is that it does not take account of the fact that the unit of analysis is the person/year and therefore the individual cases are not fully independent (as they should be for a logistic regression) but are clustered at the level of the person. Another way to understand this problem, using as an example the model estimated by Heaton and Call, is to consider that there may be a further variable (or a number of variables) which has a strong association with marital dissolution but which is not included in the model. The existence of such 'unobserved heterogeneity' will mean that those who have a greater risk of marital dissolution will tend to experience separation or divorce earlier than those at a lower risk of marital dissolution. Over time this means that the risk set will include an increasingly higher proportion of those with a *low* risk of dissolution and thus the probability of dissolution will appear to diminish with increasing marital duration. However, this effect is not a true duration effect but simply reflects the existence of unobserved heterogeneity (or unmeasured variables) for the sample. This can be understood as similar to the notion of a spurious relationship, which will be discussed in further detail in Chapter 6.

It is beyond the scope of this chapter to discuss the problems of unobserved heterogeneity in any more detail. However, it is important to be aware that there are more complex approaches to modelling, such as using fixed or random effects models that can overcome these problems and allow the researcher to produce more robust estimates of duration dependence. The STATA package is particularly good for estimating these more sophisticated models. It includes a number of modelling procedures that allow the researcher to take account of the fact that each set of person/months or person/years in the analysis can be attributed to a single individual. Some specialist software packages (e.g. SABRE) have also been developed specifically to carry out this type of analysis (Barry et al., 1990).

Discrete time event history analysis and narrative

Returning to the parallels between event history modelling and a narratively informed analytic approach, it can be seen that, in contrast to continuous time methods, discrete time methods represent a set of techniques that allow for a more explicit focus on the temporal properties of event history data. As can be seen from the example in Figure 5.2, even when the analysis involves modelling the hazard of a single event, a 'discretized' data set, which includes other time-varying covariates, preserves the sense that a narrative is a sequence of events. Each person/month or person/year can be understood as an element in the sequence, which is clearly ordered chronologically. In addition, each sequence can potentially be given coherence by the unity of the individual case, and a conclusion or resolution to each narrative is provided by the occurrence (or non–occurrence) of the dependent event, which is the focus for the analysis.

As has been demonstrated in this chapter, while it is possible to analyse longitudinal evidence in a way that takes no explicit account of the temporal nature of the data, researchers are increasingly developing and using approaches which more fully exploit the sequential and temporal qualities of the data. Discrete time methods in particular have the potential to focus on duration dependence and can allow for an exploration of how the associations between covariates and the hazard of an event occurring change over time. By including interactions between covariates and measures of duration, as well as time-varying covariates, it is possible to build up relatively complex models that attempt to capture the processual nature of individuals' behaviour and experiences. In contrast to Abbott's assertions that modelling approaches do not allow for the meaning of variables to vary with historical time and with the presence or absence of other variables (Abbott, 1990), by including interaction terms, models can be estimated that explicitly address these issues. It is therefore these types of event history models which move us much closer to being able to produce a narrative representation and understanding of peoples' lives using purely quantitative data. Quantitative approaches to research should therefore no longer be rejected for necessarily portraying an overly static view of the social world or for 'fragmenting' individuals' experiences (Bryman, 1988; Graham, 1984). Indeed it may even be claimed that for those with an interest in understanding the chronological aspects of, and temporal constraints upon, individual behaviour, these quantitative approaches will become the preferred methods. It is beyond the scope of this chapter to give a more thorough treatment of event history modelling. However, it is hoped that the above discussion has underlined that for those who are interested in understanding more about processes over time and individual careers, whether these be centred around employment, fertility, housing, health, or criminal behaviour, it is important to recognize the potential of event history analysis.

Narrative positivism and event sequence analysis

Although the event history techniques described above are powerful and flexible, they still have the disadvantage that they do not deal with sequences *holistically*. Event history modelling allows for the inclusion of duration and sequence effects so that analyses are able to preserve *some* of the temporal characteristics of the empirical evidence. However, this approach retains an analytic focus on variables and aims to uncover the underlying processes that could be used to explain the configuration of the observed data. In certain respects event history analysis could perhaps still justifiably be described as 'variable-centred' rather than 'case-centred'. As Abbott (1990; 1992a) has suggested, therefore, an alternative approach to the analysis of event history data is not to attempt to model the underlying processes, which result in particular narrative realizations within the observed data, but rather to focus on the 'narratives' themselves and to try to establish a systematic description or typology of the most commonly occurring patterns within them. This approach has been termed 'narrative positivism'. While Ragin (1987) has advocated a strategy of using truth tables and the principles of Boolean algebra to conduct a more holistic analysis of relatively small samples of cases, Abbott has demonstrated the use of optimal matching techniques to handle larger samples of sequence data (1992a; Abbott and Tsay, 2000).

Abbott introduced the set of techniques known as optimal matching analysis into sociology from molecular biology, where it had been used in the study of DNA and other protein sequences. He has applied the method to substantive issues including figure sequences in dances (Abbott and Forrest, 1986), the careers of musicians (Abbott and Hrycak, 1990), and the development of the welfare state (Abbott and DeViney, 1992). Following his lead, other sociologists have also begun to adopt this approach and in particular have found the method to be useful for the analysis of careers (Blair-Loy, 1999; Chan, 1995; Halpin and Chan, 1998; Stovel et al., 1996). However, the technique is not as well developed or as widely used as the modelling approaches described above (Wu, 2000).

The basic concept behind optimal matching analysis (OMA) is that in order to be able to produce a typology of sequences it is necessary to be able to form clusters of similar sequences, and this is only possible if a measure of the difference between each pair of sequences can be derived. In order to calculate this measure of difference OMA counts how many 'elementary operations' (i.e. substitutions, insertions, or deletions) are needed to turn one sequence into another. For example, if we consider sequences (i), (ii), and (iii) below, made up of episodes working part time (P), episodes working full time (F), and episodes looking after a young child (C), it can be seen intuitively that sequence (ii) is closer to sequence (i) than it is to sequence (iii):

(i)	F	C	P	C	P	F		
(ii)	F	C	P	F				
(iii)	P	C	P	C	P	C	P	C

In terms of OMA, two insertions are needed between episode 3 and episode 4 of sequence (ii) to transform it into sequence (i), whereas two substitutions and four insertions are necessary to transform sequence (ii) into sequence (iii). If we consider that each elementary operation incurs a cost to the pair of sequences that are being compared, then the distance between two sequences can be understood as directly related to this cost. The distance between sequence (i) and (ii) is therefore less than the distance between sequence (ii) and sequence (iii).

However, one immediate issue that researchers adopting this technique need to consider is how to calculate the cost of different types of substitution, insertion, and deletion. Once there are more than two different types of element in a sequence, as in the example shown above, it is important to decide a priori whether substituting different pairs of elements incurs the same cost. In other words, using the current example, are full-time work, part-time work and looking after children seen as equidistant from each other, or should substituting full-time work for part-time work incur a lower cost than substituting full-time work for taking care of children?[5] As Wu (2000) has argued, this problem is exacerbated by the fact that replacements, insertions, and deletions frequently do not obviously correspond to anything 'social'.

Despite these shortcomings, in a recent review of the use of these OMAs, Abbott and Tsay stress that there are two main advantages of this type of approach.

First, it allows researchers to analyse sequences of data *holistically*, instead of having to focus on specific transitions between states. Second, it makes no assumptions about what produces the regularities that may be observed among a sample of different sequences. As Abbott and Tsay emphasize:

> By not making modelling assumptions, Optimal Matching acts as a true description. It finds things we might like to explain, and it may well point the way toward explanation. (2000: 27)

The primary goal of holistic sequence analysis is not therefore to uncover the underlying processes that result in particular configurations of events, but rather to produce a systematic description of the sequential patterns that occur in the data. However, as a number of published papers have demonstrated, it is also possible to move from a detailed description of the clusters within a set of sequences to a consideration of the factors which may have produced the observed typology (Abbott and DeViney, 1992; Han and Moen, 1999; Stovel et al., 1996). As Abbott himself has argued:

> [Narrative positivism] will provide us with a method for directly addressing questions of typical sequence(s) that are central to a number of contemporary empirical literatures: life course, organizations, labor markets, and revolutions. It will uncover regularities in social processes that can then be subjected to causal analysis of a more traditional sort. (1990: 148)

It is clear therefore that although in some places Abbott appears to argue for narrative positivism and the technique of OMA as an *alternative* to the dominant variable–centred approaches within quantitative sociology, the use of this approach does not necessarily preclude an interest in causal mechanisms.

Although, as the examples given above demonstrate, a number of researchers have experimented with the use of OMA, it is still used relatively rarely and is not readily available within standard statistical packages. As Abbott and Tsay conclude in their review:

> In summary, the current prospects of OM (Optimal Matching methods for sequence analysis) are reasonably good. There is not yet any single decisive application – one that completely solves a major empirical question left untouched by standard methodology or that completely overthrows standard interpretations. But there is a modest and growing record of applications, both in areas widely studied by standard methods and outside them. (2000: 28)

It would therefore seem that although in some cases OMA may prove to be useful additional method for the exploratory analysis of sequence data, it is unlikely to replace the more widely used event history modelling techniques described above.

Creating narratives from survey data –
a person-centred strategy?

A very different method to that proposed by Andrew Abbott, but which still emphasizes the need to conduct a more holistic analysis at the level of the individual and to move away from 'variable-centred' approaches, is discussed by Singer et al. (1998). There are few examples, as yet, of people using their proposed five-stage method. However, it is worth examining the technique they suggest in some detail as it illustrates an interesting attempt to bridge the qualitative/quantitative divide as they aim to 'reject the apparent forced choice between variable-centered, quantitative nomothetic alternatives on the one hand and person-centered, idiographic, frequently qualitative alternatives on the other' (Singer et al., 1998: 5–6). In addition, Singer et al. demonstrate that the concept of narrative can be used in quantitative as well as qualitative (hermeneutic) research, although, as will be shown below, the emphasis is on the temporal or processual nature of narrative rather than its interpretive or meaning making qualities.

The full five-step method of analysis proposed by Singer et al. is relatively complex and is described fully in their 1998 paper. The aim here is therefore to outline the approach in broad terms with a particular focus on the way that narrative is used and conceptualized by these authors. They use data from the Wisconsin Longitudinal Study of individuals graduating from high schools in 1957, and their research focus is the varying pathways leading to four different mental health outcomes for middle-aged women. Specifically they aim to understand the processes that lead to women being resilient, healthy, vulnerable, or depressed in mid-life. The Wisconsin Longitudinal Study consists of three waves of data collection so that data are available on the same group of respondents for 1957, 1975, and 1992. The most innovative aspect of the approach, proposed by Singer et al. is that the analysis begins by using these three waves of survey data to piece together individual life stories. In other words, Singer et al. start with conventional quantitative data coded in terms of responses on a wide variety of variables and use the data to construct a narrative biographical story for a small subsample of individuals.

Singer et al. explain that the first step of their technique involves taking a small sample of three to six individuals from each of the four outcome groups of interest and constructing a narrative for each, based on the individual's responses to a large number of variables (approximately 250 in their example) selected as those expected to contribute to adult mental health. Their rationale for recasting the survey data in the form of a narrative is that the human mind is better suited to process the information embedded in a coherent story than to grasp long lists of variables about a single life. Constructing and reading these narratives therefore helped the research team to find similarities within and variations between the lives of those sharing one of the four mental health profiles. As the authors explain:

The purpose of Step 1 is thus to do something with survey data that rarely occurs: generate all of the information that exists about a single respondent and weave it together as a narrative account. We assert that the crafting of whole life stories is fundamental to comprehending the processes we seek to understand. New insights are obtained as detailed information about real people are brought into focus. ... Our objective is to elevate the merits of portraying 'whole lives' among survey researchers, not as an end in itself but as a crucial beginning step in generating ideas. (Singer et al., 1998: 19)

An extract from the example of a narrative life history of a resilient woman, provided by the authors in their original article, is reproduced in Box 5.1.

Box 5.1   Extract from 'Narrative life history of a resilient woman'

The respondent is one of nine children; she has two older brothers, two younger brothers, and four younger sisters. When she was in high school her father worked as a repair man for a public utility. Her mother had eight years of schooling and did not work when the respondent was in high school. ... In her senior year in high school she did not plan to go to college and said that her parents did not care whether or not she attended. She planned to get a typing job in an office, and noted that most of her friends were also planning on getting jobs after graduation. ... The month after high school graduation she took a job as a clerical worker at an insurance company. She did not take any formal business or apprenticeship training courses, yet participated in a formal on the job training program in 1965. In 1975 she was working full-time at the same job that she began in July 1957.

Source: Extract from Exhibit A, sample narrative provided by Singer et al. (1998: 14–15).

The second step of the technique proposed by Singer et al. is to increase the number of cases examined from each outcome group and to search for the commonalities and variation among the profiles from each of these four mental health groups. By developing a series of statements that summarized the essential biographical elements of each of the four groups the researchers generated what they term 'initial generic life histories' that characterized the main trajectories followed by individuals in each of the four groups. For example, Singer et al. describe how, among the ten cases of depressed/unwell respondents that they examined in detail, they found that none had attended college and none had parents who graduated from high school. Low levels of educational achievement would therefore be identified as one element in the initial generic life history. Singer et al. stress the value of working with a team of researchers in searching for the key elements that characterize the different groups; as they explain, each collaborator may 'perceive somewhat different "stories" in the raw data' (1998: 21).

The analysis then proceeds to simplify these generic life histories and aims to provide parsimonious summaries of the key biographical elements shared by women with similar mental health outcome at mid-life. By the end of the process the researchers have reduced the initial complexity represented by the 250+ variables, thought to be of relevance for mental health in mid-life, and produced a much smaller list of variables (some of them composite variables) which combine to define the main pathways followed by the women in the sample. The final stage of the analysis then consists of testing how successfully the 'life stories', based on this subsample of composite variables, distinguish the women in different outcome groups. That is, the crucial question is whether the life histories shared by women in one mental health group are not strongly evident in the other three mental health groups.

Perhaps the most obvious shortcoming of the approach advocated by Singer et al. is that, although it enabled them to suggest a small number of generic life stories which characterize one of the subgroups within their data, namely resilient women, these diverse life stories were then found to be somewhat disappointing in terms of distinguishing resilient women from the other three mental health outcome groups. In other words, although the authors successfully described what was shared by women with a similar mental health outcome, these simplified 'life stories' were not found to be unique to this group of women. As Singer et al. state: 'In sum, the preceding tests of distinguishability reveal that the life histories of the four subgroups of resilient women showed mixed distinctiveness from other mental health groups' (1998: 2). Despite what might be though of as slightly disappointing results at a substantive level, Singer et al.'s methodological approach is fascinating because of the innovative way in which they attempt to work simultaneously with qualitative narratives and quantitative information, both emanating from structured survey data. As they write:

> Constructive if not essential tensions are generated by movement back and forth between finely nuanced details of individuals' lives and thinner, less textured summaries of groups of lives. Rather than cast allegiance to an exclusively idiographic or nomothetic approach, we have tried to work in the territory between these two levels. (Singer et al., 1998: 41)

In addition, Singer et al. stress that their method requires an element of judgement and is not fully automated and computerized. They suggest that the collaboration between a group of researchers can help with this process. Although they use conventional inferential statistics and procedures such as cross-tabulation as part of their technique they stress that their methodology relies on 'a labor intensive series of mind–machine interactions'.

It is clear that in some respects the person-centred approach advocated by Singer et al. is similar to the sequence analysis suggested by Abbott and discussed above. In particular, both approaches stress the need to identify and describe common trajectories or processes that then might be found to result in specific outcomes. The emphasis is therefore on providing holistic description and retaining a focus on individual lives or careers through time rather than adopting a more variable-centred approach. Where Singer et al.'s technique differs from that proposed by Abbott is that the qualitative narratives they construct from survey data are able to incorporate a much greater diversity of information or a much higher level of dimensionality than the relatively simple sequences required for OMA. This means that the approach could be argued to be more versatile and appropriate for use with a much greater variety of data.

Summary

This chapter has introduced three approaches to the analysis of quantitative longitudinal data that can each be thought to have some narrative elements. More attention has been paid to event history modelling than the other two approaches because this is currently the most widely used in the social sciences. However, discussion of optimal matching analysis and Singer et al.'s person-centred approach demonstrates that innovative techniques for the analysis of quantitative data can begin to blur the boundaries between qualitative and quantitative approaches. In both cases the emphasis is on producing detailed descriptions of the sequences and patterns found in the data before moving on to consider the factors which might produce these patterns. In the discussions of modelling in the first half of this chapter I have deliberately avoided confronting the question of whether this type of variable analysis can be understood as providing clear evidence about causality. This will be discussed in the next chapter.

Further reading

Abbott, A. and Tsay, A. (2000) 'Sequence analysis and optimal matching techniques in sociology', *Sociological Methods and Research*, 29 (1): 3–33.

Allison, P.D. (1984) *Event History Analysis: Regression for longitudinal event data*. Beverly Hills, CA: Sage.

Singer, B., Ryff, C.D., Carr, D. and Magee, W.J. (1998) 'Linking life histories and mental health: a person centered strategy', *Sociological Methodology*, 28: 1–51.

http://tramss.data-archive.ac.uk/index.asp

This is the home page for 'Teaching resources and materials for social scientists' supported by the ESRC. The site provides a taste of statistical software applications in event history analysis and multilevel modelling.

Readings for discussion

Halpin, B. and Chan, T.W. (1998) 'Class careers as sequences: an optimal matching analysis of work-life histories', *European Sociological Review*, 14 (2): 111–30.

1   *What do Halpin and Chan identify as the main benefits of using optimal matching analysis on longitudinal data about men's careers compared with other methods?*
2   *Halpin and Chan argue that the clusters of careers identified by their analysis make sense at an intuitive level – how far do you agree?*

South, S.J. (2001) 'Time dependent effects of wives' employment on marital dissolution', *American Sociological Review*, 66: 226–45.

1   *What are the main advantages of using longitudinal data rather than cross-sectional data for addressing the research questions raised by South in his paper?*
2   *Which interaction terms does South include in his models predicting marital dissolution and what are the theoretical concerns underlying the inclusion of these terms?*
3   *Would it be possible for South to use qualitative data to address the research questions he poses? Why/Why not?*
4   *In what respects might South be described as providing a narrative understanding of the determinants of marital dissolution?*

Practical exercise: Extract some data from a longitudinal survey such as the BHPS or the NCDS and use them to try and construct individual life narratives about two different groups of people who share either a common outcome or a common starting point, e.g. women who have a child when they are young and those who do not. What are some of the differences and similarities between the narratives you have produced and the narrative that might be produced in a qualitative interview?

Notes

1   In addition to the Cox proportional hazards model there are a number of parametric continuous time event history models which *do* allow the researcher to specify the underlying shape of the hazard function – for example, the Weibull model or the log-logistic model; these are not used as frequently by sociologists and are not discussed here, but detailed discussion of these parametric models is provided by Blossfeld and Rohwer (1995).
2   Using rearrest or time to rearrest as a dependent variable is clearly not ideal as these are not direct measures of criminal activity, i.e. many crimes will be committed that remain

undetected. However, the use of official statistics in research on recidivism is typically justified on the grounds that (a) the factors associated with involvement in crime are similar to the factors predicting rearrest and (b) criminal justice agencies interested in the success and cost-effectiveness of their programmes hold official measures to be of particular relevance.

3   A good practical discussion and example of the use of logistic regression is provided by Morgan and Teachman (1988).

4   However, this coefficient needs to be interpreted with great caution because of the way the model has been specified, as will be discussed in more detail below.

5   It should be noted that there are a number of other methods for the analysis of these types of sequential data, but as Halpin and Chan have argued, they are less general than the optimal matching algorithm (Halpin and Chan, 1998). It is beyond the scope of the current discussion to explore further the technical or statistical aspects of this type of method.

Uncovering and understanding causal effects and processes

In the previous four chapters, detailed consideration has been given to the role of narrative in shaping methods of data collection and analysis in both quantitative and qualitative approaches to research. The emphasis has therefore been on the way that an interest in narrative has contributed to the development of specific techniques within research. For example, in Chapter 2 it was suggested that over the past two decades there has been a growing interest in allowing and encouraging respondents to tell stories about their lives and experiences within qualitative interviews, while in Chapter 5 it was demonstrated that innovative approaches to the analysis of longitudinal quantitative data have developed out of the recognition that it is important to reach an understanding of how processes unfold over time and can shape outcomes for individuals. The remaining chapters of this book move on to examine some of the recent methodological debates in social research and how they too might be understood as informed by an interest in narrative. The main questions discussed in this chapter are what is meant by 'causality' in social science research and whether narrative and causal explanations should be viewed as alternative or perhaps even contradictory ways of understanding the social world.

The way that social scientists use multivariate quantitative analysis to try to establish causal links between variables will be discussed and the advantages of longitudinal data over cross-sectional data will be highlighted. It will be argued that statistical associations and statistical models can never be a sufficient basis for establishing causality and that there is an increasing awareness of the need for theory to explain and underpin the results of quantitative analyses. Although the chapter focuses on the conceptual issues surrounding causality and does not require any technical statistical background on the part of the reader, the discussion does assume a basic understanding of the principles of statistical modelling. Introductory material on this, with a specific focus on longitudinal methods, is provided by Dale and Davies (1994) and Elliott (1999; 2002a).

Narrative and causality: two modes of explanation?

A distinction is frequently made by authors with an interest in narrative between 'narrative' explanations as opposed to causal explanations (Abbott, 1990; 1992a; 1998; Bruner, 1986; Hinchman and Hinchman, 1997; Polkinghorne, 1988; Zukier, 1986). Indeed, just as the differences between qualitative and quantitative approaches to research are frequently treated as if they are self-evident, the distinction between narrative and causal explanations or accounts is also thought to be obvious. Bruner underlines this with the following quotation from William James:

> To say that all human thinking is essentially of two kinds – reasoning on the one hand and narrative, descriptive, contemplative thinking on the other – is to say only what every reader's experience will corroborate. (James, cited by Bruner, 1986: 4)

Causal explanations are frequently thought of as sharing the logical–scientific heritage of the natural sciences, and as aiming to fulfil the ideal of a formal or mathematical system for prediction. In contrast, narrative explanations are understood as embedded in the realm of literature and history (Bruner, 1986; Polkinghorne, 1988). As Bruner has argued, 'a good story and a well-formed argument are different natural kinds. Both can be used as a means for convincing another. Yet what they convince of is fundamentally different: arguments convince one of their truth, stories of their lifelikeness' (1986: 11). In addition, several authors argue that an important feature of the difference between narrative modes of explanation and causal (or paradigmatic) explanations is that, whereas narrative explanations remain rooted within the *particular*, causal explanations aim for applicability beyond the individual case – that is, they are more generalizable. This has been termed the distinction between 'ideographic' and 'nomothetic' explanations. As Baumeister and Newman have argued: 'Narrative thinking sacrifices the generality of the paradigmatic mode in favour of comprehensiveness. Rich accounts can encompass many features, and so narratives are more flexible and can accommodate more inconsistencies than paradigmatic thinking' (1994: 678). By definition, therefore, a narrative explanation is context specific. As was discussed in Chapter 1, in relation to Labov and Waletzky's structural analysis of narrative, narratives typically include an orientation that provides information about the time and place in which the events recounted unfolded. Causal theories have been described as attempting to 'capture and elaborate some timeless essential reality "behind" the world of human events, whereas narratives organize and render meaningful the experiences of the narrator in that world' (Hinchman and Hinchman, 1997: ix). This emphasis on narrative as providing a focus on individual cases, as highlighting the importance of context, and as a tool for understanding the meaningful qualities of human experiences, can perhaps be seen as linked to a hermeneutic approach to methodology. As Polkinghorne has argued:

> narrative is a scheme by means of which human beings give meaning to their experience of temporality and personal actions....Thus the study of human beings by the human sciences needs to focus on the realm of meaning in general and on narrative meaning in particular. (1988: 11)

As was discussed in Chapters 2 and 3, there is a clear affinity between narrative and qualitative approaches to research. Quantitative approaches are frequently viewed as very different because they attempt to achieve an understanding of *causal* relationships. However, not all social scientists with an interest in narrative could be described as adopting a hermeneutic or interpretative approach to research. Although Andrew Abbott uses the concept of narrative to argue for a return to sociological explanations that are firmly situated in time and space (Abbott, 1997), and that treat cases holistically, he does not emphasize the hermeneutic qualities of narrative to the same extent. Indeed he explicitly states that:

> Thinking about things narratively means thinking along cases rather than across them....It does not necessarily involve a turn to interpretive methods, although the two have shown an elective affinity in the past. (Abbott, 1990: 148n.7)

There is also a subtle difference between Abbott's injunction that we should think 'along cases rather than across them' and the link made by authors such as Bruner between narrative and ideographic methods. This is perhaps best exemplified by Abbott's chapter 'What do cases do?' in which he argues that it is important not to conflate narrative analysis with single-case analysis (Abbott, 1992b: 75) and that what is needed is a methodology that allows consideration of multi-case narratives. Abbott's conception of 'narrative positivism' therefore shifts the concept of narrative away from hermeneutics and attention to the individual case, and emphasizes temporality, context, and contingency. In some senses therefore he should not be aligned with the other apologists for narrative cited above. While he apparently shares their enthusiasm for a move away from the 'causal paradigm' that has been influential within sociology for several decades, and proposes narrative as a promising way forward, the way that he conceptualizes this dichotomy is rather different. Indeed, as will be shown later in this chapter, there is perhaps a greater affinity between Abbott's arguments and those of authors such as Ragin (1987), Hedstrom and Swedberg (1998), and Sorensen (1998). Although these authors do not explicitly talk about narrative methods, many of their arguments resonate with Abbott's call for 'narrative positivism'. They too emphasize the need critically to re-examine the established practices of quantitative sociology and its unhealthy preoccupation with relationships between variables that frequently obscure the relations between people. As I will demonstrate below, the argument that we need a greater focus on social *mechanisms* as 'plausible accounts of how an input and outcome are linked to each other' (Hedstrom and Swedberg, 1998: 7) has clear parallels with Abbott's interest in narrative.

Establishing causality in quantitative research

It is widely recognized that establishing a statistically significant association between two variables in quantitative analysis is not the same as establishing a causal relationship between them. Indeed, even texts on quantitative analysis that avoid an extended discussion on causality invariably include a reminder than an association between two variables is not equivalent to a causal relationship (Gorard, 2003). While the appropriate scientific technique for establishing causality is usually thought to be the experiment, it is rarely practical or ethical to conduct experiments within the social sciences. For example, if we are interested in the consequences of parental separation and divorce for the well-being of children it is clearly not possible to assign families randomly to two groups and force couples in the experimental group to divorce and couples in the control group to stay together. However, without such an experimental research design we should be very cautious about making statements about the *effects* of parental divorce on children. Once we are reliant on observational data we cannot be sure that there is not some prior factor, such as economic hardship or severe conflict within the marriage, which both increases the propensity for a couple to divorce and has negative consequences for the children (Ni Bhrolchain, 2001).

Given the difficulty of conducting experiments in the social sciences and the reliance on observing rather than manipulating the behaviour of individuals and their social context, researchers usually adopt a pragmatic approach to the analysis of survey data, which at least goes some way towards establishing causal relationships. This can be traced back to the work of the American sociologist Paul Lazarsfeld in the 1950s but has evolved into the standard custom and practice adopted by many of those analysing quantitative data in the social sciences. This pragmatic approach relies on three key criteria for establishing that a variable X *causes* a second variable Y. First, the cause must precede the effect in time. For example, parental social class may have a causal influence on a child's educational outcome but a child's qualifications are unlikely to have an impact on the parents' social class. Second, the two variables must be correlated or associated so that variation in one variable predicts variation in the other. And third, the association cannot be explained by a third variable that influences both of the variables of interest. If the association between two variables X and Y is found to be the result of a third variable W which is affecting both of them, then the relationship is said to be *spurious* and the possibility that the observed relationship between X and Y is causal can be discounted. An example of this would be if we let N represent the number of fire engines attending a fire and D represent the amount of damage caused by a fire; then we would not be surprised to observe a relationship between N and D, such that as the number of fire engines increases the amount of fire damage also increases. However, to suggest that there is a *causal* relationship between number of fire engines and degree of fire damage would be nonsensical. Instead we would explain this relationship by the antecedent variable, S, 'severity of fire'. This is likely to have an impact on both the number of fire engines that are needed to control a blaze and also the eventual amount of damage done.

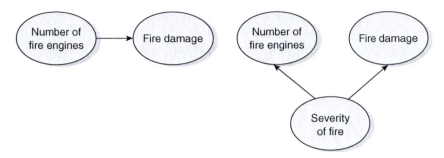

Figure 6.1 *Example of a spurious association*

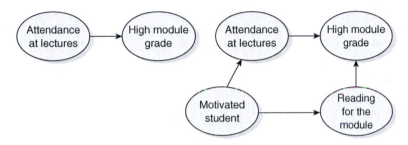

Figure 6.2 *Example of a partially spurious relationship*

A slightly more complex case of the issue of spurious relationships is provided if we consider the relationship between the number of lectures attended by students and their subsequent grades or marks for a module. As a lecturer, I might hope that there is indeed a straightforward causal link here, such that attendance at lectures improves students' understanding of the subject and thereby improves their grades. However, an alternative explanation for the association could be that motivated students attend lectures and also do a great deal of reading for the module. In this case, part of the link between attendance at lectures and final grade will be spurious because motivated, well-read students both attend lectures and do well in the module assessment. However, there is also likely to be some residual causal relationship between attendance at lectures and module grade. In this case, if we only focused our analysis on the relationship between attendance at lectures and module grade we would be likely to overestimate the causal link between them. These two examples are illustrated in the simple path diagrams shown in Figures 6.1 and 6.2.

Interaction effects

In addition to attempting to understand more about the causal relationships between variables by elaborating the analysis to check for spurious relationships, another important element of multivariate analysis is the investigation of possible interaction terms. An interaction effect is said to exist when the association between two variables is modified by the status of a third variable. For example, in their recent topical research on entry to higher education, Gayle et al. (2002) have demonstrated that although there is a positive link between attending an independent school and going to university, this association is only significant for those whose parents *did not* go to university. This indicates that there is an interaction effect between the type of school attended and parental education. Attending an independent or a state school did not appear to have a large effect on the likelihood of a young person with graduate parents studying for a degree. As one newspaper report on the research succinctly put it in a headline: 'School fees a waste for graduate parents'. In other words, the link between the variable 'school attended' and the dependent variable 'progression to higher education' is contingent on the level of a third variable, namely parents' education. In this example the interaction effect was described as a moderating effect by the authors because parental education was understood to moderate the influence of schools attended on outcomes for children.

In the same way that multivariate modelling can be used to check for spurious effects, so that the researcher tests whether there is still a significant relationship between the two variables of interest once other variables are included in the model, modelling is also used to test for interaction effects. In practical terms, a new variable, or set of dummy variables, can be created to represent each interaction and these are then included in the model together with the original variables. However, once we start to include interaction terms in a model, in addition to the main effects, the number of possible combinations of covariates (and therefore the number of possible models) rapidly escalates. For example, with only four covariates there are $3 + 2 + 1$, i.e. six, two-way interaction terms. This is demonstrated in Table 6.1 using variables from Gayle et al.'s research. With eight covariates, however, there are twenty-eight two-way interaction terms that could be tested. So, even with a relatively small number of variables, there are a large number of different models that could be tested. However, good models should be closely related to tests of substantively important hypotheses and the researcher therefore needs to make a series of decisions about which interaction terms are worth testing based on substantive theory.

Table 6.1 *Illustration of possible two-way interaction effects between four variables*

Main effects	Interaction effects		
Parental education	Parental education by school type	Parental education by gender	Parental education by ethnicity
School type	School type by gender	School type by ethnicity	
Gender	Gender by ethnicity		
Ethnicity			

Direct and indirect causes: using quantitative analysis to understand causal processes

In addition to elaborating the analysis of variables to check for spurious relationships and interaction effects, it is generally recognized that an observed association between two variables does not always provide immediate and direct evidence of a causal link and that it may be necessary to consider additional intervening variables or factors that help to explain the association. For example, as Esser (1996) argues, the discovery of a relationship between variables such as income and voting does not constitute the discovery of a causal law. Rather there are a series of implicitly assumed dispositions and sets of economic interests linked to different income groups that are used to 'explain' typical voting behaviour. A further, more detailed, example of the need to elucidate the intervening variables which may help to explain the link between two other variables is provided by Balnaves and Caputi in their discussion of a study of Australian National University students reported in an article in *Higher Education Research and Development* (2001). In this research, age was found to be the best predictor of academic performance among students studying the behavioural sciences. More specifically, it was found to be the mature students who obtained the best results. Just as in the example provided by Esser above, it does not make sense to suggest that age 'causes' students to obtain better results. Rather a number of intervening factors were suggested by the researchers to help explain the observed link. For example, the mature students were found to be more likely to have made personal sacrifices in order to be able to return to education and they were more likely to have self-selected their courses. These factors both made them more highly motivated and gave them greater determination to succeed, leading them to study hard and perform better than younger students. In addition, the older students were likely to have more accumulated knowledge and life experience leading to better performance, and a higher proportion of them were part-time students, a further factor that was associated with high attainment. The relationships between these different variables are illustrated in Figure 6.3. This conceptualization demonstrates that age does not have a direct effect on students' performance, rather age is linked to a number of intervening factors and dispositions which themselves have an impact on performance.

One way of understanding these different types of links between variables is in terms of 'distal' and 'proximal' factors. A variable such as age might be thought of as a distal factor because there are important mediating factors that explain the raw distal association between age and the outcome variable. Variables such as 'level of motivation' are proximal factors. They are closer to the lived experience of the individual and impact more directly on the outcome of interest. The distinction between 'proximal' and 'distal' processes originated in developmental psychology and more specifically in ecological models of development. However, as Feinstein et al. (2004) have emphasized, the framework is generic in that it can be applied to many different research topics.

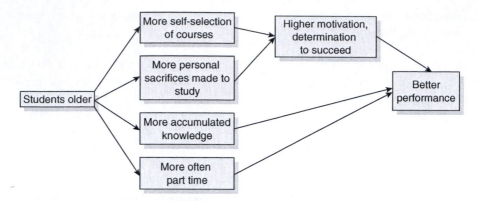

Figure 6.3 *A diagram of possible causal linkages between age of students and academic performance*

Source: Reprinted by permission of Sage Publications Ltd from © Balnaves and Caputi (2001: 43)

Research carried out by Savage and Egerton (1997) further illustrates how multivariate analysis enables us to go beyond simply identifying and quantifying the associations between pairs of variables and can move us towards a better understanding of causal processes. Savage and Egerton's research is interesting because they use longitudinal cohort data to examine the relative importance of 'primary' and 'secondary' class effects in facilitating social mobility (1997). Using data from the National Child Development Study (NCDS), a British cohort study started in 1958, Savage and Egerton examine the role of ability measured at age 11 in mediating the relationship between father's social class and individuals' class position at age 33. The argument is that if the higher social class position of those from middle-class backgrounds can be solely attributed to the fact that they have higher measured ability and therefore obtain higher levels of educational qualifications, this is evidence of a 'primary' social class effect. However, if parental social class has an effect on occupational outcome even once measured ability is taken into account, this suggests the presence of 'secondary' social class effects operating at later stages of the educational process, e.g. facilitating young adults progressing into higher education despite relatively poor academic performance or obtaining good employment. A number of sociologists argue that secondary effects are more significant than primary ones (Boudon, 1974; Goldthorpe, 1996) and Savage and Egerton's research confirms this. They found clear evidence that class advantages are transmitted through both primary and secondary effects. While some of the advantages of children from middle-class homes can be explained in terms of their ability to score higher in ability tests and therefore to succeed in the education system, there were also found to be other mechanisms at work that tended to reproduce class inequalities. In particular, the analyses showed that for boys from middle-class backgrounds, secondary class effects played a major role in shaping their final class destination. This study therefore provides an excellent example of the way that detailed quantitative data, and in particular longitudinal cohort studies, can be used to gain an understanding of the pathways that lead to different social outcomes. As the authors themselves state, 'the range of individual level information included in surveys such as the NCDS can be valuable in unpacking the "black box" of process' (Savage and Egerton, 1997: 649).

Proximate causes and basic causes

In contrast to the three examples discussed above, where the emphasis was on understanding the processes that lead to the association between two variables, and thereby, in some senses, bridging the explanatory gap that often seems to be left in quantitative analysis, there are other occasions where it has been argued that the most immediate or the apparent 'cause' of a particular outcome is misleading. For example, Reskin (1998) highlights the fact that although occupational segregation is frequently cited as providing a large part of the explanation for the disparity between male and female wages, it is important to recognize that if occupational segregation was eradicated this would not necessarily lead to women's wages increasing to match those of men. Rather, Reskin argues that the causes of pay inequality should be understood as operating at a deeper level and as being due to the power disparities between men and women and society. Although occupational segregation can be understood as one of the mechanisms by which women's wages are depressed, it is only a 'proximate' cause. In other words, if the 'problem' of occupational segregation was solved the patriarchal nature of society would result in some other mechanism to ensure that men maintained their economic advantage. As Reskin states in her conclusion:

> Integrating men's jobs and implementing comparable worth programs have helped some women economically and, more fully implemented, would help others. But neither strategy can be broadly effective because both are premised on a flawed causal model of the pay gap that assigns primary responsibility to job segregation. A theory that purports to explain unequal outcomes without examining the dominant group's stake in maintaining them is incomplete. Like other dominant groups, men make rules that preserve their privileges.' (1988: 73)

Reskin bases her critique of existing research that focuses on segregation as the explanation of the gender wage gap on the methodological work of Lieberson (1985). He makes the distinction between *superficial* causes that appear to produce a particular outcome and basic or underlying causes that are actually responsible for the outcome and argues that if the causal models constructed by social scientists are incorrect then the remedies they imply are likely to be ineffective (Lieberson, 1985: 185).

Lieberson and Silverman (1965) make a similar point in relation to understanding the race riots in American cities during the first half of the twentieth century. They describe the incidents that have precipitated riots in these cities as highly charged offences committed by one racial group against another, such as attacks on women, police brutality and interference, murder and assault. However, they highlight the fact that in comparison with riots, this type of event is relatively common and therefore it is clear that a riot does not ensue in every case. In other words, these events might best be understood as *necessary* but not *sufficient* conditions to spark off a riot. For a cause to be necessary and sufficient no riots would occur without these precipitating factors and a riot would ensue every time such an offence was committed. By making comparisons between the cities in which riots *did* occur and a matched sample of cities of similar size and location where riots *did not* occur, Lieberson and Silverman provide evidence that the functioning of local community government, in terms of the number of 'negro policemen' employed and the responsiveness of local council members to the interests and concerns of their constituencies, is important in determining whether a riot will follow a precipitating incident. They argue that: 'Populations are pre-disposed or prone to riot; they are not simply neutral aggregates transformed into a violent mob by the agitation or charisma of individuals' (Lieberson and Silverman, 1965: 897). Lieberson and Silverman therefore suggest that the incident that sparked off a particular riot in a specific place and time might best be conceptualized as no more than a 'random event', so that the 'causes' of riots are more properly understood as the structural underlying conditions.

A further example of a similar methodological point is nicely exemplified in the work of Hilary Graham, who has used both qualitative and quantitative research to examine women's health and their caring and health behaviour. Graham argues that the stress on the importance of health behaviour that emerged as a theme in government documents on health inequalities in the 1980s places the emphasis and therefore the responsibility for poor health on the health behaviour of individuals. To underline this point she quotes Edwina Currie as having said that northerners were dying of 'ignorance and chips' while 'Independent and Guardian readers have bean sprouts coming out of their ears' (Graham, 1990: 204). Graham contrasts this 'individual/behavioural' framework with what she calls the 'structural/material' framework which pays greater attention 'to the adverse effects of material deprivation on health: to the physical environment of the home and the workplace, and to the restrictions on diet and heating that poverty brings' (1990: 204).[1] Drawing on qualitative interviews with mothers caring for pre-school children, all of whom were either living on benefit or had incomes at or below the level of benefits, Graham demonstrated how smoking cigarettes had developed as a coping strategy for many of these women. Although they were well aware of the health risks attached to smoking, cigarettes represented a small, readily accessible, luxury that they could afford, and taking a short break to smoke a cigarette provided a means of structuring time and reasserting control over their busy and disordered lives. In some senses then, using Lieberson's terms, smoking behaviour and poor diet could be understood as the 'precipitating factors' of poor health, while economic deprivation and social inequalities are the more 'basic causes'. However, what makes this example rather different is that it cannot be denied in medical terms that smoking is a real and direct cause of ill health in that it has been shown to have a direct effect on lung cancer and heart disease. Rather, the implications of Graham's methodological argument is that instead of targeting resources only on health education to try and prevent people from engaging in behaviour that is detrimental to their health, it is important also to try and tackle the economic deprivation and social inequalities that give rise to this behaviour. Her qualitative research suggests that the problem is not that women are ignorant about the health risks associated with their behaviour, but rather that smoking is such a fundamental part of their coping strategy in the face of the profound hardship of everyday life that it is very difficult for them to give up.

Causality in cross-sectional and longitudinal research

As was emphasized at the beginning of this chapter, information about the temporal ordering of events is generally regarded as essential if we are to make any claims about a causal relationship between those events. In other words, if X is to be understood as a cause of Y, then it is necessary for X to precede Y. Claims about causal linkages therefore require an essential asymmetry between cause and effect which is most clearly established when there is a strict temporal ordering such that the cause occurs before its effect (Cox, 1992: 293). Given the importance of establishing the chronology of events in order to be confident about causality, it can be seen that longitudinal data are frequently to be preferred over cross-sectional data. As was discussed in Chapter 4, it is important to make a distinction here between cross-sectional data and the collection of data (some of which may be longitudinal) at a single point in time. In some substantive examples even when data are collected in a cross-sectional survey, it is clear that one event or variable precedes another. For example, in an analysis that focuses on the impact of school-leaving age on occupational attainment there is unlikely to be confusion about the temporal ordering of the variables. However, there are a number of examples where the use of cross-sectional survey data prevents researchers from determining the causal ordering of variables. For example, there is a considerable body of research that has shown a strong association between unemployment and ill health. This can be interpreted to imply either that unemployment causes poor health or that those who are in poor health are more likely to become unemployed and subsequently find it more difficult to find another job, i.e. there is a selection effect such that ill health might be described as causing unemployment (Bartley, 1991; Blane et al., 1993). This question about the direction of causality cannot be answered using cross-sectional data. In this case, longitudinal data would be needed to follow a sample of employed individuals and determine whether their health deteriorated if they became unemployed, or conversely whether a decline in health led to an increased probability of becoming unemployed.

In addition to providing clear evidence about the temporal ordering of variables and therefore the appropriate type of causal explanation, longitudinal data are also valuable for overcoming the problems of disentangling maturational effects and generational effects. As Dale and Davies (1994) explain, cross-sectional data that examine the link between age and any dependent variable confound, i.e. confuse, cohort and life course effects. For example, if analysis of a cross-sectional survey demonstrates a link between age and preference for a particular political party it is possible that it is the life experiences of different cohorts, who have grown up and reached maturity in rather different historical contexts, that lead individuals of different generations to form distinct and enduring party loyalties. An alternative explanation of the observed association, however, would be that individuals change their political allegiances as they grow older, as suggested by the oft-quoted adage: 'Not to be a socialist at twenty is proof of want of heart; to be one at thirty is proof of want of head' (Georges Clemenceau, 1841–1929).

Omitted variables

Although it is not yet fully recognized by the majority of British social scientists, perhaps the major advantage of longitudinal data over cross-sectional data in understanding the possible causal relationships between variables is the ability to take account of omitted variables. Longitudinal data enable the construction of models that are better able to take account of the complexities of the social world and the myriad influences on individuals' behaviour. This is best demonstrated by means of an example provided by Dale and Davies (1994). They highlight the fact that because of our limited ability accurately to model human behaviour, there will always be considerable remaining variation in the response or outcome variable even among subgroups of our sample with the same characteristics on all the explanatory variables. For example, research on women's employment behaviour demonstrates that educational levels, number of children, and marital status are all factors that are strongly associated with women's employment status. This means that women with low levels of qualification, who are caring for dependent children, and who are not married or cohabiting, are unlikely to be in paid employment. However, even among subgroups of women with the same levels of education, the same number and age of children, and the same marital status there will remain differences in their levels of labour market participation. This is likely to be because of other influences and characteristics of these women that have not been observed in research and therefore cannot be included in the model. The omission of these variables potentially leads to misleading results, particularly if the missing variables are associated with one of the explanatory variables. This is similar to the problem of checking for spurious relationships discussed at the beginning of the chapter. However, when longitudinal data are used there are specific statistical techniques (known as random effects and fixed effects models) that enable the researcher to make allowance for potential omitted variables and therefore ensure that the model is not misspecified. As was partially discussed in Chapter 5, the ability to take account of potentially omitted variables is particularly important when the focus is on how the length of time in a particular state or situation might influence the chances of leaving that state, i.e. when we are interested in what have been termed 'inertia' or duration effects. For example, we might be interested in the question of whether women who have been out of the labour market for many years caring for young children have a lower probability of re-entering the labour market than women who have only spent a few months out of paid employment. If we simply focus on the fact that women who have long durations out of the labour market have a lower probability of re-entering the labour market we run the risk that there is some antecedent variable such as 'motivation to work' or 'availability of jobs in the local labour market' which is both increasing the women's duration out of the labour market and simultaneously reducing the probability of getting a job. However, by estimating models that use longitudinal data on women's work histories, some of which include a number of spells out of the labour market, it is possible to disentangle duration effects from the influences of omitted variables or 'unobserved heterogeneity'. Indeed it has been shown that duration out of the labour market *does* have a negative impact on a woman's chances of returning to full-time or part-time work in Britain, but that this effect is much weaker once omitted variables are taken into account (Elliott, 2002a). It is beyond the scope of this chapter to provide details of the statistical techniques used; however, Davies (1994), Blossfeld and Rohwer (1997), and Elliott (2002a) provide accessible introductions to the types of models that focus on duration effects and fully exploit these advantages of longitudinal data.

Optimism about causality based on longitudinal data

The increased availability of longitudinal data in the social sciences coupled with the development of high-powered computers and new statistical techniques for dealing with temporal data has lead to optimism, among some authors, about the advances in the ability of social scientists to make strong claims about causality. For example, Tuma and Hannan conclude that:

> Event histories provide rich opportunities for answering fundamental socio-logical questions....The procedures we have outlined permit analysis of causal effects on the rates at which events occur and of time dependence in such rates....Event history analysis offers substantial advantages over other common approaches to the study of causal effects on changes in qualitative variables. (1979)

While Blossfeld and Rohwer explicitly state that:

> Event history models provide a natural basis for a causal understanding of social processes because they relate the change in future outcomes to conditions in the past at each point in time and enable to researcher to predict future changes on the basis of past observations at each moment of the process. (1997: 381)

However, at other points in their article Blossfeld and Rohwer are more guarded in their characterization of event history analysis as the appropriate approach for

109

uncovering causal relationships: 'Although longitudinal data are no panacea, they are obviously more effective in causal analysis and have less inferential limitations' (1997: 376).

While, for the reasons discussed above, it is undeniable that longitudinal data can lead to the construction of better models than those which can be estimated using cross-sectional data, it should also be recognized that there is a growing body of research that stresses that social scientists should be cautious in assuming that constructing a good model is equivalent to establishing causality, even when detailed longitudinal data are available. There are two main strands to this litera-ture. The first is rooted in statistical theory and stresses the problems of 'model uncertainty'. The second is more dominated by social scientists and empha-sizes the need to move away from simply describing or documenting linkages between variables towards understanding the mechanisms or processes that give rise to the statistical regularities that are observed. These will be briefly discussed in turn.

Model uncertainty

Alongside an enthusiastic literature which highlights the explanatory or 'causal' potential of longitudinal research and event history techniques, there are a grow-ing number of papers by authors who argue that statistical modelling, *of all kinds*, falls far short of providing the causal explanations that we might hope for within the social sciences (Chatfield, 1995; Clogg and Haritou, 1997; Cox, 1992; McKim, 1997). It is important to be clear that in the following brief discussion of the causal deficiencies of modelling, the focus is not exclusively on event history models per se. However, the arguments outlined below can be applied to event history models and therefore cast doubt upon the assumption, made by authors such as Tuma and Blossfeld (above), that such models represent a major advance in understanding *causal* processes within the social sciences.

As McKim (1997) has argued, with reference to statistical modelling in general, it is important to be aware that when using observational (rather than experi-mental) data, models cannot in themselves be understood to provide information about the *causal* links between variables. This is because for any given set of vari-ables, the number of distinct models consistent with the observed data will be large, and clearly once interaction terms are considered for inclusion, together with non-linear forms of interval-level data (e.g. the square of age or the log of income), the number of models that could possibly be used to describe the data becomes enormous. In practice it is very unlikely that a researcher will attempt exhaustively to test every model. In many pieces of research only a dozen or so of the multitude of possible models are likely actually to be estimated and com-pared in order to ascertain which provides the best fit to the data. This leads American sociological methodologists such as Clogg and Haritou and statisticians such as Chatfield to emphasize that the uncertainty due to model selection will be much greater than that due to sampling error in many of the standard uses of regression-type modelling. As Clogg and Haritou write:

> Finding models that predict well or fit the data well has little or nothing to do with estimating the presence, absence or size of *causal* effects. The uncertainty in making causal inferences from regression-type models needs to be appreciated more fully. (1997: 110, my emphasis)

In other words, given the problems of model uncertainty we should perhaps understand models as representing *plausible accounts* of how variables might be linked rather than as providing definitive evidence of causal linkages between those variables (Elliott, 1999). As Marsh emphasized more than twenty years ago: 'No body of data suggests a unique model of its structure and no one model can ever be shown to be the one and only way to make a good fit to the data' (1982: 72). To be cautious we might therefore argue that a statistical model can never be more than a provisional description used to make sense of a set of data values. Although the precision of the numeric coefficients presented in statistical models has a rhetorical force that suggests that a definitive solution has been obtained, statistical models might be better understood as providing narratives about the factors that probably contribute to a particular outcome.

Mechanisms

A second issue in relation to the causal powers of statistical modelling takes us back to the arguments discussed at the beginning of this chapter about the problems with mainstream quantitative approaches to sociology, where it was suggested that the existence of a correlation or association between two variables represents a rather weak conception of causality. Even if we could overcome some of the problems of model uncertainty, outlined above, a model which shows a statistically significant association between a group of independent variables and an outcome or particular event could still be argued to fall short of a causal explanation as it omits to provide an account of *how* the prior variables affect the outcome. As Gorard argues:

> If causation is a generative process then something must be added to the statistical association between an intervention and an outcome for the model to be convincing. The cause must be tied to some process that generates the effect. (2003: 158)

A similar point was made by Harré in 1970, when he argued that causal laws should describe the manner and mechanism by which a cause generates its effect. Harré suggested that the proof of a causal law requires two criteria: firstly 'favourable instance statistics' and secondly a 'plausible generative mechanism'. While statistical models, such as the event history models described in Chapter 5, can provide the first of these, it is unlikely that they can provide direct evidence of a generative mechanism. This same argument is taken up by Sayer when he states that:

> Merely knowing that C has generally been followed by E is not enough: we want to understand the continuous process by which C produced E. (1992: 107)

Sayer then goes on to suggest that the search for statistical regularities is relevant to causality in so far as such regularities may draw attention to factors which might be responsible for the process whose outcome has been observed. He stresses, however, that more qualitative techniques are needed to gain an understanding of how the process operates.

A useful distinction can perhaps be made here between 'causal description' and 'causal explanation' (Shadish et al., 2002). Shadish et al. argue that experiments are useful for discovering the consequences of deliberately varying some factor or 'treatment'. This can be thought of as 'causal description'. However, it is much more difficult to use experimental methods to understand the mechanisms through which the relationship between two variables operates or the context in which the causal relationship holds. This might be thought of as 'causal explanation'. Shadish et al. use the example of turning an electric light on and off to illustrate the difference between causal description and causal explanation. Whereas we quickly learn the relationship between flicking a switch and lighting up a room (i.e. the causal description), very few people could fully explain why the light goes on, i.e. they would find it difficult to provide a full causal explanation for the observed effect. This is partly because the cause of the light going consists of a relatively complex set of factors. Of course, it is when the light fails to work, and in particular when the problem is not simply solved by replacing a damaged bulb, that the practical importance of causal explanation is most keenly felt. It is due to the importance of causal explanations that once a relationship between two variables is established, attention rapidly turns to trying to go beyond causal description and to understand the processes through which one variable affects another. However, Shadish et al. caution against over-emphasizing the distinction between causal description and causal explanation. As they state:

> If experiments are less able to provide this highly-prized explanatory causal knowledge, why are experiments so central to science, especially to basic social science, in which theory and explanation are often the coin of the realm? The answer is that the dichotomy between descriptive and explanatory causation is less clear in scientific practice than in abstract discussions about causation...many causal explanations consist of chains of descriptive causal links in which one event causes the next. Experiments help to test the links in each chain. (Shadish et al., 2002: 11)

In the social sciences, where experiments are rare and research frequently relies upon observational data, we might conceptualize causal description as akin to establishing statistically significant associations between variables, whereas causal explanation might be thought of as equivalent to specifying the mechanisms or producing the theories which give rise to those associations. Goldthorpe (2001) has also drawn attention to the fact that many quantitative social scientists have traditionally been content to understand causality as 'robust dependence' in that they have used multivariate analysis and modelling techniques to eliminate spurious relationships and establish 'real' associations between variables. However, he argues that causal explanations cannot be developed using statistical methodology alone. Rather, background knowledge and theory about the substantive focus of the research is essential in order to form hypotheses about the generative processes that might be thought to constitute the causal relationships observed.

If causality is to mean more than the regular observation of one event following another, we therefore need to introduce the concept of a mechanism. As Hedstrom and Swedberg have argued:

> The search for mechanisms means that we are not satisfied with merely establishing systematic covariation between variables or events; a satisfactory explanation requires that we are also able to specify the social 'cogs and wheels' that have brought the relationship into existence. (1998: 7)

In the same volume, Sorensen defines a mechanism as 'an account of how change in some variable is brought about – a conceptualisation of what goes into a process' (1998). What is particularly interesting here is that Sorensen's use of the word 'account' points towards a link between the concept of mechanism and the concept of narrative. Whereas the idea of causality, as it is routinely used in the social sciences, is suggestive of a covering law that can be generalized to many different contexts, the notion of causality as a generative process entailing a mechanism suggests that causality is actually closer to the idea of narrative as a representation of a series of important or significant events linked together with an explicit temporal component. To use Goldthorpe's terminology, causality in the social sciences is little more than 'robust dependence' unless a 'narrative of action' can be obtained that provides as 'explicit and coherent formulation as possible of the generative processes that are proposed' (2001: 12).

In addition to understanding narrative as underpinning the mechanisms that are theorized to explain the links found between variables in statistical models, however, we can also turn the link between causality and narrative on its head by recalling that, owing to the problems of model uncertainty, any model should be understood as a provisional account of how variables may be linked rather than a final or definitive statement. A statistical model itself may therefore be thought of as akin to a narrative, particularly since a well-specified model requires the selection of the most salient variables for inclusion and also an appreciation of the temporal ordering of those variables.

It could therefore be argued that the concepts of narrative and causality are too interdependent to act as opposite poles of a dichotomy, and that the corollary of this is that, in contrast to authors such as Bruner, Polkinghorne, and Abbott, it is unhelpful to characterize any particular technique or method within the social sciences as being either 'causal' or 'narrative'. Indeed rather than contrasting or dichotomizing these approaches it would seem to be more productive to focus on both the narrative and causal aspects of any explanation or model that is produced as a result of a piece of research. There is more to be gained from exploring the narrative potential of statistical modelling techniques, such as event history analysis, than in trying to uphold a rigid distinction between 'causal approaches' and 'narrative approaches' to research.

Summary

This chapter has provided an overview of some of the strategies and techniques used to establish causality using multivariate statistical analysis. In particular it has highlighted that longitudinal data have clear benefits in allowing social scientists to develop a better understanding of causal processes operating in society. Although it started by outlining the arguments of those who suggest that narrative and causal explanations should be seen as very different ways of describing the social world, this chapter has suggested that far from being seen as alternative and radically opposed ways of describing the social world, 'causal' and 'narrative' understandings should be seen as mutually dependent. As was discussed in Chapter 1, and as has been further highlighted in the work of Baumeister and Newman, narratives depend on causal structures to give them coherence and to provide the foundations for events that are not simply temporally ordered but linked together like the cogs and wheels of a mechanism. In addition, in the same way that a narrative involves selection and provides a simplified account of events and experiences, a statistical model can be understood as a simplified representation of the structure of a set of data that aims to make sense of the evidence within it. Recent literature stressing the importance of acknowledging model uncertainty further contributes to the idea that a model is more properly thought of as a possible account of the relationships between variables rather than a definitive statement about causal relationships. This argument is important in that it leads on to the suggestion that by paying greater attention to the narrative properties of event history analyses, we can be more reflexive about the way that individuals are represented or even constituted by research accounts. This will be discussed in more detail in Chapters 7 and 10.

Further reading

Abbott, A. (1992) 'What do cases do?', in C. Ragin and H.S. Becker (eds), *What is a case?* Cambridge: Cambridge University Press. pp. 53–82.

Davies, R.B. (1994) 'From cross-sectional to longitudinal analysis', in A. Dale and R.B. Davies (eds), *Analyzing Social and Political Change: A Casebook of Methods.* London: Sage. pp. 20–40.

Goldthorpe, J.H. (2001) 'Causation, statistics, and sociology', *European Sociological Review*, 17: 1–20.

Lieberson, S. and Lynn, F.B. (2002) 'Barking up the wrong branch: scientific alternatives to the current model of sociological science', *Annual Review of Sociology,* 28: 1–19.

Reading for discussion

Ni Bhrolchain, M. (2001) '"Divorce effects" and causality in the social sciences', *European Sociological Review*, 17: 33–57.

1 *Would it ever be possible to design a piece of quantitative research to test whether divorce has a causal effect on poor educational outcomes for children?*
2 *How might you design a qualitative piece of research with the aim of understanding more about the mechanisms that may result in poor outcomes for children with divorced parents?*

Note

1   Similar arguments, but with reference to health inequalities in the United States, can be found in the work of Link and Phelan (1995).

Narrative and identity: constructions of the subject in qualitative and quantitative research

A man is always a teller of tales;
He lives surrounded by his stories and
The stories of others; he sees everything
That happens to him through them,
And he tries to live his life as
If he were recounting it.
(Jean-Paul Sartre, *Nausea*)

Whereas the previous chapter examined the multiple understandings of causality to be found within qualitative and quantitative methodologies, the aim of this chapter is to explore conceptualizations of the individual within different approaches to research. A key argument in this chapter will be that once we look beyond the technical differences between particular methodologies, we find not only episte-mological, but ontological differences. That is, differences in theories about iden-tity, and about what it means to be an individual in society. Once again it will be stressed not only that differences are to be found *between* quantitative and qualita-tive approaches, but rather that there are also major ontological differences *within* the broad field of qualitative research.

As will be discussed below, a number of authors have written about the fact that quantitative methods, and particularly structured cross-sectional surveys, tend to obscure the individual. Indeed, one common distinction that has been made between qualitative and quantitative research is that qualitative methods are ideographic: that is, they focus on understanding the individual case and build up from that, whereas quantitative methods are characterized as nomothetic in that they are concerned with establishing generalizations or law-like statements that apply to large groups of cases (see e.g. Becker, 1996). However, this chapter moves beyond this conceptualization of the differences between qualitative and quantitative approaches to suggest that the key question is not simply whether the individual is obscured in quantitative research, but rather what *type* of individual is implied or constructed in different approaches to research. Indeed, is the word 'individual' used to mean different things in different contexts? In particular a distinction will be made between the common-sense, or traditional, notion of an individual as having a stable set of characteristics, traits, or dispositions and the concept of the *reflexive* individual which has been discussed by qualitative researchers influenced by more post-modern or deconstructionist theories of the self (e.g. Chase, 1995b; Gubrium and Holstein, 1995; Hollway and Jefferson, 2000; Holstein and Gubrium, 2000).

The main aim of this chapter is therefore to highlight and discuss the ontological assumptions embedded within different research paradigms. To begin with, the criticisms of quantitative work as obscuring the individual will be outlined. It will be demonstrated that *cross-sectional* data limit the analysis that can be carried out at the level of the individual. It will then be shown that *longitudinal* quantitative data, however, allow for a greater focus on the individual and a number of examples will be given of researchers who have used longitudinal quantitative data to build rudimentary individual biographies. The chapter will then move on to show how the very concept of the individual has become problematic for social scientists in recent years. The post-structuralist challenge to the modernist conception of the unified self will be outlined and then the recent philosophical and psychological literature that emphasizes the importance of narrative for providing a temporal unity for the self will be discussed. The work of Ricoeur and MacIntyre is of particular relevance here. Literature on narrative and identity can be found within the disciplines of philosophy and psychology as well as in sociology and it is beyond the scope of this chapter to provide a thorough review. However, the aim will be to highlight key features of the writing within these three areas. In the final part of the chapter the methodological implications of this 'narrative' understanding of individual identity will be discussed in relation to both qualitative and quantitative approaches.

The individual in quantitative research

A number of authors have argued that a major shortcoming of quantitative approaches to research, and in particular cross-sectional surveys, is that they do not pay enough attention to individual cases (Abbott, 1992a; Bertaux, 1981; Farran, 1990; Pugh, 1990). However, as will be discussed below, these criticisms all take rather different forms. There are several respects in which quantitative research can be said to neglect the individual and, although some of these are closely linked, they can helpfully be listed as follows:

1   Quantitative research neglects the individual as a unique and complex case.
2   Quantitative research neglects the biographical trajectories of individuals.
3   Quantitative research neglects the individual as an active agent.

4   Quantitative research neglects the conceptual schema held (and meanings made) by individuals.
5   Quantitative research neglects the reflexive work carried out by the individual in establishing and revising his or her own identity.

Whereas the first four of these are relatively straightforward in that they do not disrupt a common-sense notion of the individual, the fifth is rather more problematic in that it raises questions about what is meant by the individual. The following discussion will therefore start by considering the first four criticisms of quantitative research as neglecting the individual. However, before tackling the fifth issue it will be necessary briefly to rehearse some of the recent post-modern writings, which have called for the deconstruction of the stable and immutable self, and to discuss the concept of narrative identity.

Neglect of the individual as a unique and complex case

At the simplest level, quantitative analysis can be understood to obscure the individual because it aims to provide a summary description of the characteristics of a group or aggregation of people rather than focusing on the unique qualities of each case in the sample. To illustrate this, both Farran (1990) and Pugh (1990) provide interesting accounts of their personal experiences of producing statistics in research reports and their dissatisfaction with the way that these reports represent the experiences of the individuals who constituted their samples. The research projects which each of these two authors describe involved the semi-structured collection of data from a relatively small sample of individuals (i.e. the research involved less than 500 individuals). In Pugh's project, statistics were constructed from examination of the log-book from a youth advice and counselling service. In Farran's research, information was collected using semi-structured interviews with young people using a water adventure centre. The aim of both studies was therefore to provide a description of the use made of a particular service. Both Farran (1990) and Pugh (1990) write about their misgivings about the internal validity of their statistical reports because of the problematic connection between the statistics they produced and the individual lives they aimed to represent. In her chapter, entitled 'Seeking Susan: producing statistical information on young people's leisure', Farran gives a careful description of how the interviews she conducted were coded and transformed into statistical data. As she writes: 'I have entitled this section "Seeking Susan" because, paradoxically, once a statistical table is produced there is no way in which the ordinary reader can seek and find the individuals and their experiences which are what the table is supposedly "about"' (Farran, 1990: 93). Later in the chapter she goes on to comment that:

> During the coding process a sociological vanishing trick has occurred wherein the uniqueness of what Susan has said has disappeared in the final format. All the things that were interesting about her have been removed: her experience has been sieved through my classificatory schema. (Farran, 1990: 100)

For both Farran and Pugh, the main problem encountered when producing reports that prioritized statistical (i.e. quantitative) descriptions of groups of people was that they felt these accounts did not do justice to the vibrant and unique individuals they had met during the process of research.

This can also present a problem for those reading research reports based on statistical aggregations. Lay audiences and those wanting to use research to inform policy can find descriptive and multivariate statistical analyses rather dry and impenetrable. For this reason, some sociologists have experimented with providing case studies of individuals to illustrate or augment the results of their research. For example, Bynner et al. (1997) provide descriptions of trajectories followed by a number of 'typical' individuals from the 1958 and 1970 British cohort studies to complement their statistical descriptions of the longitudinal data.

Neglect of the biographical trajectories of individuals

Linked to this notion that quantitative research neglects fully to represent the complexity of unique individual cases is the problem that cross-sectional surveys, and in particular repeated cross-sectional surveys, used to analyse and describe social change at the aggregate level, *obscure the biographical trajectories of individuals*. A good illustration of this methodological point is provided by Walby (1991) in her chapter 'Labour markets and industrial structures in women's working lives'. Using data from a study of the Lancaster travel to work area, conducted in the early 1980s, Walby demonstrates that at a structural level there was clear evidence of a decline in manufacturing industry between 1960 and 1980 accompanied by an expansion in the service sector. However, as Walby highlights, this aggregate-level data cannot reveal whether individuals themselves experience de-industrialization in their own work lives. It is longitudinal datasets on life histories and employment that contain data at the individual level. Indeed, by using data from a longitudinal dataset of women's work histories, she shows that this marked change in the structure of the economy did not necessarily result in a large proportion of women moving from jobs in the manufacturing sector to jobs in the service sector. Rather, it was new entrants to the labour market who took the new jobs in the expanding service sector, while those workers who had been in the manufacturing industry gradually retired or became unemployed. The majority of individuals therefore did not directly experience de-industrialization in their own employment histories. As Walby states: 'The strengths are that life histories enable us to understand the implications of structural change *at the actual individual level*, and prevents false assumptions that the individual experience is represented by aggregate change' (Walby, 1991: 185, my emphasis).

Clearly, although, as Walby has demonstrated, longitudinal life histories go some way towards allowing us to look at change at an individual rather than an aggregate level, there remains a sense in which the individual is concealed by statistical summaries even if these are based on longitudinal data. Quantitative analysis still works by putting people into groups rather than examining individual cases. It could therefore be argued that the focus in quantitative approaches is still on relationships between variables rather than on relationships between people. This has prompted a few researchers to adopt innovative approaches to the analysis of longitudinal quantitative data and to use the rich detailed information collected in a longitudinal study to construct individual biographies. These techniques seem almost to belong within the umbrella of qualitative methods because of their focus on the particular rather than on groups of cases. However, they are clearly not based on the close analysis of textual material from in-depth interviews that is more usually associated with qualitative research. As was discussed in Chapter 5, Singer et al. (1998) have used this approach with data from the Wisconsin Longitudinal Study to try to understand which combinations of factors result in different mental health outcomes for women in mid-life. They describe a method of weaving together data from all waves of the study to create a more narrative or coherent life story for three or four individuals with a similar outcome. These constructed life histories are then used as a starting point for identifying common processes resulting in a particular mental health outcome, such as resilience or depression.

Although the statistical techniques used are rather different, a similar approach to examining quantitative longitudinal data *holistically*, i.e. in terms of trajectories or sequences, has been adopted by Andrew Abbott. As was discussed in some detail in Chapter 5, rather than focusing on a few individual cases, Abbott advocates a technique known as 'optimal matching analysis' to search for clusters of patterns or sequences across large samples of data (Abbott, 1992a; Abbott and Tsay, 2000). This move from a 'variable-centred' approach to quantitative research, which became dominant in sociology in the 1950s and 1960s, towards a more case-centred approach, based around longitudinal data, demonstrates that quantitative approaches can be used to explore individual biographies or trajectories.

This emphasis on the importance of understanding individual trajectories is also exemplified by the work of Sampson and Laub, who have carried out extensive research on turning points in criminal careers. They have used life history data from a longitudinal study on delinquency, started by the Gluecks in the 1940s, in order to try and illuminate the processes of criminal offending (Sampson and Laub, 1993). In particular they are interested in factors which lead to desistance and those associated with continued offending behaviour. Sampson and Laub's approach is similar to that of Singer et al. in that they develop complex profiles of individuals based on combinations of variables. They describe this as a shift from a 'variable orientation' to a 'person orientation' and, consonant with Singer et al.'s work, their aim is to illuminate the *processes* that result in either persistence or desistance. Where Sampson and Laub's approach differs from Singer et al.'s method, however, is that they start by carrying out more traditional 'variable-centred' quantitative analysis and use this to identify some individuals whose outcome is successfully predicted by their statistical models and some whose outcome is unexpected. These separate groups of individuals are then examined in more detail by using the quantitative data to construct individual case histories.

A further difference between the approaches to constructing individual case histories used by Singer et al. and by Sampson and Laub is that the data used by

Singer et al. from the Wisconsin Longitudinal Study are all highly structured and quantitative, whereas Sampson and Laub are able to draw on detailed handwritten interviews with the respondents and their families conducted by the original research team together with interviewer narratives produced for each respondent at each interview. This means that Sampson and Laub are able to access information about the respondents' own perspectives on their lives and on the factors which the respondents themselves believe have led them either to persist in or to desist from criminal and delinquent behaviour. For example, they quote one respondent who described the combination of influences that had led him to 'go straight':

> Well for one thing I got out of Boston. I began to work steadily, and now I have a family – a son whom I always wanted. My father helped me to get back on the road to respectability and he has lived with us since we moved here. My wife always wanted me to do the right thing, and I try to follow her advice. I got away from the old gang and the bookie racket, which my uncle runs in the city. In a small town like this you have to go straight. (Laub and Sampson, 1998: 223)

However, although Laub and Sampson do have access to rich qualitative material from the Gluecks' longitudinal study their approach to the qualitative analysis of this material is to focus on the *content* rather than the *form* of the narratives. They emphasize the value of the qualitative data as lying in the rich detail and the attention to process rather than in understanding criminal careers from the perspective of the respondents. Their approach is therefore somewhat similar to that taken by Bertaux and Bertaux–Wiame in their study of the careers of French bakers as discussed at the beginning of Chapter 3 (Bertaux and Bertaux–Wiame, 1981). As Laub and Sampson explain, 'qualitative data expose human agency in the processes leading to individual change. … At the same time qualitative data can help uncover the developmental sequences underlying patterns of continuity found in quantitative data' (1998: 229).

It is important to stress that the techniques used by Singer et al. and by Laub and Sampson are relatively unusual. They represent isolated examples of researchers who use quantitative data to construct individual life histories and who attempt to integrate this case-based approach with more conventional quantitative or 'variable-centred' analysis. However, what makes this work particularly interesting from a methodological point of view is that it begins to blur the boundaries between qualitative and quantitative approaches. It demonstrates that quantitative research, and particularly longitudinal studies, can collect very detailed information about individuals and that this can potentially be presented in the form of individual trajectories, case histories, or biographies as well as analysed using more conventional statistical techniques. As Laub and Sampson write in explaining the rationale for their approach: 'We believe that merging quantitative and qualitative data analyses provides important clues for explaining the processes of continuity and change in human behavior over the life course' (1998: 214). However, this also underlines the fact that there are many very different approaches to research that are described under the umbrella of qualitative research but which have a very different focus in terms of both the type of research questions they address and the methods they use. Although Laub and Sampson describe some of their analysis as qualitative, it is quite distinct from the type of *qualitative* analysis of in-depth interviews described by authors such as Hollway and Jefferson (2000) or Gubrium and Holstein (1998). As was discussed in detail in Chapter 3, these authors highlight the importance of attending to the way in which individuals talk about their experiences, i.e. analysing the *form* of interview data rather than just focusing on the *content* of what is reported.

Neglect of the individual as an active agent and of the conceptual schema held by individuals

A further respect in which quantitative research can be criticized for obscuring the individual is its lack of attention to the motives and values that guide the actions of individuals in specific cultural contexts. As has been stressed by many authors discussing the distinctive features of qualitative and quantitative research, one of the main aims of qualitative methods, such as in-depth interviews and focus groups, is to try to gain an understanding of the social world from the perspective of the individuals being studied. This understanding can then be applied to help explain why people make a particular decision or follow a particular course of action.

For example, in the research by Duncan and Edwards (1999) on lone motherhood they have explicitly moved away from the 'rational economic man' models for explaining women's decisions about working full time or part time. Rather they have used in-depth qualitative interviews to concentrate on lone mothers' own understandings and agency. In particular they have focused on how lone mothers socially negotiate understandings about the extent to which being a good mother is compatible with taking up paid work. Duncan and Edwards argue that by examining individual cases in depth, and taking account of the holistic character of lone mothers' lives, they are able to provide an insight into how lone mothers' social networks are related to their conceptualization of what it means to be a good mother, and how this in turn influences their decisions and choices around paid work. Duncan and Edwards contrast their approach with that adopted in the majority of studies on lone mothers which use the statistical analysis of large datasets to try and determine how a range of different attributes or variables (such as education, age, region, age of youngest child, housing tenure, etc.) predict lone mothers' propensity to participate in paid employment.

In a very closely focused qualitative study on how at-risk individuals decide to request predictive testing for Huntingdon's disease, Cox (2003) also moves away from understanding decision making through the framework of rational choice. In contrast to the research on lone motherhood and employment by Duncan and Edwards, Cox's focus is as much on the process of *how* individuals come to make decisions as it is on *why* they make those decisions. As was discussed in Chapter 3, by attending to the narratives individuals told in interviews, about the decision to request the genetic test for Huntingdon's disease, Cox demonstrates that while some interviewees described decision making as an evolving or gradual process, others simply assumed that they would have the test and did not perceive or describe themselves as making an active or rational decision. This type of in-depth qualitative research therefore not only seeks to understand how individuals' perspectives shape the decisions they make, but also tries to provide a rich descriptive account of how individuals experience the decision-making process itself. Both these examples of research therefore demonstrate how qualitative research can potentially provide an insight into the individual as decision maker and active agent that is fundamentally different from the perspective provided by quantitative studies.

Problematizing the individual

In discussing the place of the individual in different quantitative and qualitative approaches to research, the discussion so far has implied that the term 'individual' is relatively unproblematic and has a clear and precise meaning. However, in recent years the very notion of 'the individual' has become something of a contested concept. Post-modern writers such as Foucault, Lyotard, and Harraway have questioned the traditional assumption that the individual should be understood as the creative force behind society, and in response to these writers there has been something of a decline in the belief in a unitary and coherent self. Indeed, one of the major themes of the post-modern turn has been the decentring of the human subject (Seidman, 1994). As will be discussed in the next section of the chapter, a more post-modern understanding of the self can perhaps be accommodated within qualitative research and, indeed, has engendered qualitative analysis that emphasizes the role of narrative in the formation and maintenance of the self. However, the individual within quantitative research has remained relatively impervious to post-modern deconstruction. Even when detailed longitudinal studies are used to construct case histories or biographies of individuals, the assumption is that those individuals have a clear, stable, and coherent identity. Perhaps what is most important is that in quantitative research the description of the individual is provided by the researcher and the resources available are variables which apparently allow no scope for ambiguity or inconsistency. This point will be returned to below.

Changing conceptions of the individual: the self in post-modern thought

To attempt a description of the defining features of post-structuralism and to offer a brief account of how it has been taken up with respect to concepts of personal identity and the self is an almost impossible enterprise. In the context of the argument of this chapter, however, the key contribution of post-structuralist or 'post-humanist' writers such as Foucault, Derrida, and Nietzsche is to suggest that the concept of the authentic human subject, autonomous from society and existing

123

beneath a cultural overlay, should be understood as merely an effect, or a 'fiction', which emanates from humanist discourse itself. The notion that we can 'lift the veil of the social and reveal the reality beneath' is mistaken (Annandale and Clark, 1996: 19). In other words, individuals cannot be understood as having a fixed identity that is ontologically prior to their position in the social world. Identity is not to be found inside a person (like a kernel within a nut shell) but rather it is relational and inheres in the interactions a person has with others.

In contrast to the humanist notion of the individual as having an authentic core and an essential identity, the post-modern conception of the self therefore stresses the continual production of identity within specific historical and discursive contexts. Whereas a modernist approach to understanding social life would view the individual as an agent responsible for social transformation, post-structuralism turns this on its head and examines how subjectivity itself is shaped and maintained within a social world. In post-modern thought the self is deconstructed in that the linguistic sources of the self are emphasized and identity therefore becomes much more fluid and determined by context. In his inaugural lecture, Foucault spoke of subject positions that were only created by discourse. For Foucault and Derrida, the notion of a unified self is mistaken; the self is better understood as multiple and continually under construction rather than being a fixed set of characteristics or traits. This leads to an interest in a radically new set of research questions, and a turn to the analysis of language, literature, and discourse as central to understanding social life. For example, drawing on the work of Foucault, Judith Butler argues for a post-modern feminism that concentrates on producing a 'genealogy' of gender. She suggests that the central task is to work at uncovering the multiple processes by which the category of woman is made to seem real while simultaneously being inferior to the category of men. With reference to de Beauvoir's edict that 'one is not born but rather becomes a woman', Butler suggests that 'women itself is a term in process, a becoming, a construction that cannot rightfully be said to originate or to end. As an ongoing discursive practice, it is open to intervention and resignification' (1990: 33).

In its most radical form, post-modern thinking might be understood to undermine empirical research in the social sciences, or at least to redirect its attention towards the analysis of texts. However, post-modern scepticism about the existence of an unproblematic, unified, and coherent self has also opened up new possibilities for qualitative research to focus on the everyday practices by which individuals constantly construct and reconstruct their sense of individual identity. As will be discussed in the section that follows, much of this work uses the concept of the narrative constitution of identity to suggest an identity that is grounded in experience and temporality and has coherence without being static and fixed.

The narrative constitution of identity: stability and change

Perhaps one of the most influential writers to have made a major contribution to the notion of the narrative constitution of identity is the French philosopher

Paul Ricoeur. In his later writings, *Oneself as Another*, and the three-volume *Time and Narrative*, Ricoeur uses narrative in two ways (Ricoeur, 1984; 1988; 1992): first, as a means of understanding how people make sense of time at a human level; and second, of suggesting how individuals can be conceptualized as having a continuous presence through time without becoming fixed or essentialized, representing a completely stable set of characteristics and dispositions. Ricoeur highlights the fact that the term 'identity' can be understood in two different ways. On the one hand there is the notion of identity as *exactly* the same, equivalent, or identical (the Latin *idem*). Alternatively, identity can be used to refer to continuity or something that can be traced through time. The Latin *ipse* or 'selfsame' (*soi-meme*) conjures up this sense of identity as permanence through time without sameness through time. Narrative fits with this conceptualization of individual identity as 'selfsame' in that it provides the practical means by which a person can understand themselves as living through time, a human subject with a past, present, and future, made whole by the coherence of the narrative plot with a beginning, middle, and end. As Gubrium et al. have argued: 'Much of the work of assembling a life story is the management of consistency and continuity, assuring that the past reasonably leads up to the present to form a life line' (1994: 155). In other words, a conception of the self as 'selfsame' arises by applying a narrative account of human time to personal identity. Ricoeur argues that a narrative understanding of identity avoids the choice between continual flux and instability and the stasis of absolute identity. The narrative constitution of the self suggests that subjectivity neither is an incoherent stream of events – a sense of life as 'one damned thing after another'[1] – nor is it immutable and incapable of evolution (Ricoeur, 1991). An account of narrative identity can therefore avoid the extremes of both essentialist and constructivist views of the self.

As Ricoeur explains:

> Without the recourse to narration, the problem of personal identity would in fact be condemned to an antimony with no solution. Either we must posit a subject identical with itself through the diversity of its different states, or, following Hume and Nietzsche, we must hold that this identical subject is nothing more than a substantialist illusion, whose elimination merely brings to light a pure manifold of cognitions, emotions and volitions. This dilemma disappears if we substitute for identity understood in the sense of being the same (idem), identity understood in the sense of oneself as self-same [soi-meme] (ipse). The difference between idem and ipse is nothing more than the difference between a substantial or formal identity and a narrative identity. (1988: 246)

The tension between the need to understand ourselves as relatively stable over time, as maintaining the same characteristics, while also wanting to incorporate an element of change, progress, and development, has also been discussed within social psychology (Gergen and Gergen, 1988; Smith, 1994). Personal identity is created through the process of managing the opposing forces of change and continuity (Smith, 1994: 388). Narrative is one of the few resources we have for organizing long sequences of occurrences involving our own experiences and activities, as well as the actions of those who are close to us (Bruner, 1990). As Lynch has argued: 'For us to be continually experiencing, in the present moment, a range of thoughts and feelings, or for us to be engaging in a range of actions, with no sense of what had preceded these thoughts feelings and actions, would be a bewildering existence devoid of any clear meaning' (1997: 355). The ability to form narratives therefore enables an individual to organize his or her experiences in a way that provides that individual with a sense of him- or herself as an intentional agent with continuity through time.

A similar point about the individual's need simultaneously to manage stability of identity and change over a major life transition was made over four decades ago by Berger and Kellner (1964). They argued that, when a couple get married, the identity of each takes on a new character as it needs constantly to accommodate to that of the other. However, this process is not perceived as such by the individuals involved; instead 'the reality that has been "invented" within the marital conversation is subjectively perceived as a "discovery". Thus the partners "discover" themselves and the world, "who they really are", "what they really believe", "how they really felt, and always have felt, about so and so"' (Berger and Kellner, 1964: 63–4). In other words, once the couple are married: 'Reconstructed present and reinterpreted past are perceived as a continuum, extending forwards into a commonly projected future' (Berger and Kellner, 1964: 63). In a similar vein, Gergen and Gergen suggest that:

> Functioning viably in a relationship often depends on one's ability to show that one has always been the same and will continue to be so and yet, contrapuntally, to show how one is continuing to improve. One must be reliable but demonstrate progress: one must be changing but maintain a stable character. Achieving such diverse ends is primarily a matter of negotiating the meaning of events in relationship to each other. Thus with sufficient skill one and the same event may figure in both a stability and a progressive narrative. (1988: 36–7)

The activity of narrating a life therefore involves the restructuring or reconfiguring of past events in the light of the present. In particular, by structuring events and experiences into a narrative whole, a biography produces a sense of temporal unity for the self (Lloyd, 1993; Polkinghorne, 1988; Ricoeur, 1984). It is this continuity or identity of the self through time that makes us accountable for our past actions but also means that we can expect others to account for their actions (MacIntyre, 1981).

Narrating the self in social context

As well as creating an internal or private sense of self, narrative provides a means by which we can convey and negotiate our sense of self with others (Linde, 1993). There are two important and related ways in which ontological narratives will be shaped by the social world: first, through the audiences which each individual encounters; and second, through the cultural repertoire of stories to which each individual has access. It is these social influences that will be discussed here before returning to a consideration of the active and reflexive individual narrator.

As was highlighted in Chapter 1, one of the defining features of narrative is that it is a *social* activity. Narratives are a means by which individuals translate knowing into telling (White, 1987) and oral narratives can helpfully be understood as in some senses 'joint actions' requiring the co-operation of a conversational partner or audience (Plummer, 1995). Focusing on the importance of the context and the audience for the performance of a narrative acts as a reminder that our 'self-narratives' must be supported or at least tolerated by those around us. Personal stories are embedded within a variety of social relationships (Gergen, 1992). Ideally the stories of individuals will be complementary with those of at least some other individuals. Siblings, married couples, school or college friends will all expect to have something of a shared history. We will all have attended social gatherings where stories that are shared by an intimate group are retold as a collaborative enterprise in a way that reaffirms the bonds between those individuals. In addition to some of the broader cultural resources for narrative practice, which will be described below, narrative models may also therefore be provided and maintained by more intimate social groups.

'Ontological narratives' and 'public narratives'

Narrative identities should not be understood as free fictions. Rather, they will be the product of an interaction between the cultural discourses which frame and provide structure for the narrative, and the material circumstances and experiences of each individual (Bruner, 1987; Ezzy, 1997; Gergen, 1992). In other words, while each person has the capacity to produce a narrative about themselves that is creative and original, this narrative will take as its template existing narratives which each individual has learned and internalized. How a narrative is told will depend crucially on the cultural resources available (Kelly and Dickinson, 1997). One way of understanding these culturally specific narrative resources is in terms of 'genres'. As was discussed in Chapter 3, genre can be defined as a narrative pattern that has become established through repetition. It is because they are familiar and easily recognized that genres act to shape the expectations of the audience while also providing a template for the author. An obvious and simple example is the children's fairy story. From the opening phrase 'Once upon a time' the audience know to expect a particular type of story with a happy ending. Familiarity with, and tacit knowledge of, established literary genres such as the comedy, the tragedy, the romance, and the satire shape the kind of stories that are told by individuals in their daily lives.

Institutional settings can also be understood as providing resources for constructing narratives, as well of course as restrictions on what should be told. As Gubrium and Holstein argue:

> Schools, clinics, counseling centers, correctional facilities, hospitals, support groups and self-help organizations, among many other sites for storying existence, provide narrative frameworks for conveying personal experience through time, for what is taken to be relevant in our lives, and why the lives under consideration developed in the way that they did. (1998:164)

These 'narrative frameworks' may be more or less restrictive and may be managed and maintained in very different ways. For example, Denzin (1989) describes how an alcoholic's story about his life can be understood as located within the cultural texts and shared experiences of 'Alcoholics Anonymous'. Gubrium and Holstein (1998) also suggest that in the context of a self-help group such as a support group for the caregivers of Alzheimer's disease sufferers, the members of the group actively monitor each other's narratives and prevent each other from deviating too far from what is considered to be relevant and acceptable. However, in other support groups the formats for story-telling are much more rigidly defined. In these contexts narratives are expected to follow a typical course mapping the progress of the disease together with the adjustment of the caregiver (Gubrium and Holstein, 1998).

Other more formal settings may provide even more explicit control of the way in which personal narratives can be told. Medical consultations, job interviews, and research interviews are all examples of occasions where particular types of stories are required, and there may be a variety of procedures in place to ensure that the appropriate narratives are elicited.[2] There are clear links here with the work of authors such as Foucault and Rose on the institutional settings that contribute to the shaping of the modern regulated self (Foucault, 1990; Rose, 1989). As Foucault has stressed, the west has become a 'singularly confessing society. The confession has spread its effects far and wide. It plays a part in justice, medicine, education, family relationships and love relations. ... Western man has become a confessing animal' (1990: 59).

Although some traditional narratives or 'public narratives' may be maintained and remain stable over relatively long periods of time, they also have a capacity for change. Genres of the past are replaced by new genres, stories breed new stories, narrative structures metamorphose into new narrative structures (Todorov, 1990 [1978]). As Plummer (1995) highlights, the rape narratives and 'coming out' stories that have a well-recognized form in the 1990s would not have been possible just thirty years ago. Chase (1995b) also notes that although previous researchers have stressed the ways in which successful women's life narratives have been constrained by the cultural idea that achievement and power are unwomanly, in her own interviews with women superintendents in the 1980s these women were able to 'speak forthrightly about their accomplishments' (Chase, 1995b: 9). Chase attributes this difference, at least in part, to the historical context in which the narratives were produced:

> When Heilbrun describes the dearth of narratives in which women assume power over their lives, she is speaking in broad terms about the nineteenth

and twentieth centuries. While that long history certainly continues to exert weight, it makes sense that successful women in the late 1980s would not be as burdened by it as women in earlier decades. (1995b: 11)

There are therefore many different established narrative forms, sedimented at different depths, within a culture to which individuals can turn in order to make sense of their own experience and communicate that experience to others. It is the interplay between these existing cultural discourses or 'public narratives' and the production of new individual or 'ontological' narratives that makes the idea of the narrative construction of identity particularly compelling within sociology.

The active narrator

Having discussed some of the ways in which individuals may be constrained to tell particular types of stories about themselves, depending on the social or institutional context, the audience, and the cultural narrative resources available, it is necessary also to consider the extent to which individuals are *active* narrators. It is important to recognize that individuals are not 'cultural dopes' (Garfinkel, 1967). This means that each individual is able to 'artfully construct' a story based on his or her interpretations and experiences (Faircloth, 1999). Gubrium and Holstein (1998) argue that cultural resources may provide guidelines that help individuals to recount their stories but cannot determine the content of each individual's narratives. They go on to cite Chase's work on the narratives of women superintendents (Chase, 1995b) as an example of how, although the women interviewed all talked of their power and success as well as describing their experiences of discrimination in an occupation dominated by white men, the stories produced in the research interviews were nevertheless individual and distinctive. Gubrium and Holstein also use the concept of 'narrative editing' to underline the reflexivity of individual narrators: their ability to manage actively their own narrative performances and to suggest appropriate ways in which their stories may be heard and interpreted. They argue that 'As much as the storyteller can be the author of his or her narrative, he or she is also an editor who constantly monitors, manages, modifies, and revises the emergent story. …Editing confirms that storytellers are never narratively "frozen" as authors of the texts they produce' (Gubrium and Holstein, 1998: 170).

This view of the individual as an active narrator has implications for the way that social scientists might analyse narrative material (Johnstone, 1997). Whereas one approach within socio-linguistics has been to try to link or correlate the social characteristics of narrators with the characteristics of their narratives, an alternative is to understand socio-linguistic variation in narrative as a 'resource for self expression rather than as the result of pre-existing social facts about speakers' (Johnstone, 1997: 316). In other words, to focus on *how* individuals constitute themselves through their use of narrative rather than assuming that they have fixed identities, which can be understood as determining the narratives they produce or, conversely, which can be simply read off from those narratives. This alternative approach suggests that identity is not some kind of 'static essence' but is instead a dynamic accomplishment (Cohan, 1997).

A good example of research that focuses on the way that individuals actively narrate and shape their own identities is provided in a fascinating paper by Ronai and Cross (1998) on the narrative resistance strategies of male and female striptease artists. In this research ten men and fourteen women, who all worked in the south-eastern United States, participated in tape-recorded 'life history' interviews. Ronai and Cross describe the strategies of narrative resistance that the male and female striptease artists employed to distance themselves from the negative societal view of striptease (and particularly female performers). By close analysis of the bio-graphical accounts provided in the research Ronai and Cross demonstrate that by setting up 'straw men' and 'straw women' in the form of other dancers who were prepared to strip completely, have sex with clients, or perform in grossly sexually explicit routines, the interviewees practised 'biographical work' in defining them-selves as exceptions to the average striptease dancer. In conjunction with 'sleaze', gender was also used as 'a biographical resource, a category on which dancers draw to construct deviant exemplars' (Ronai and Cross, 1998: 116). Ronai and Cross found that both the men and women in their sample reflected dominant concep-tions of the difference between male and female sexuality by specifying male dancers as more 'sleazy' (or explicitly sexual) than female dancers. The white males in their sample resisted this attribution of sleaze, in turn, by setting up black male strippers as the sleaze exemplar. By demarcating a position for themselves distant from that of others who are described as deviant, the striptease dancers who were interviewed therefore managed to create and maintain a positive sense of their own identity. This research therefore provides an excellent example of how attributes such as gender and race, that routinely appear as *variables* (i.e. stable characteristics) in quantitative research, are actively manipulated by respondents in a qualitative study and used as resources as they construct biographical identities. This further underlines the potential of qualitative research to explore and demonstrate the reflexive nature of the self in contrast to quantitative methods that depend upon an understanding of the individual as having fixed characteristics.

As is evident from the material reviewed above, the notion of the narrative con-stitution of the self has been discussed by authors across a range of disciplines. Its particular value within sociology is that it simultaneously refuses the humanist tendency to assert the primacy of individual experiences and understandings while also avoiding the pitfalls of a structuralist view, which offers an over-deterministic account of society and does not allow a space for individual agency. Similar arguments for the importance of understanding identity as narratively constituted have been made by Somers and Gibson (Somers, 1994; Somers and Gibson, 1994). They argue that the ability of sociologists to build adequate under-standings of why individuals choose to act in the way that they do has been ham-pered by their inattention to issues around identity and ontology. They suggest that it is important not to view theories about identity as the province of philosophers and psychologists, but rather to allow a focus on the social constitution of iden-tity to inform the development of sociological interpretations and understandings of social action. The implication is that just as it is impossible to make sense of action without focusing attention on structure, it is also unlikely that sociologists will be able to interpret social action if they fail to take account of ontology, social being, and identity. Whereas a categorical or 'essentialist' approach to identity presumes that individuals within a particular category (defined by race, class, or sex, for example) will have stable characteristics, which in turn will lead them to act predictably, the narrative approach allows for a more active, processual view of identity that shifts over time and is more context dependent.

Returning to the discussion begun in the first paragraphs of this chapter, it is clear that although quantitative longitudinal research has the potential to provide very detailed information about individuals, what is lost in this approach to research are the narratives that individuals tell about their own lives. While researchers such as Sampson and Laub and Singer have demonstrated that complex biographical case studies can be developed from survey data, these accounts are clearly authored by the researcher and do not allow any access to the reflexivity of the respondents themselves. This can be contrasted with the qualitative research by Ronai and Cross where the whole emphasis of the study is on understanding the identity work accomplished by individuals. It is important to be clear therefore that whereas the criticism that quantitative research is less detailed than qualitative research is often misplaced, there is a sense in which, in contrast to some qualitative approaches, quantitative research can never provide access to the *reflexive* individual. The identity of individuals, and the meaning of variables such as gender and social class, in quantitative research therefore remain relatively fixed. Paradoxically, therefore, it could be argued that while longitudinal approaches to analysis, such as event history modelling discussed in Chapter 5, appear to give a more processual or even narrative understanding of the social world, they do so at the expense of setting up an overly static view of the individual. It is not so much that quantitative research obscures the individual but rather that there is no scope within quantitative research for understanding the ways in which individuals use narrative to construct and maintain a sense of their own identity. Without this element there is a danger that people are merely seen as making decisions and acting within a predefined and structurally determined field of social relations rather than as contributing to both the maintenance and metamorphosis of the culture and community in which they live.

Summary

This chapter started by suggesting that longitudinal quantitative data might go some way to answering the criticisms made of much quantitative research, namely that it is concerned only with aggregations and thus obscures the individual. In particular it was demonstrated that longitudinal panel data can be used to examine individual trajectories in a way that repeated cross-sectional designs cannot. In other words, longitudinal research could be understood as potentially bridging the gap between qualitative and quantitative approaches. Indeed examples were given of researchers who have explicitly used longitudinal quantitative data to construct individual biographies that are more akin to the cases analysed by many qualitative researchers. However, an important distinction was made between using the term qualitative to mean detailed and using the term qualitative to indicate that the respondent's own perceptions and conceptual schema are taken into account.

This chapter has also outlined the post-modernist challenge to the conception of the unified self. It has introduced some of the recent philosophical and social psychological literature that emphasizes the importance of narrative in providing a sense of self as continuous through time and as contributing to an individual's sense of having a coherent personal identity. In this context, research has been discussed which highlights the way in which autobiographical narratives might be thought of as constituting rather than simply representing individual identities.

In conclusion, it has been shown that while a more processual, narrative understanding of the self is consonant with at least some approaches to qualitative analysis, it clearly cannot be readily accommodated within traditional quantitative methods. As will be discussed in more detail in the chapters which follow, this can either lead to the position that quantitative and qualitative approaches are fundamentally incompatible, or more helpfully suggest that while they cannot be integrated in any straightforward way, this in itself makes it all the more important that as social scientists we engage with both approaches to research.

Further reading

Gergen, K.J. and Gergen, M.M. (1997) 'Narratives of the self', in L.P. Hinchman and S.K. Hinchman (eds), *Memory, Identity, Community: The Idea of Narrative in the Human Sciences*. New York: State University of New York. pp. 161–84.

Holstein, J. and Gubrium, J. (2000) *The Self We Live By: Narrative Identity in a Postmodern World*. New York: Oxford University Press.

Ricoeur, P. (1991) 'Life in quest of narrative', in D. Wood (ed.), *On Paul Ricoeur*. London and New York: Routledge.

Somers, M.R. (1994) 'The narrative construction of identity: a relational and network approach', *Theory and Society*, 22: 605–49.

Readings for discussion

Ezzy, D. (1998) 'Theorizing narrative identity: symbolic interactionism and hermeneutics', *The Sociological Quarterly*, 39: 239–52.

Lucius-Hoene, G. and Deppermann, A. (2000) 'Narrative identity empiricized: a dialogical and positioning approach to autobiographical research interviews', *Narrative Inquiry*, 10: 199–222.

1 *What practical tools is an interviewee likely to use in the context of a research interview to establish his or her personal identity (see pp. 118–19)?*

2 *In what specific ways might an interviewer be understood to 'co-author' an autobiographical narrative produced by an interviewee in a research interview (see pp. 120–1)?*

3 *Why do Lucius-Hoene and Deppermann stress that analysis of interview narratives must attend to the performative and situational aspects of the interview as well as the content of the interview?*

4 *Should interviewers reveal anything about their own identities and life experiences in a research interview or should they be reticent and refrain from 'communicating [their] own experiences, opinions, and feelings'?*

Notes

1 There are a number of different people who are quoted as saying something along the lines that life is just one damned thing after another. For example, 'Life is just one damned thing after another' (Elbert Hubbard), 'It is not true that life is one damn thing after another, it is the same damn thing over and over' (Edna St Vincent Millay).

2 An example of this can be found in the work of Mishler who describes the way in which researchers may in a sense 'train' individuals to give appropriate responses at the beginning of research interviews (Mishler, 1986).

8

The ethical and political implications of using narrative in research

The wisest know that the best they can do…is not good enough. The not so wise, in their accustomed manner, choose to believe that there is no problem and that they have solved it. (Malcolm, 1990: 162, quoted by Josselson, 1996)

Any research that involves the participation of human subjects requires consideration of the potential impact of that research on those involved. There are now a number of ethical guidelines and codes which researchers in the social sciences can use to inform their practice. For example, the British Sociological Association and the British Psychological Society both have a statement of ethical practice, and in the United States the American Psychological Association and the American Sociological Association have a set of ethical principles and code of conduct that their members are expected to follow (American Psychological Association, 2003). However, as yet there has been relatively little discussion of the specific ethical issues that are raised by the use of narrative in research (although Smythe and Murray (2000) provide one notable exception). This chapter therefore considers the ethics and politics of narrative research. In this context, the term 'ethical' is used to describe those issues that relate to the relationship between the researcher and the research subjects or participants, and the impact of the research process on those individuals directly involved in the research, while the term 'political' is used to describe the broader implications of research in terms of the impact it may have on society or on specific subgroups within society. Although, in practice, ethical and political considerations may be linked, for the purposes of this chapter they will be treated separately. The first part of the chapter will therefore explore the ethical implications of using narrative in research while the second part of the chapter will move on to consider the more political aspects of using narrative in research.

The ethics of using narrative in research

As is helpfully highlighted by the British Sociological Association's (BSA's) *Statement of Ethical Practice*, 'Sociologists, when they carry out research, enter into personal and moral relationships with those they study.' This is perhaps most evident in the data collection stages of qualitative research when the researcher is likely to come into direct contact with the research subject. However, this relationship arguably continues throughout the analysis and dissemination stages of research. This discussion of the specific ethical implications of using narrative in research will therefore start by focusing on issues raised by the use of narrative in the process of data collection in terms of the interaction between the researcher and research subject, issues around informed consent and the potential impact of the research encounter on the respondent, and will then move on to consider the implications of using narrative when trying to preserve the confidentiality or anonymity of the research subject during analysis and dissemination.

The ethics of narrative interviewing

During the 1980s, a number of researchers emphasized that the movement away from structured interview schedules towards giving research respondents more opportunity to provide narratives about aspects of their lives and experiences was a way of empowering the subjects of their research (Graham, 1984; Kleinman, 1988; Mishler, 1984; 1986). For example, in line with other researchers advocating qualitative methods in the early 1980s (and in particular feminist writers such as Anne Oakley (1981) and Janet Finch (1984)), Graham (1984) highlighted the exploitative nature of a great deal of survey research. She suggested that story-telling provides an alternative to more structured interviews, whose format is determined by the researcher. Graham therefore advocated stories as the basis for informant-structured interviews, which 'more effectively safeguard the rights of informants to participate as subjects as well as objects in the construction of sociological knowledge' (1984: 118) and argued that because the narrator is aware that he or she is providing information, the 'story marks out the territory in which intrusion is tolerated' (1984: 107). More recently, Ochberg has made a similar point in relation to the use of narrative in research, stating that 'questionnaires limit our informants to narrow menus of pre-selected questions and answers', whereas 'interviews let informants choose the events that matter to them and put their own construction on them' (1996: 97). The use of narrative within research interviews clearly does give informants more opportunity to become active subjects within the research process, to select what they believe to be the most salient information, and to 'build up and communicate the complexity of their lives' (Graham, 1984: 119). However, as will be discussed in more detail below, the *potential* for exploitation is just as great as in structured interviews and survey approaches. Graham's assertion that attending to women's stories *necessarily* allows researchers to establish a more equal and reciprocal relationship with their informants is therefore, perhaps, misplaced.

In the same volume as Graham's chapter, Finch (1984) also discusses the ethical issues that arise in the context of conducting in-depth interviews with women. Based on her own experience of interviewing two very different groups of women, in her research on the wives of the clergy and interviews with working-class women involved in running and using pre-school playgroups, Finch argues that interviews carried out in an informal manner, in the setting of the respondent's own home, easily take on the character of an intimate conversation between friends. She suggests that it is the very effectiveness of this type of interview technique that leaves women open to exploitation. Finch writes: 'I have…emerged from interviews with the feeling that my interviewees need to know how to protect themselves from people like me. They have often revealed very private parts of their lives in return for what must be, in the last resort, very flimsy guarantees of confidentiality' (1984: 50).

The BSA statement of ethical practice (British Sociological Association, 2002) acknowledges that 'social research intrudes into the lives of those who are studied' and that 'while some participants in sociological research may find the experience a positive and welcome one, for others, the experience may be disturbing. Even if not harmed, those studied may feel wronged by aspects of the research experience.' This can be a particular issue in research that encourages individuals to construct and share narratives about their lives and experiences in the context of a research interview. Research subjects may be prompted to reflect on areas of their lives that they have not explicitly thought about before. Indeed the style of 'active interviewing' advocated by Gubrium and Holstein, and discussed in Chapter 2, specifically encourages the researcher to work with the respondent to produce new data and conceptualize and reflect on the research topic in innovative ways (Gubrium and Holstein, 1995). As Hollway and Jefferson (2000) discuss in relation to their qualitative narrative research on people's feelings about crime and risk, although the criterion of avoiding harm is a basic ethical principle, the topics discussed by respondents frequently involve some danger of psychological distress as research is likely, at times, to focus on unpleasant or disturbing topics. For example, they describe an interview with 'Fran', a 35-year-old divorced mother, in which she gave an account of her relationship with her ex-husband, a childhood dominated by her violent father, together with her current fears about rape and sexual assault.

Even when research focuses on a topic that might not be expected to be sensitive or disturbing for respondents, once interviewees are given the space to provide stories about their experiences some unexpected distressing accounts can emerge. For example, Parr (1998) describes a qualitative interview study with forty-nine mature women students in which she interviewed them about their experiences of going back into education. As she explains:

> Over half of the students interviewed spoke of painful life experiences which could be significantly linked with their education, both past and present. This is not what I anticipated would come out of the interviews and these stories were certainly unsolicited….I was surprised at the way these

clearly painful experiences tumbled out with no prompting. I found these accounts very stressful and this was accompanied by a mixture of conflicting emotions: anger and distress at the women's experiences, but also excitement that they were actually telling me about them. (Parr, 1998: 94)

Lieblich (1996) also writes about narrative interviewing as similar to 'opening a Pandora's box' and describes how in her research collecting the life stories of the members of a kibbutz her opening questions elicited painful accounts of past experiences. As she writes: 'I was constantly tormented with the sense of opening my interviewee's wounds and (as I thought then) leaving them with the pain' (Lieblich, 1996: 177).

Of course it is not necessarily harmful for research subjects to experience distress in the course of an interview, and it may in fact be therapeutic or reassuring for a respondent to be given a safe space in which to talk about an upsetting event or experience (Hollway and Jefferson, 2000). This, however, does require that the interviewer is experienced enough to manage the interaction in such a way as to minimize any long-term negative effects of the research experience on participants and, as Parr's quotation above demonstrates, the interview experience can also be a troubling one for the interviewer. It is important, however, not to overstate the possibility that qualitative narrative interviews may have a disturbing or negative impact on the interviewee. People can also benefit from being given the opportunity to reflect on and talk about their lives with a good listener.

In a paper on the effects of participating in semi-structured interviews on the interviewees, Proctor and Padfield report that most of their forty-seven research participants claimed to have little recall of earlier interviews when they were re-interviewed a couple of years later. However, they did broadly remember them as being both interesting and enjoyable (Proctor and Padfield, 1998). The two main reasons for respondents' positive evaluations of their interview experiences were first that they felt the research (on the work and family experience of young women) was a worthwhile project to contribute to and be part of, and second that they enjoyed the rather unusual opportunity to talk at length, to someone who was interested, about their lives and experiences. Proctor and Padfield also emphasize that the research interview did not have the same impact on all respondents. While some of the women they interviewed found the research experience personally helpful in that it gave them a chance to reflect on their lives and make decisions about future plans, in at least one case the interview made clearer to the interviewee her own (self-defined) failures and in particular her inability to stick to things she was aiming for. What this paper also highlights is that, despite the burgeoning literature on qualitative methods and reflexivity, there are very few published empirical accounts documenting the way that interviewees perceive and experience interviews. As has been discussed in Chapter 2 and Chapter 7, it is widely acknowledged that the account or the 'self' presented in an interview will partly be a function of the interview interaction itself. However, within the existing literature there is little evidence provided to suggest the *extent* of the effect of the interview.

The ethics of postal questionnaire studies

Of course, it is not only qualitative interviews that raise ethical issues. Although rarely discussed in the methodology literature, quantitative methods of data collection, such as postal questionnaire studies, can also have an impact on research subjects and elicit narratives from individuals that speak directly of the physical or psychological pain in their lives. For example, in a longitudinal, prospective study of women's experiences of pregnancy, labour, and childbirth, which sent a series of self-completion questionnaires to over 800 women, the researchers received several questionnaires with extensive comments written on them from women who were depressed or severely troubled about their pregnancy and family life (Green et al., 1988). Green et al. do not describe or discuss their study in terms of 'narrative research'. However, it is interesting to reflect on the fact that this type of quantitative *longitudinal* research, based on self-completion questionnaires, does enable researchers and research participants to build up more of a relationship than would be likely to be established in a *cross-sectional* survey. In particular, this type of panel study requires that each questionnaire can be linked to a specific respondent so that when the results are collated, the whole series of questionnaires from the same individual can be matched together. This means that when respondents complete the questionnaire and return it they know that the research team is fully aware from whom each response has come. In this context, if an individual records severe psychological distress it raises ethical issues for the research team as to how to respond to that distress. In the maternity services research, discussed above, the researchers resolved this issue by writing to any individual who expressed severe problems to acknowledge their feelings and by suggesting sources of help and support.

This research study also provides some rare evidence about the impact of the questionnaires on the women involved. In response to the concerns of a general practitioner (advising on the project) that the postal questionnaires might alarm some women, the researchers included two specific questions in the second antenatal questionnaire about how the research had affected respondents. While only 2% of the women in the sample indicated that they had been worried by the questionnaire, nearly 40% of women felt that the questionnaire had made them think about new issues. For example, one woman added the comment that 'I have been forced to think of labour and birth – not particularly pleasant', while another wrote: 'It has made me feel that I haven't had much opportunity to discuss what I would like during labour' (Green et al., 1988: Appendix D). Many women clearly enjoyed completing the questionnaires, however, and were particularly enthusiastic about the postnatal questionnaire stating that they found it a useful way of reflecting on the birth and their feelings about it. The researchers explained that:

> In some cases the questionnaire provided a 'listening ear' to women who felt that no-one else was interested. One woman who thanked us for inviting her to participate in our study wrote:
>
> "It seems that I am the only one that really loves and wants [the baby]. I have felt so unspecial during this pregnancy that it has hurt me very deeply and made me very sad."

> Another woman who had been widowed at 6 weeks of pregnancy wrote:
> "I'd just like to say when I answered your questions, I felt as though I was
> talking directly to someone. Well done."

A longitudinal study in the United States that followed a sample of approximately 100 women, who were college seniors at Mills College in 1958 and
1960, through adult life into middle age, also provides some insights into the
impact of a more quantitative longitudinal survey on the lives of those involved.
Members of the study were recruited in their final year at college in the late
1950s, contacted a second time at about age 27 in 1963 or 1964, a third time in
1981 (at approximately age 43), and finally at age 52 in 1989 (Helson, 1993). In
addition, in 1990, when a report of the preliminary results of the 1989 survey
was sent to participants, women were also sent a very brief questionnaire about
their experiences of being part of the study. Agronick and Helson (1996) provide a useful discussion of women's responses to this questionnaire. Seventy-two
women responded and in answer to a fixed choice question, twenty-two indicated that the study had affected them 'quite a bit', thirty-four indicated that the
study had affected them 'some', and fourteen indicated that the study had
affected them 'not very much'. Two women did not respond to this question.
A total of thirty-eight women made some further comments about the impact
of the study and most comments contained one or more of four main themes:
twenty-two women stated that the study had given them psychological insight;
fourteen said it had provided support and validation; seven stated that it
had increased their awareness of social change; and four said that it had given
them a chance to contribute to useful research. Agronick and Helson (1996)
provide some examples of the type of comments written by women that reveal
the emotional impact that research can have on some participants even when
data collection is carried out using postal questionnaires rather than in-depth
interviews:

> It was quite valuable to pause during several points of my life to take a
> longer view of directions. This process gave a perspective to my progress
> and regresses I would not normally have had.
>   [The study] has always generated feelings as I have reviewed where I've
> been and where I am going – precipitated some grieving.
>   Learning about the group has made me realize my life is on course.
>   I am glad to know [from the reports] I'm quite normal and much happier
> than many of my classmates.
>   (Agronick and Helson, 1996: 84–5)

These examples demonstrate that any research that asks respondents to reflect in
detail on their lives and experiences is likely to have an impact on respondents
and that it is difficult for researchers to predict in advance what issues will be
raised by research. A major advantage of working as part of a research team is that
such issues can more easily be discussed and dealt with sensitively, drawing on the
support of others directly involved with the research.

Ethics, narrative identity, and informed consent

An approach to the analysis of interview material, which is informed by the notion (discussed in Chapter 3 and Chapter 7) that autobiographical or ontological narratives do not merely describe a world already made but are inseparable from the self, raises additional ethical problems for the researcher. As Smythe and Murray have emphasized, the traditional conception of the research participant in the social sciences is that of a source of data, a repository of information that can be tapped by the researcher, or 'a locus of variables to be observed and manipulated for the purpose of establishing general laws' (2000: 317). This model of the research process gives rise to a set of ethical principles that have to do with obtaining people's voluntary consent to 'give away' their data to the researcher and with the researcher's obligation to treat participants respectfully in the process. However, once narrative is understood as not simply descriptive but constitutive of the self, the potential of research to be a significant transformative experience must also be recognized. The fact that individuals are likely to have a great deal of personal investment in the stories and accounts they provide in a research interview makes it more problematic for participants simply to relinquish such information to the researcher. Unlike data such as reaction times or scores on memory tests that are routinely collected in psychological research, or information about occupation, hours worked, marital status, etc., that is elicited in sociological surveys, personal narratives deal with the meaning of one's own life experiences and thus touch on issues of personal identity. As Smythe and Murray argue, 'research in the narrative study of lives yields information that cannot be dissociated so readily from one's fundamental human values and meaningful life experiences' (2000: 318). This therefore requires a rather different approach to the ethics of data collection and analysis. Narrative studies could be argued to have components of both research and therapy, so that it is not possible simply to apply the ethical regulations that pertain to one or other of these rather different fields (Lieblich, 1996: 173). As will be discussed below, the recognition that personal narrative is firmly bound up with individual identities raises important questions about the analysis of this narrative material and the impact of the analysis on the research participant.

As Mishler has argued: 'Through their narratives, people may be moved beyond the text to the possibilities of action…to apply the understanding arrived at to action in accord with one's own interests' (1986: 119). Indeed, one view of therapy is that it precisely consists of the (re)formation of a client's self-narratives according to certain normative resources (Lynch, 1997). It could be argued that a similar process takes place within qualitative research interviews and a number of researchers have noted the almost therapeutic nature of narrative biographical interviews (Collins, 1998; Parr, 1998; Riessman, 1990). In her research on divorce Riessman (1990) explicitly recognizes that interviewing has potentially therapeutic effects. One man in her study even said that the interview 'felt like therapy'. However, researchers do not always address the ethical implications of the therapeutic potential of interviews. If narrative interviews have 'therapeutic' overtones then we also need to acknowledge the possibility of less positive outcomes. The effects of interviewing on the self-concept of both the interviewer and the interviewee must be considered (Day-Sclater, 1998b).

Ethics and narrative analysis

It is clearly not only the interview itself that may have an effect on the research subject. The way in which the researcher interprets and analyses the narratives produced in the interview also may have an impact (either positive or negative) on the interviewee. If the production of personal narratives is seen as a central process by which people comprehend their own lives and establish a unified and coherent sense of self, a researcher's deconstruction and interpretation of those narratives, if not presented sensitively, may undermine the work being done by the interviewee to maintain his or her ontological security (Borland, 1991). As Smythe and Murray have argued:

> The problem is that, once the researcher's account is taken as the authoritative interpretation of an individual's experience, the individual's own understanding of their experience inevitably is compromised. Narrative research in this way can become intrusive and subtly damaging, even when participants respond positively to the researcher's account. (2000: 321)

Interviewees may also perceive an element of dishonesty or duplicity here. If the research subjects believe that the purpose of an interview is for the researcher to gather information or 'facts' about a particular aspect of their life or experience, but the analysis and interpretation of the interview focuses not on the content but rather on the structure or form of the narratives provided by the interviewees, and particularly if the analysis includes discussion of the interviewees' identity, they may rightly feel that they have been deceived. The BSA *Statement of Ethical Practice* states that 'As far as possible participation in sociological research should be based on the freely given informed consent of those studied. This implies a responsibility on behalf of the researcher to explain in appropriate detail and in terms meaningful to participants, what the research is about.' However, once there is a move away from a naturalistic or humanistic approach to research towards an interest in constructivism, it becomes more complex for the researcher to explain the nature of the research and the research questions to the research subject. Indeed, even in the context of naturalistic research, if the aim is to try to understand a topic from the perspective of the respondent rather than setting out clear research questions in advance of data collection, it can be difficult to provide potential respondents with a detailed description of the nature of the research project. This extract from Hollway and Jefferson's discussion of their research highlights the complexity of the ethics of consent in narrative interviews:

> We were also aware of a (more) intractable issue concerning informed consent. We felt that it was impossible to inform participants in advance in ways that would be meaningful, about the experience of our kind of

interviews. Their experience of researchers (if any) was based on market and survey researchers who would ask structured questions and tick boxes on forms. The questions would be about specific behaviours or opinions.... It was only through the experience of the first interview that they would come to realise what telling stories about their experiences to people like us could entail. (2000: 86)

Confidentiality

An additional issue that is raised by the use of narrative and a focus on 'the case' in sociological research is the problem of preserving individuals' anonymity or confidentiality. It is a key ethical principle that the anonymity and privacy of those who participate in the research process should be respected; however, once a combination of attributes and experiences is ascribed to a particular case in a research report it can be very difficult to ensure that the case does not become recognizable. The information collected in a narrative interview with an individual may not be any more detailed than that collected in a quantitative longitudinal study such as the National Child Development Study or the Panel Study of Income Dynamics. However, the commitment to understand and represent cases holistically, in much research informed by an interest in narrative, means that case histories are frequently provided when the research is written up. It is the unique nature of these case histories, the specific constellation of attributes, which means that individuals are likely to be identifiable by those who know them. Lieblich's research, which focused on people's experiences of living on an Israeli kibbutz (Beit Hashita), provides a clear example of the problems of maintaining anonymity in narrative research. As she wrote:

> [T]he final outcome was well forseen. Israeli gossip identified the kibbutz quite soon after the publication, and the guess was validated by a smart reviewer in the daily paper. The personal identity of the protagonists was, then, a simple game for all interested. Members of Beit Hashita itself could naturally identify each other with almost no difficulty. Although most of the individuals were rather pleased with their sections, a few were distressed. (Lieblich, 1996: 176)

In this type of case–study research it is clear that even if a few details are changed and a pseudonym is used to 'disguise' the individuals involved, it is likely that they will be recognized by family and friends.

Clearly, given the very probable risk of lack of anonymity once research is written up, it is important to discuss the dissemination of the research with the respondents involved. Indeed, Lieblich (1996) describes how she sent a draft personal narrative to each of the sixty-one individuals whose stories she was hoping to include in her book. Although the majority of research participants were happy for their accounts to be included, two of the women asked her to withdraw their entire stories from the research. Once the book was published, and read by members of the kibbutz community, however, further unanticipated ethical issues emerged. As Lieblich explains, she had been concerned to protect each of the individuals within the research process but she could not foresee the implications of the publication of the research for relations between family members. In particular she gives the example of a mother who was deeply upset by the stories of her two daughters. Both of them had described how their mother had dedicated much of her time to the kibbutz during their childhood and had left them feeling neglected.

In addition to sharing research findings with the research participants and gaining their explicit approval for their stories to be made public, there are perhaps two approaches to the ethical problem of preserving individuals' anonymity in narrative research. One is to focus on the analysis and interpretation of narrative material that is already in the public domain. William James used this approach in his influential book *The Varieties of Religious Experience* (1952). As Bakan explains:

> The fundamental data for that book were provided by the narratives of religious experience that James found among the books in the library. He collected lengthy passages of narrative, studied them carefully, and provided a series of extraordinary observations and reflections in connection with them. It is a model of the use of narrative material in the field of psychology. (1996: 6)

A similar approach has been used by a number of psychologists interested in narratives and lives over the past twenty years. For example, Gergen (1992) focuses on a comparison of the autobiographies of notable men and women while Hollway and Jefferson (1998) deconstruct press accounts of a specific date rape case in their research on the nature of gendered identities involved in heterosexual relationships. An additional approach to this problem of preserving the anonymity of those who provide their stories in narrative research is to construct a fictionalized account. However, the production of fictional 'composite' characters using elements from several different life stories may give researchers licence to 'cheat' in that they can choose only those elements which support their hypotheses (Hollway and Jefferson, 2000).

Confidentiality is usually less of an issue when conducting large-scale quantitative surveys. For example, Bakan (1996) reports that Alfred Kinsey used very large samples of respondents when carrying out his research on sexual experiences and sexual behaviour, in order to conceal the identity of the individuals who provided him with details of their sexual histories. Problems of anonymity do not only arise when material has been collected using in-depth interview techniques, however. The type of case history produced using longitudinal quantitative data by researchers such as Singer et al. (discussed in Chapter 5) also runs the risk that it may breach the anonymity of the individual involved. In some cases, of course, individuals may be happy to be identified within the research and it is more honest to discuss this possibility with them than to promise levels of anonymity that are impossible to ensure in practice. Indeed, as Mishler (1986: 124–5) has argued, confidentiality and anonymity may not always be a good thing if individuals feel that they have been deprived of the chance to have their voices heard within the context of a piece of research.

It is for all these reasons, then, that in-depth interviewing, which gives individuals an opportunity to provide narratives about their lives and encourages interviewers to elicit and attend to these personal stories, entails as many if not more ethical considerations than structured survey interviews. Indeed within a structured survey interview the contract between interviewer and respondent is much clearer: there is less ambiguity about what type of information is being elicited and what is being provided. This clearly problematizes Graham's assertion that the 'story marks the boundary of what the individual is prepared to tell' (1984: 120). Indeed the analytic boundaries around fixed choice questions are much more clearly defined than those attached to a narrative. This is not, of course, to argue that we should avoid the use of in-depth interviews. They clearly provide an extremely good basis for sociological research. However, encouraging respondents to become more active participants in the research process does not automatically result in a more ethical methodology and indeed leads to the need for a *greater* sensitivity to the ethical issues raised by research.

Narrative and the politics of research

Having discussed the ethical implications of carrying out research informed by an interest in narrative, this second main section of the chapter moves on to consider the broader political ramifications of using methodologies that make explicit use of narrative. Attention to narratives within research can be understood as congruent with a wish to develop methodologies that give a voice to the most marginalized groups within society. For example, in their work on the sociology of illness and medicine, both Mishler (1984) and Kleinman (1988) advocate the use of narrative and argue that it provides evidence about patients' insights into their own problems and can be empowering. The popularity of narrative approaches among many social scientists may also lie in its potential to be subversive or transformative. By providing a means through which the experiences of individuals can be represented in their own words, 'narrative scholarship participates in rewriting social life in ways that are, or can be, liberatory' (Ewick and Silbey, 1995: 199). In contrast to large-scale surveys and other quantitative approaches, research informed by an interest in narrative places the individual and his or her personal biography centre stage. An interest in the narratives produced in research makes it more likely that 'the voices, feelings and meanings of persons are heard' (Denzin, 1983).

Among feminist researchers there has traditionally been a particular interest in documenting individual women's stories. As Maynard (1994) has discussed, in the 1970s and 1980s there was a specific focus on qualitative in-depth interviews as the appropriate 'feminist method' within social science. While surveys were often criticized for imposing the researcher's agenda and understandings on the respondents, the focus on subjective meanings and experiences within much qualitative research was seen as more appropriate by feminist researchers. The material produced in these interviews corresponded more closely to the type of knowledge they wanted to make available and the possibility of a close relationship between researcher and interviewee was more in keeping with feminist ideals concerning the ethics of research (Oakley, 1981). In addition, some feminist theorists, in particular Hartsock (1997), Harding (1992), and Smith (1987) have gone as far as asserting that qualitative approaches, which attend to the accounts that women give of their experiences, represent the most appropriate methodology for understanding gender inequalities in society. Their argument is that it is the members of the most marginalized and subordinated sections of a society who can provide the most useful evidence of the oppressive structures that maintain the power differentials within that society.

However, it can be very difficult for women and members of other disadvantaged groups to see and understand general systems of inequality from the perspective provided by their own everyday lives. As Mott and Condor have argued: 'Social facts – including facts about gender inequality – often exist at a level of statistical abstraction to which the individual subject may have no direct access' (1997: 64). While the existence of gender discrimination may become apparent when aggregate data are available, it may not be so evident when individual cases are examined separately. It is therefore important to be aware that individuals' narratives are not always subversive or transformative of existing power differentials in society. Neither do they necessarily illuminate structural explanations for inequalities or the external constraints that shape people's lives. People are not always conscious of the aspects of their life histories that they share with others, or of the common patterns that underlie what appear to be very individual experiences. Although, as has been discussed in previous chapters, there are good reasons for sociologists to attend to the accounts that people give of their lives, a methodology informed by an interest in narrative should not be thought to provide some kind of simple panacea. In particular the existence of 'public narratives' and genres, discussed in Chapter 3, and the inherently social nature of narrative – the need to make narratives comprehensible within specific social contexts – mean that stories never communicate raw experience. As Atkinson has argued:

> Autobiographical accounts and self-revelations are as conventional and artful as any other mode of representation. We sell short ourselves and the possibility of systematic social analysis if we implicitly assume that autobiographical accounts or narratives of personal experience grant us untrammelled access to a realm of hyperauthenticity. The collection and reproduction of narratives and the celebration of voices through that work are not guarantees of anything. (1997: 331)

However, it is not just that individual narratives may not provide ready insights into structural inequalities in society, or that we need to be aware that they do not simply provide a transparent window onto people's lives and experiences. Indeed the inherently social nature of narrative means that even the narratives of the least powerful members of a society may contribute to, rather than undermine, existing inequalities. As Ewick and Silbey have stressed:

> Because of the conventionalized character of narrative, then, our stories are likely to express ideological effects and hegemonic assumptions. We are as likely to be shackled by the stories we tell (or that are culturally available for our telling) as we are by the form of oppression they might seek to reveal. In short, the structure, the content, and the performance of stories as they are defined and regulated within social settings often articulate and reproduce existing ideologies and hegemonic relations of power and inequality. (1995: 212)

In this context 'the hegemonic' is understood as those ideas, power differentials, and structural arrangements that are so securely embedded in the social fabric that they literally 'go without saying'. The hegemonic therefore represents those aspects of social life that are 'taken for granted' and are seen as so natural that they require no comment or explanation. Ewick and Silbey stress that a hegemonic tale should be understood as doing more than simply reflecting current dominant ideologies. Rather, the narratives that individuals tell can be understood as profoundly implicated in constituting and reinforcing the hegemony, which in turn shapes individuals' lives and behaviour. It is for this reason that we should be cautious about assuming that research methods resting on the collection and analysis of individuals' narratives and life stories will necessarily be emancipatory.

It could, of course, be argued that all forms of discourse will to some extent necessarily reflect and maintain the hegemonic within society, and that therefore research which does not specifically focus on narratives will also be in danger of supporting and reproducing existing power differentials. However, there are some specific features of narrative that make it particularly central to the maintenance of the hegemony. First, the sequential or chronological aspect of narrative and the expectation of coherence mean that narratives tend to include implicit assumptions or claims regarding causal links. As was discussed in Chapter 1, readers will tend to assume causality when a sequence of events is recounted as a narrative (Chatman, 1978). The fact that these causal links are not made explicit makes it hard for them to be openly challenged or debated. Second, narratives simultaneously use general understandings of the social world while depicting specific individuals in specific contexts. They therefore reproduce without making manifest the connections between specific events and cultural assumptions or social structures. Once again this means that many of the assumptions underlying a narrative will remain unacknowledged and unchallenged. For example, the following extract is taken from a biographical interview I carried out with a graduate woman in her early forties. Right at the beginning of the interview she provided the following narrative explanation of the way she had combined motherhood with her career over the last few years, since the birth of her third child, and her plans for the immediate future:

1. Workwise, I'm just about to give up my job,
2. at the end of August.
3. I was appointed on um a full-time, permanent contract
4. for *** University in 1993,
5. and I got pregnant
6. um by a series of strange coincidences [laughs]
7. in 1994,
8. and when I had the baby in 1995
9. I um decided to go part-time.
10. So I was part-time, point five, until now.
11. I'm still part-time.

12. And um I'm giving up,
13. er, because he's going to school in Manchester,
14. and I can't face the thought of being so far away from him,
15. because I have to go up and down the M6,
16. and although it's only actually forty miles, forty-five miles away,
17. and it can be done in three-quarters of an hour,
18. often it takes me two hours, at least once a week.
19. And so I wouldn't like to be that far away from him
20. if he's at school and I'm called because he's ill or something.

21. Plus I want to um-
22. I've learned from the other children
23. that there's more to life than work,
24. and I want to spend some time with him
25. and try and give him a solid grounding. (Cecilia's story)

These three stanzas can be seen to form a narrative in their own right (with an abstract, complicating action, and evaluation) but were also expanded by other narratives later in the interview. In this section, Cecilia apparently feels that she does not need to justify her decision to 'go part-time' when she had her baby in 1995, and indeed she does not provide further explanation of this later in the interview. In contrast, even in this summary narrative, in the second stanza, Cecilia elaborates her reasons for deciding to give up work at the point when her son is starting school. The implicit message here is that while it is considered 'normal' for a woman to start working part time rather than full time when she has a baby, it is unusual for her to give up work once her child starts school. This therefore is an example of the way in which assumptions about conventional ways of combining motherhood and paid employment structure a woman's narrative account of her own experiences. The way in which this narrative extract subtly incorporates hegemonic assumptions can perhaps be most clearly grasped if a thought experiment is carried out in which the narrator of the second two stanzas is a man rather than a woman. In other words, although the interviewee here is ostensibly giving a very specific account of her own choices, preferences, and employment behaviour and the links between this and the life stage of her youngest child, her narrative is simultaneously reinforcing a set of gendered expectations about the normal and appropriate behaviour of mothers in British society.

Although Ewick and Silbey's work is specifically focused on narratives in the socio-legal context it is relevant for the present discussion because of the distinction they make between 'hegemonic tales' and 'subversive stories' (1995). The core of their argument is that narratives that obscure the linkages between particular individual experiences and broader social structures can be understood as hegemonic tales. These are narratives that reinforce and support the status quo. They present a version of the world in which individuals' behaviour can be understood completely in terms of their own motivations and local conditions. As other authors have cautioned, there is a tendency for individuals' accounts to be somewhat 'voluntaristic' (Bearman et al., 1999). In contrast Ewick and Silbey's 'subversive stories' are those that 'recount particular experiences as rooted in and part of an encompassing cultural, material, and political world that extends beyond the local' (1995: 219). They suggest that it may be those who are at the margins of society and who feel most excluded from the plots and characters that constitute the culturally available narrative resources, who are most likely to produce these 'counterhegemonic' narratives. In addition, Ewick and Silbey argue that a 'condition for generating subversive stories derives from understanding how the hegemonic is constituted as an ongoing concern. In other words knowing the rules and perceiving a concealed agenda enhance the possibilities of intervention and resistance' (1995: 221).

These suggestions about the possibilities for producing 'subversive stories', i.e. narratives which challenge rather than maintain power differentials in society, are helpful in that they suggest that even where research participants may provide 'hegemonic tales' there is scope for the researcher to use these to produce a 'collective narrative' which reveals rather than maintains what is taken for granted in a society.[1] While it may be the case that some individuals can provide accounts about their lives that offer insights into structural power differentials within society, it seems more valuable to recognize that *the researcher* is responsible for providing an analysis of narratives which makes explicit that which has gone without saying, and which makes linkages between particular cases and underlying social conditions. As Chase explains in relation to her research on the biographies of women school superintendents in the United States:

> As I analyzed the narratives, I focused on a set of language processes that are taken for granted in everyday speech: the use of cultural discourses for making sense of individual experience; the development of narrative strategies in relation to conflicting cultural discourses; and the communication of meaning through linguistic features of talk....The aim of narrative analysis is not to impose immutable or definitive interpretations on participants' stories or even to challenge the meanings participants attach to their stories. Rather, its goal is to turn our attention elsewhere, to taken-for-granted cultural processes embedded in the everyday practices of storytelling. (1996: 55)

It is therefore perhaps by analysing individual narratives in order to expose or reveal the 'taken-for-granted' or hegemonic and how it operates, that research can truly provide a subversive story about people's lives and experiences. In other words, qualitative research informed by an interest in narrative is about more than just allowing the voices of respondents to be heard. Respondents' words will always be edited by the researcher and filtered through his or her theoretical framework. The researcher therefore has a responsibility to do more than valorize the narrative voice of respondents, rather to conduct an analysis which places narratives firmly within their social and cultural context and which makes explicit the available resources which have been used to structure them. As Smythe and Murray have argued:

> It is incumbent on the narrative researcher, as a social scientist, to relate the meanings of an individual's story to the larger, theoretically significant categories that they exemplify, an objective quite foreign to that of the individual telling a purely personal narrative. (2000: 325)

In this context, Smythe and Murray's concept of the 'typal narrative' is useful. They argue that the most familiar form of narrative is the personal narrative, which focuses on the individuality of a central person or main character. However, the narratives that social scientists construct bear on broader psychological and social themes and 'attempt to subsume individuals and their life experiences within broader types that are of theoretical interest to social scientists' (Smythe and Murray, 2000: 327). For this reason they are termed typal narratives. They will not be as individually specific as personal narratives but will provide concrete examples of the theoretical constructs developed by social scientists. Smythe and Murray use this difference between the typal narrative and the personal narrative to understand why, as was discussed earlier, research respondents may feel that the research accounts produced by researchers do not adequately do justice to them as complex and unique individuals.

What is interesting here is that in the context of a more quantitative approach to research, individuals would have no expectation that their life or experiences would be represented holistically in the context of a research report. Perhaps the tension emerges in qualitative work in part because the sample is smaller. This means that the researcher is likely to develop a closer relationship with each participant, and the participants may therefore be led to believe that the integrity of their accounts will be preserved and that it is the manifest content of their narratives that will be presented as part of the research findings. In contrast to these not-unreasonable expectations, narrative researchers such as Ochberg have stated that:

> When I interpret a life story, I try to show what an informant accomplishes by recounting his or her history in a particular fashion. To succeed, I must undermine the usual assumption: that people say what they mean and mean only what they say. I lead a reader through the account showing how everything that has been said has other meanings, ulterior purposes. (1996: 98)

This analytic approach returns us directly to the question of ethical issues in narrative research, in that if interviewees have one set of expectations about how their stories are going to be used then it might be seen as problematic to conduct a rather different type of analysis. In particular, interviewees might reasonably expect the researcher to be primarily interested in the *content* of what they are saying and may well be disquieted to discover that the focus is instead on 'cultural discourses' or 'narrative strategies'. This is in no way to argue that the type of analysis advocated by Chase or Ochberg is inherently unethical or that it should be avoided. An appreciation of narrative as an artful form, as a self-construction, and as a tool for persuading an audience does not necessarily demean or diminish the narrator in any way (Ochberg, 1996). However, the challenge for researchers who are concerned to demonstrate the rhetoric at work in the narratives of their respondents is how to collect this narrative material without exploiting the individuals who have consented to provide detailed biographical accounts of their lives and experiences.

Summary

In this chapter it has been argued that many researchers have advocated the use of narrative within qualitative interviews on the grounds that it is more ethical and more empowering than more traditional structured interview methods. However, the appreciation that interviews are not merely a means for collecting but also a site for producing data, coupled with the concept of the narrative constitution of identity, underlines the fact that the use of narrative in interviews may demand consideration of additional ethical issues. It has been suggested that the use of narrative not only has implications for the impact of the interview on a research participant, but can also raise questions about how to secure informed consent, how to share the results of analysis with respondents, and how to preserve the confidentiality and anonymity of those involved in research. The intention has been not to suggest that the use of narrative raises ethical questions which are insurmountable, but rather to avoid a simplistic understanding of qualitative research as providing some kind of panacea for the power differentials and ethical problems that ensue from more structured or quantitative methods of data collection and analysis.

The second half of the chapter provided a reflection on some of the more political implications of using narrative in research. In particular, Ewick and Silbey's conception of 'hegemonic tales' and 'subversive stories' was found to be helpful in that it disrupts the notion that research which allows the stories of the oppressed or least powerful in society to be heard is *necessarily* emancipatory. It was argued that the process of analysis and interpretation has the potential to reveal the social and structural influences that have an impact on the shape of individuals' lives and also on the way they make sense of and narrate those lives. It is therefore the researcher's responsibility to attend to the interpretive narrative produced as a result of the research. In the next chapter, the role of the researcher as narrator, and the reflexivity encouraged by the use of narrative in research, is discussed in more detail.

Further reading

Ewick, P. and Silbey, S.S. (1995) 'Subversive stories and hegemonic tales: toward a sociology of narrative', *Law and Society Review*, 29 (2): 197–226.

Finch, J. (1984) '"It's great to have someone to talk to": the ethics and politics of interviewing women', pp. 70–87 in C. Bell and H. Roberts (eds), *Social Researching*. London: Routledge & Kegan Paul.

Josselson, R. (1996) 'On writing other people's lives: self-analytic reflections of a narrative researcher', in R. Josselson (ed.), *Ethics and Process in the Narrative Study of Lives*. Thousand Oaks, CA: Sage.

Smythe, W.E. and Murray, M.J. (2000) 'Owning the story: ethical considerations in narrative research', *Ethics and Behaviour*, 10: 11–36.

Reading for discussion

Chase, S.E. (1996) 'Personal vulnerability and interpretive authority in narrative research', in R. Josselson (ed.), *Ethics and Process in the Narrative Study of Lives*. Thousand Oaks, CA: Sage. pp. 45–59.

1   *What were Chase's main reasons for*

   (a)   *Sending copies of their interview transcripts to the women in her study?*
   (b)   *Not sharing her interpretations and work in progress with research partici-pants prior to publication?*

2   *Do narrative researchers have an ethical responsibility to tell participants that their experiences will be reframed through the methods of narrative analysis?*

Note

1   Laurel Richardson's idea of the 'collective narrative' is perhaps helpful here. In her research on 'the other woman' which involved interviewing single women who had had or were having affairs with married men, she discusses analysing the individual narratives produced by her interviewees and producing a collective narrative demonstrating the similarities and themes that emerged as a result of the research.

9

The researcher as narrator: reflexivity in qualitative and quantitative research

> In our work as researchers we weigh and sift experiences, make choices regarding what is significant, what is trivial, what to include what to exclude. We do not simply chronicle what happened next, but place the next in meaningful context. By doing so we craft narratives; we write lives. (Richardson, 1990: 10)

Much of this book so far has focused on the narratives produced by the subjects of research, the 'respondents' who provide accounts about their lives in qualitative interviews or who complete structured work histories and life histories in more quantitative studies. This chapter redirects the spotlight to illuminate the role of the researcher as narrator. Once we start attending to the narrative features of the data produced by respondents it is, perhaps, inevitable that we should also become more attuned to the narrative quality of research accounts. For researchers who work on the analysis of individual life stories and examine the structure of those narratives, it is difficult to ignore the fact that they themselves are also narrators who must convince and persuade their readers. As Richardson has highlighted, 'social science writing, like all writing, depends on literary and rhetorical devices to articulate its ideas and make its point convincingly, credibly and cognitively' (1990: 17). An approach to qualitative analysis informed by an interest in narrative is therefore frequently accompanied by a more reflexive methodology. However, for those working with quantitative data, language is more usually treated as simply a tool for the collection and presentation of information. The narratives that inhere within quantitative research accounts and the roles that those narratives play in shaping our understanding of individual identities remain largely hidden or implicit and are therefore rarely discussed. One of the aims of this chapter will therefore be to consider some of the ways in which a focus on narrative in longitudinal *quantitative* research might also encourage researchers to be more reflexive about their analyses and research accounts.

The chapter will begin by discussing what is meant by reflexivity in the context of recent debates about research practice. In particular, this section of the chapter will explore how the concept of reflexivity has been used by those who want to rescue qualitative work from the more 'extreme' excesses of relativism and post-modernism, while also rejecting a naive naturalist approach to describing the social world and 'writing up'[1] research. The chapter will then consider what has been written about reflexivity in the context of data collection, data analysis, and 'writing up'. Clearly these three facets of the research process are not necessarily discrete or easy to separate, particularly in qualitative research, but the distinction between these different but linked research activities provides a helpful way to structure a discussion of reflexivity in practice.

Defining and understanding reflexivity

As was discussed in Chapter 7, in relation to individual identity, in the simplest terms, reflexivity might be understood as a heightened awareness of the self, acting in the social world. Various theorists have stressed the reflexive nature of late–modern identities. Individuals can no longer simply assume comparatively stable identities, they have to be actively constructed (Beck, 1992; 1994; Beck and Beck-Gernsheim, 2002; Giddens, 1991; 1994). For example, Giddens (1991) emphasizes that what characterizes the self in late–modern society is the ability to reflect on personal identity, coupled with an awareness that one's identity is chosen and constructed. As he explains:

> Self-identity is not a distinctive trait, or even a collection of traits, possessed by the individual. It is *the self as reflexively understood by the person in terms of her or his biography*. Identity here still presumes continuity across time and space: but self identity is such continuity as interpreted reflexively by the agent. (Giddens, 1991: 53, original emphasis)

We are more aware of ourselves and of our place in society than we have been in the past and the notion of identity as a reflexive achievement emphasizes the autonomy of individuals in making choices and shaping their own lives. This is known as the 'reflexive modernization thesis', the argument that identity is now both increasingly flexible and individualized.

In the context of research methodology, the notion of reflexivity is used more specifically to indicate an awareness of the identity, or self, of the researcher within the research process. Reflexivity means the tendency critically to examine and analytically to reflect upon the nature of research and the role of the researcher in carrying out and writing up empirical work. As Alvesson and Skoldberg explain: '[I]n reflective empirical research the centre of gravity is shifted from the handling of empirical material towards, as far as possible, a consideration of the perceptual, cognitive, theoretical, linguistic, (inter) textual, political and cultural circumstances that form the backdrop to – as well as impregnate – the interpretations' (2000: 6).[2]

For the most part, reflexivity is discussed by those adopting *qualitative* rather than quantitative approaches to research and, with a few notable exceptions, is more often emphasized in the context of the collection of data and the relationship of the interviewer to the respondents than in relation to data analysis, interpretation, or the 'writing up' of results. The aim here therefore is to broaden the discussion to think more about reflexivity in analysis and the presentation of results. In particular, the emphasis will be on the implications of understanding both qualitative and quantitative research accounts as narratives for encouraging greater reflexivity across qualitative and quantitative research. This next section of the chapter will discuss the ways in which reflexivity has been proposed as a way forward, given the crisis of representation that has influenced qualitative research methods in recent decades.

Reflexivity and the crisis of representation

As was discussed above, in Chapter 3, over recent decades qualitative researchers have become more methodologically self-conscious. A growing emphasis on the constructed nature of the social world as the subject of research has provoked something of a troubled response from the research community. There is now awareness that the process of research itself does not simply produce descriptions of reality but should also be understood in some senses to construct reality. If the narratives produced by research respondents in interviews are to be understood as 'accomplishments' rather than unproblematic descriptive accounts, this suggests that the 'realities' reported by researchers should also be understood as accomplishments. As Gubrium and Holstein ask: 'What is the basis for treating research reports as authoritative? How can they be authentic if they too are merely representations of experience, themselves grounded in particular places and perspectives?' (1997: 10). In other words, once we become aware that when the subjects of our research provide us with narratives, they are not merely reporting their experiences but rather are engaged in an activity that makes sense of those experiences, we are obliged to admit that our own research narratives are also constructed. Research is frequently a frustrating and messy enterprise with false starts, and blind alleys to negotiate, but in published work it is more often presented as a logical progression of stages. Taken to the extreme, this 'crisis of representation' could clearly lead to researchers abandoning any attempt to engage in real-world research. As an exasperated postgraduate student once asked me at the end of a seminar on post-modernism and research methodology, 'What's the point in doing research at all then, why don't we just all go away and write fiction?'

For a number of qualitative researchers with a commitment to producing research that has a capacity to make a difference in the social world (research that illuminates inequalities in society, for example), the adoption of an explicitly reflexive approach to research provides a way through this crisis of representation. While acknowledging that all research accounts will be partial and will be shaped by the intellectual biography of the author, there is a desire to make those accounts as informative as possible and to provide insights into the means and circumstances of their production. An approach to conducting and writing up research which makes clear the perspective of the author and describes the practicalities of how the research has been conducted is therefore advocated. As Edwards and Ribbens have written:

> Rather than relativistic despair, we need high standards of reflexivity and openness about the choices made through any empirical study, considering the implications of practical choices for the knowledge being produced. (1998: 4)

Although a reflexive approach to research, and to writing up research, is acknowledged to be important by many adopting qualitative approaches to empirical work, discussions of reflexivity are especially prominent amongst those who situate themselves within feminist methodology. In particular, there has been an emphasis on the need to be explicit about the operation of power in the process of researching and representing people. Well-known and frequently cited examples of this can be seen in the work of Finch (1984), Oakley (1981), Stanley and Wise (1983), and Stanley (1990). In more recent years the literature on feminist methodology has also discussed reflexivity in relation to the interpretation and analysis of qualitative evidence and specifically to the representation of women in research accounts. For example, as was discussed at the end of Chapter 3, the process of transcribing, and questions about how best to preserve the nuances of spoken language on the page, also raise issues about power differentials between researchers and their research subjects (Standing, 1998). Although this chapter is not written from an explicitly feminist perspective a great deal of the material that I draw upon is therefore from the feminist canon. Debates about producing research accounts and appropriate strategies for 'writing up' research have also been running through the anthropological and ethnographical literature since at least the mid-1980s (Atkinson, 1990; Clifford, 1986; Geertz, 1988; Okley, 1992; Van Maanen, 1988). Many of the arguments in these texts can be applied to the representation of sociological work more generally and need not be restricted to the writing of ethnographic accounts.

In summary, by developing a reflexive awareness and becoming open to new ways of writing and reading texts, qualitative researchers need not abandon hope of providing useful empirical descriptions of the social world. However, it should also be acknowledged that 'unfettered reflexivity' risks diverting all attention away from the subjects and subject matter of research and onto the researcher. The aim is therefore for researchers not simply to provide their readers with detailed confessional accounts of their experiences of conducting research, but rather to produce an analytic discussion of how their own theoretical and biographical perspective might impact on their relationships with research subjects, their interpretation of research evidence, and the form in which the research is presented.

Reflexivity and data collection

Some of the earliest reflexive accounts of the research process focus on the experience of interviewing and the relationship between the interviewer and the interviewee. Perhaps the most well known is Oakley's (1981) chapter which describes the problems she had in trying to apply the usual rules about the way to conduct a research interview in the context of her study of the transition to motherhood. In particular, she highlights the fact that the women she interviewed had important questions to ask her as the interviewer. These questions frequently demonstrated unexpected levels of ignorance and fear among women expecting their first babies. Oakley therefore made the decision that it was more ethical to respond honestly to the requests for information, rather than preserving the detached objective role called for by contemporary manuals on research interviewing. The more reciprocal relationship, which developed as a result of Oakley's approach to interviewing, meant that she became friends with some of the women who were part of her study. She describes how some women cooked meals for her and several took the initiative in contacting her to provide extra pieces of information about their antenatal care between interviews, which they thought would be helpful for the research. Four years after the conclusion of the research Oakley reported that she was still in touch with more than a third of the women she had originally interviewed. Oakley concluded that: '[I]n most cases, the goal of finding out about people through interviewing is best achieved when the relationship of interviewer and interviewee is non-hierarchical and when the interviewer is prepared to invest his or her own identity in the relationship' (1981: 41).

Much less has been written about the power relations inherent in the collection of quantitative data. One of the distinguishing features of quantitative research is that the relationship between the researcher and the respondent tends to be much more distant than in qualitative studies (Bryman, 1988). Indeed, when social scientists carry out secondary analysis of large-scale datasets (as is often now the case for more sophisticated statistical modelling) it is likely that they will never meet the subjects of their research or even see the physical questionnaires they completed. In addition, data are now overwhelmingly available from data archives in electronic form and are increasingly being collected using computer-assisted interviewing procedures. This means that little trace can be left of the broader response of the research subject to the structured interview or questionnaire. There is no space for marginalia, or evidence of answers being revised, when data are captured electronically. This will make it increasingly difficult for researchers using quantitative data to reflect on how the methods of data collection may have shaped the responses of individuals in their sample.

As was discussed in Chapter 4, there is a growing body of empirical work that focuses specifically on this issue of how individuals' responses in structured interviews and self-completion questionnaires may be influenced by the design of the survey instrument. In particular, there is an interest among those using longitudinal data in how different research designs may have an impact on the quality of the data collected. For example, reported levels of women's unemployment have been shown to be different, depending on whether data are collected prospectively or retrospectively (Dex and McCulloch, 1998; Jacobs, 2002).

In addition, even when the aim is to collect detailed life history data about the month-by-month events shaping individuals' lives in terms of family, employment, fertility, housing, and education, the need to simplify the data and make them tractable, inevitably results in the distortion of at least some people's experiences (for further discussion of this see Chapter 4). All large-scale quantitative surveys will have been developed after numerous discussions about question wording and extensive piloting, so that social scientists involved in the design of this type of research will be only too aware of the difficult decisions and compromises made before the data collection could take place. However, the chapters and papers that report analysis of such data rarely provide any insight into this process. Instead variables are frequently presented as though they reflect unproblematically the concepts of interest to the researcher. This is not to be overly critical of such work, indeed the word limits imposed by publishers and editors of journals often make it impossible to do justice to the intricacies of both data analysis and data collection. However, if those working with quantitative methods want their work to be read and taken seriously by colleagues more familiar with qualitative techniques, it is important that more space is given to a discussion of how quantitative evidence is 'constructed' and not simply 'collected'.

Reflexivity and the analysis of data

Reflexivity and qualitative analysis

Writing about the importance of a reflexive approach to the analysis of narratives produced in interviews, Mauthner and Doucet (1998) stress that, compared with the wealth of literature that has now been written about the *collection* of qualitative material, there is much less written about how to go about the practical process of analysis. Even when clear guidelines are available (e.g. in relation to grounded theory, or the Biographic–Narrative–Interpretive Method discussed in Chapter 3) it is not always clear to what extent individual researchers actually follow those guidelines in practice. Mauthner and Doucet suggest that the latter stages of qualitative analysis, which may involve examining each interview in turn for the occurrence of a particular theme or concept, may become routinized, and are therefore relatively straightforward to document. However, the early or preliminary stage usually relies on the individual researcher's intuition and this is much more difficult to document or explain. Alvesson and Skoldberg (2000) also emphasize the intuitive nature of much analysis that is rooted within the hermeneutic tradition. They argue that insight is achieved 'not by laborious pondering, but rather at a stroke, whereby patterns in complex wholes are illuminated by a kind of mental flashlight, giving an immediate and complete overview' (Alvesson and Skoldberg, 2000: 52).[3] Some might question whether it is possible for a researcher to document this intuitive process so that it is transparent and available to others' scrutiny – in other words, for researchers to be fully reflexive about the analysis stage of research.

Mauthner and Doucet (1998) argue that although this has been a neglected area in the past, it is important for researchers to be more methodologically explicit about the 'nitty-gritty' of the analytic process in relation to qualitative research. In particular they advocate the voice–centred relational method as a set of strategies for the qualitative researcher that can lead to greater reflexivity and openness about the analysis of biographical narratives. The first stage of this method consists of a series of four close readings of interview transcripts:

1 Reading for the plot and the researcher's own response to the narrative.
2 Reading for the active 'I' who is telling the story.
3 Reading for the respondent's relationship with family and close friends.
4 Reading for the broader social and cultural context of the respondent.

The first reading has two components because the researcher both reads for the overall story, i.e. what happens, and also explicitly attends to his or her response to the narrative. It is this latter element that distinguishes this approach from other methods of qualitative analysis. As Mauthner and Doucet explain:

> In the second 'reader-response' element of this first reading, the reader reads for herself in the text in the sense that she places herself, with her own particular background, history and experiences, in relation to the person she has interviewed. The researcher reads the narrative on her own terms – how she is responding emotionally and intellectually to this person. (1998: 126)

This then is the most explicitly reflexive stage of the analysis process and it is noteworthy that it is introduced in the first reading of the transcripts. In other words, the researcher starts by acknowledging his or her own perspective in relation to the evidence collected. By paying attention to his or her emotional response to the narrative, together with considering his or her social relation to the respondent and by writing notes on this in the first stage of analysis, the aim is to 'retain some grasp over the blurred boundary between their narratives and our interpretation of those narratives' (Mauthner and Doucet, 1998: 127). Stanley (1992) similarly encourages sociologists to make their own 'intellectual autobiography' clear in their analytic writing. This does not simply mean providing the reader with personal data about the researcher, but rather providing an analytic account of how the researcher's personal and academic history, together with theoretical perspective, lead him or her to approach the evidence in a particular way. As Gill has cautioned:

> Too often – and I have been guilty of this – papers start with what seems to be little more than a ritual incantation of the identities occupied by the author – with little or no attempt to reflect on the significance of those positions for the research. It is as if by simply stating them that one has been reflexive and eradicated their effects. (1998: 32)

Although they do not use the framework supplied by the voice-centred relational method, Hollway and Jefferson (2000) describe a reflexive approach to the analysis of biographical interview data about the fear of crime which is very similar to that advocated by Mauthner and Doucet. They suggest that there are four questions that must be asked in relation to the analysis of any qualitative data:

- What do we notice?
- Why do we notice what we notice?
- How can we interpret what we notice?
- How can we know that our interpretation is the right one?

The first question relates to the initial intuitive stages of qualitative analysis. Listening to recorded interviews or reading transcripts, certain elements and phrases stand out and become embedded in our minds. It is the second question that highlights the reflexivity that can be incorporated within qualitative analysis. That is, we step back from the material itself and attend to ourselves as individuals doing the analysis and responding to the narratives that have been collected. In order to explain the process of analysis in relation to his own research on the fear of crime, Tony Jefferson describes in detail his personal response to one interviewee's (Tommy's) account of his childhood. In particular Jefferson focuses on the parallels between Tommy's story and his own memories of his father (Hollway and Jefferson, 2000: 65–7). This then is an example of Mauthner and Doucet's suggestion that we should be explicit about our own emotional response to qualitative material and the way that it resonates with aspects of our own personal biographies.

Reflexivity and quantitative analysis

This discussion of reflexivity in relation to *qualitative* analysis clearly also raises questions about whether it is possible to be reflexive about quantitative analysis. In some senses it could be argued that it is much easier to be explicit about the practical steps that are undertaken in the analysis of quantitative data. This is perhaps because statistical analysis is more akin to the routinized procedures that comprise the final stages of qualitative analysis. For example, consider the following extended extract from a journal article describing the quantitative analysis of data on recidivism:

> We used logistic regression to predict whether or not the offender was arrested for a new offense, and a Cox Proportional Hazards model to predict time until a new arrest was made....Although event history analyses have gained wide-spread popularity, especially for analyzing recidivism data, there is some debate about the best model to use. Researchers have been encouraged to test the assumptions of the model in use (see Schmidt and Witte, 1988). Following Allison's (1995) recommendations, we tested the assumption of the proportional hazards model first by visually inspecting

> the hazard rate across groups of select independent variables (e.g. sex and offense types). The proportional hazards model seemed to be supported by visual inspection. Then we reran the main effects model 13 times; each time we included a different interaction term created by multiplying each of the independent variables by time....We also reran the models using different functional forms of the baseline hazard: Weibull, exponential, gamma, log-logistic, and log-normal. The substantive findings were not sensitive to the form of the baseline hazard. (Gainey et al., 2000: 741–2)[4]

On first reading, this description of the statistical techniques used certainly appears to meet Mauthner and Doucet's criterion that researchers should describe the 'nitty-gritty' of the analytic process. The authors not only provide very specific information about the statistical models they have applied, but also describe in detail the way they checked that the proportional hazards assumption was correct when using the Cox model. The persuasive power of this description rests in the fact that it disrupts the notion that statistical analysis requires that the 'appropriate' type of analysis is straightforwardly chosen and then applied. Instead it portrays the researchers as thoroughly checking that the substantive results of their analysis would not be unduly affected by the way they formulated the model. What is emphasized, in this description of the methods used, is the *type* of model that was estimated and, within this focus, the researchers provide a thorough description of the choices made and paths followed during the analysis stages of their research.

However, it is important to be aware that there are numerous other decisions embedded in the analytic process that are not documented for the reader in the extract above. For example, thirteen variables are included in the analysis, obtained from the case files of offenders (see Chapter 5 for a full list of these). These include a number of demographic variables such as gender, race, employment status, and marital status. What the researchers do not make clear is whether the variables included represent all the data available or whether decisions were made about which variables to incorporate in the analysis and which were deemed irrelevant (presumably on theoretical grounds). In addition, all the models discussed in the analysis section are 'continuous time models' (see Chapter 5 for a discussion of this approach). This means that variables such as employment status and marital status, which may well have varied over the course of the study (if someone got divorced or moved from unemployment into a new job, for example), are included in the model as though they do not change over time. It could be argued therefore that the emphasis in this paper is not on conducting an analysis to achieve a broad understanding of the many different factors that may impact on recidivism, but rather there is a narrow focus on the effectiveness of electronic monitoring to delay or prevent reoffending. Indeed the language used to describe the variables included in the model is reminiscent of the vocabulary used in experiments. The authors describe the measures of recidivism as 'dependent variables', the sentence length, time served in jail, and time on electronic monitoring as 'independent variables', and the demographic variables (such as gender, marital status, etc.) as 'control variables'. The primary concern is therefore whether electronic monitoring is effective, once other background characteristics have been controlled. This is not to argue that this paper or the analysis within it is fundamentally flawed, but rather to illustrate that despite its codified and routinized nature, quantitative analysis, no less than qualitative analysis, requires researchers to make decisions about how to approach their data and how to frame their research questions. Of course this raises questions about how productive and realistic it is to expect quantitative researchers to preface their analyses with a thorough reflexive account of the decision-making processes that have preceded the final analyses presented. It would, however, be helpful if more of the contingent aspects of quantitative analysis were revealed.

If the focus is on the collection of data, it could be argued that the role of reflexivity is very different depending on whether qualitative or quantitative methods are being used. The relationship between the researcher and the respondent or participant is likely to be much closer in the case of qualitative research and the identity or personal characteristics of the researcher are therefore likely to have a much greater impact on the process of collecting *qualitative* data than on the process of collecting *quantitative* data. However, with respect to the analysis of data the theoretical perspective and intellectual autobiography of the researcher is likely to be just as relevant whether qualitative or quantitative analysis is undertaken. Although the intuitive and interpretive aspects of qualitative analysis are already widely acknowledged (Alvesson and Skoldberg, 2000; Mauthner and Doucet, 1998), there needs to be greater recognition that quantitative analysis is by no means a completely routinized and codified process, but rather is also shaped by the decisions made by individual researchers.

Reflexivity and longitudinal analysis

In the example discussed above, the focus was on the process of modelling multivariate data. Although the research discussed used longitudinal data, the emphasis was not on change over time or duration effects. Once these additional elements are included in the process of quantitative analysis I would suggest that the need for reflexivity with respect to the analysis of data becomes even more important. This section will therefore briefly discuss the ways in which different approaches to longitudinal analysis, such as event history modelling, can have implications for the construction and understanding of the social world.

As was discussed in Chapter 5, event history models focus on predicting the probability of the occurrence of a specific event. For example, the probability of individuals reoffending following their release from prison (Gainey et al., 2000), the probability of marital dissolution among married couples (Heaton and Call, 1995), or the probability of individuals' re-employment following redundancy (Rosenthal, 1991). It was also suggested that the temporal nature of the longitudinal data needed for this type of modelling means that there are some parallels between these statistical models and narratives. As was discussed in Chapter 1, the basic structure of a narrative is that it has a clear beginning, middle, and end. It is the bounded nature of the narrative, or its configurational dimension, to use Ricoeur's term, that distinguishes it from a chronicle. That is, the beginning and end are not arbitrary: a narrative does not simply represent 'a slice of life' but rather it adds up to something – the meaning of each element is dependent on its place within the whole. The start and end points of the narrative are therefore crucially important in that they contribute to its significance or meaning. The parallel in terms of event history modelling is that the choice of the starting point for the analysis can have important implications for the meaning that is communicated through the analysis.

For example, as has been discussed in more detail elsewhere (Elliott, 2002b), analyses of women's employment behaviour that capitalize on the increasing availability of longitudinal data in Britain, mainland Europe, and the United States typically take as their starting point the birth of a woman's first child and focus on the length of time until she returns to paid employment. Although there is nothing technically or statistically amiss with such models, the risk is that by adopting this approach the employment behaviours of *women* and *mothers* is conflated. This is compounded when the terms 'mothers' and 'women' are used interchangeably in the description of such analyses. This slippage between the categories of 'women' and 'mothers' can lead to a conceptualization of gender and gender differences as emanating from women's biological capacity to bear children and therefore as relatively fixed and immutable. Longitudinal analyses that take the birth of a first child as their starting point therefore run the risk of reifying the concept of gender.

An alternative approach, and one that I have used in my own research (Elliott, 2002b), is to model the duration of *all* episodes out of the labour market over a woman's life history. This means that women who never become mothers are not excluded from the analysis and such analyses can more properly be understood to focus on *women's* employment behaviour rather than more narrowly examining *mothers'* employment trajectories. This has the additional merit that it avoids the danger of selection biases, which can be shown to distort the coefficients in statistical models (Berk, 1983). In addition, by analysing data from specific cohorts of women such as the National Child Development Survey (1958 cohort) or the British Cohort Study 1970, and highlighting the limited generalizability of the findings, it is possible to present analyses which are clearly situated in a specific geographic and historical context and do not make claims for the timeless nature of the gendered division of labour and the resultant gender inequalities in the labour market. In this way we can move towards a better understanding of gender inequalities within society without reifying gender in a way that potentially contributes to the perpetuation of those inequalities.

Reflexivity and writing

If it is rare to find reflexive discussions of the process of analysis in research accounts it is perhaps even more unusual for social scientists to be reflexive about the experience of writing up their research results. Van Maanen is one of the very few authors to provide a detailed analysis of different approaches to writing about research. He delineates three main types of account: the realist tale, the confessional tale, and the impressionist tale. These are discussed in relation to ethnographic work and therefore Van Maanen frequently makes reference to 'the fieldworker', 'the native', and 'culture' rather than the researcher, the respondent, and the research topic. However, as will be discussed below, elements of Van Maanen's typology can usefully be applied across a wide range of different substantive topics and it does not need to be restricted to anthropological studies.

The realist tale is perhaps the most common type of research account. It is described by Van Maanen as having four main elements. The first and most striking is the absence of the author from the text – only those who are being studied appear in the account, what they say and what they do.[5] Having completed the fieldwork, the researcher in effect is erased from the text. The implication of this is that the identity of the researcher is irrelevant to the process of research. What has been observed and recorded is exactly what would have been observed and recorded by any competent fieldworker. As Van Maanen emphasizes:

> Ironically, by taking the 'I' (the observer) out of the ethnographic report, the narrator's authority is apparently enhanced, and audience worries over personal subjectivity become moot. (1988: 46)

In addition, Van Maanen describes how realist tales tend to focus on concrete details of daily life and aim to display the thoughts, feelings, and perceptions of the members of the culture being studied. Finally, the realist tale presents a single, unambiguous interpretation of the culture under investigation. The researcher therefore has 'Interpretive omnipotence'. As Van Maanen writes:

> Realist tales are not multivocal texts where an event is given meaning first in one way, then another, and then still another. Rather a realist tale offers one reading and culls its facts carefully to support that reading. Little can be discovered in such texts that has not been put there by the fieldworker as a way of supporting a particular interpretation. (1988: 52)

Van Maanen argues that it is partly the need for short monographs and research articles that exacerbates these tendencies for researchers to prioritize a single theme or interpretation in their writing. There is not space to discuss ambiguities, puzzles, or other possible solutions to questions raised by the researcher. In addition, many students are trained, at least implicitly, to use the realist account and to structure their writing around a clear, single message.

In contrast to the realist tale, the confessional tale is an attempt to demystify the process of fieldwork (or research more generally) by documenting the practical elements of the research process. The author as an active agent of the research is highly visible within the text: the account is laced with autobiographical information. The perspective of the fieldworker/researcher is emphasized so that: 'The omnipotent tone of realism gives way to the modest, unassuming style of one struggling to piece together something reasonably coherent out of displays of initial disorder, doubt, and difficulty' (Van Maanen, 1988: 75). Although Van Maanen does not choose to call these confessional tales 'reflexive accounts', and indeed the word 'reflexivity' does not appear in his index, there are clear parallels here between his characterization of 'confessional tales' and the reflexive discussions of qualitative research within edited collections such as *Feminist Dilemmas in Qualitative Research* (Ribbens and Edwards, 1998) and *Feminist Praxis* (Stanley, 1990). Interestingly, however, despite the contrasts that Van Maanen makes between realist and confessional tales, he stresses that the main aims of these two different accounts may overlap as he explains:

> Confessionals do not usually replace realist accounts. They typically stand beside them, elaborating extensively on the formal snippets of method description that decorate realist tales. They occasionally appear in separate texts and provide self-explanatory and self-sealing accounts of how the author conducted a piece of work reported elsewhere. (1988: 75)

Confessions about the messy and contingent nature of much research fieldwork therefore invariably end up supporting the realist tale that described the results of the research: 'it often boils down to the simple assertion that even though there are flaws and problems in one's work, when all is said and done it still remains adequate' (Van Maanen, 1988: 79). Clifford has also written about the emergence of this subgenre of ethnographic writing in which 'Ethnographic experience and the participant–observation ideal are shown to be problematic' (1986: 14). In these new reflexive accounts previously neglected topics that were deemed irrelevant within realist tales become the central themes. Confusions, difficulties, and the fieldworker's relationship with informants are no longer edited out but rather structure the plot of confessional tales.

The final type of research account described by Van Maanen is the impressionist tale. This is clearly the type of writing he prefers. Impressionist tales are perhaps closest to narratives in their form. That is, they follow the chronology of the research. Events are recounted in the same order that they occurred and to bring the text to life they are accompanied by the kind of vivid concrete details that provide substance to the remembered events: 'The idea is to draw the audience into an unfamiliar story world and allow it, as far as possible, to see, hear, and feel as the fieldworker saw, heard, and felt' (Van Maanen, 1988: 103). In choosing the term 'impressionist tales' Van Maanen draws a parallel with impressionist painters who experimented with new techniques and used their materials in an innovative way in order to startle their audience and 'evoke an open, participatory sense in the viewer' (1988: 101). In contrast to confessional tales or realist tales, which focus exclusively on either the researcher or the subject of the research, impressionist tales focus on the 'doing of the fieldwork'. As Van Maanen explains:

> The story itself is a representational means of cracking open the culture and the fieldworker's way of knowing it, so that both can be jointly examined. Impressionist writing tries to keep both subject and object in constant view. The epistemological aim is then to braid the knower with the known. (1988: 102)

Examples of impressionist tales in sociology provided by Van Maanen include Reinharz (1979) *On Becoming a Social Scientist*; Beynon (1973) *Working for Ford*; and Krieger (1983) *The Mirror Dance*. In contrast to realist tales, the aim in impressionist tales is not to foreground the researcher's interpretation but rather to present the reader with a vibrant account that invites participation in the interpretive process. This also means that there is something of an open-ended character to impressionist tales: 'The magic of telling impressionist tales is that they are always unfinished. With each retelling we discover more of what we know' (Van Maanen, 1988: 120). Van Maanen therefore advocates the explicit use of narrative to communicate the whole process of research to an audience. The researcher or fieldworker should appear in this narrative, not as the central character, but as one of the key protagonists alongside the subjects of the research. By showing the audience the relationship between the actors in the story, Van Maanen suggests that the interpretive omnipotence of the researcher will be undermined and the readers will be encouraged to form their own interpretations. McCormack (2004) makes a similar point in relation to her own qualitative research on women students' experiences of leisure. She describes the process of 'storying stories' as presenting the analysis of a series of in-depth interviews in the form of narratives that include the multiple voices of the participant and the researcher and which provide the reader with the opportunity to make new interpretations (McCormack, 2004: 222).

An additional text that explicitly engages with the process of writing, rather than simply doing research, is Richardson's useful book *Writing Strategies* (1990). This book is helpful on two levels. First, it demonstrates the possibility of creating a reflexive account of the writing process and provides a discussion of the issues of authority and authorship in light of post-modern writings on representation and texts. Second, it offers some practical insights into the practice and process of writing for different audiences.

Richardson argues that as sociologists it is important to be aware that all texts run the risk of reproducing existing power relationships. As researchers we are frequently called upon to write about social groups to which we do not belong. As was discussed in Chapter 8, and in particular when our research focuses on vulnerable, oppressed, or disenfranchised groups within society, issues are raised about our authority to speak for these constituencies. In response to the dilemma about how to face our political and ethical responsibilities, Richardson (1990) advocates 'a merging of progressive and post-modernist thinking about authors and authority'. As has been argued in previous chapters, one of the distinctions that has been made between narrative approaches to knowledge and more 'scientific' or 'paradigmatic' approaches is that narratives are always firmly rooted in a particular time and place (Hinchman and Hinchman, 1997). Richardson's suggestion that we explicitly view our research accounts as *narratives* therefore serves to underline the fact that we are writing as 'situated, positioned authors' with a specific perspective.

To acknowledge that what we are writing is a narrative, and not simply a transparent representation of the realities of the research process, is also to foreground the role of the imagined audience in shaping that narrative. As was highlighted in

Chapter 1, narratives are a social product whose form is necessarily shaped by the relationship of the author to his or her audience and, as Van Maanen reminds us:

> The categories of readers an author recognizes and courts help shape the writing. In this sense, the narrative tricks the ethnographer uses to claim truth are no less sophisticated than those used by the novelist to claim fiction. Writing of either sort must not mystify or frustrate the audience an author wishes to reach. (1988: 25)

Richardson uses the term 'collective story' to suggest a type of research account that represents the common experiences of a group of people who are typically marginalized, silenced, or excluded from more dominant narratives and discourses in society. From her own research she gives the example of the 'new other woman' collective story which focuses on the experiences of single women in relationships with married men. Richardson argues that the common cultural narratives about infidelity cast 'the other woman' as the villain and as in competition with another woman for the love of a man. However, in her own research the aim is to restructure this narrative so that 'the other woman' becomes the central character and becomes recognizable as part of an identifiable social category.

In the second half of her book, Richardson (1990) describes strategies for writing three different types of research narratives intended for very different markets. In particular, she gives a detailed account of how she wrote up her research, on single women in long-term relationships with married men, as a trade book with the aim of appealing to, and communicating with, a wide audience. In this account the techniques Richardson describes are very reminiscent of Van Maanen's discussion of the elements that go into producing an impressionist tale. For example, she describes how the book is structured around two interlocking narratives – a sociological narrative and the other woman's collective story:

> but because I wanted the sociologist's narrative and the Other Woman's collective story to be interlinked, the sociological narrator appears in the Other Woman's chapters, and their lives appear in the first and last bracketing chapters, rather than adapting the social scientific writing convention of separating data from theory and implications. (Richardson, 1990: 37)

In Van Maanen's terms, then, Richardson is describing a technique for 'braiding' knower and known so that both appear in the text for the reader to evaluate. In addition, Richardson explains that the use of short, eye-catching quotations are more likely to attract the reader's attention than longer indented passages that readers may well be tempted to skip. It is the use of brief quotations embedded within the text that are likely to disrupt the flow of the text, surprise and startle the reader, and evoke the kind of participation and range of emotional responses that is hoped for by those producing an impressionist tale.

Both Richardson and Van Maanen focus on the process of writing up qualitative research and emphasize the way that narrative can be explicitly used to structure these accounts. However, an overlapping set of arguments is made by Aldridge (1993) but in relation to *quantitative* research, and more specifically to her own experiences of research using survey data. Although Aldridge does not refer to Van Maanen's work, what she is clearly describing in her account of producing a report of quantitative survey research is the production of a realist tale. In particular, she highlights the way that by apparently removing the author from the text a particular type of disembodied, omnipresent, and properly 'scientific' author is constructed. Aldridge emphasizes that the convention in scientific accounts is not to write in the first person. Rather than 'I used a random sampling procedure' we find phrases such as 'a random sampling procedure was employed' in the text. For example, in a guide for students writing up research, Anderson and Poole advise:

> Scientific writing is not of a personal or conversational nature and for that reason the third person is commonly used. As a general rule, personal pronouns such as I, we, you, me, my, our and us should not appear, except in quotations. (1994: 6)

Aldridge argues that by removing the actual author from within the text a detached and impersonal author is thereby constructed behind the text. This textual disembodiment of the author is also accomplished by the narrative structure of reports of quantitative research. Aldridge explains that in her own experience of research, the specific research method (of analysing survey data) was prescribed by the culture of the department in which she was studying. She therefore started the research process by analysing survey data, informed by her own hunches as to interesting research questions that could be addressed using that particular method. Her task was then to go back to the existing research literature to find a way of framing her analyses and results. Although her description of her own experiences of conducting research for her Masters dissertation could be seen as something of an extreme example, it is certainly the case that research rarely follows the neat progression implied by the sequence of literature review, hypotheses, methods, results, conclusions. Indeed, one of the recurrent problems that I have encountered in writing empirical research papers is that it is often difficult in practice to separate the methods and results because the preliminary results obtained in analysis of data influence decisions about the most suitable type of subsequent analysis. There is therefore a kind of iterative feedback loop between methods and results that cannot readily be represented by constructing them as two distinct elements of a sequence. However, as Aldridge writes:

> The standard ordering in which research must textually be seen to be done takes creativity, insight and intelligence from the hands of the researcher and places the guiding force of scientific inquiry squarely in the hands of scientific method and technique. It is by excising the sociologist and his or her personal experience from the textual account of it that we are seen to be doing science *best*; indeed that we are seen to be doing science *at all*. (1993: 62)

Chapters on the experiences of doing research, such as those produced by Aldridge (1993) and Mauthner and Doucet (1998), are instructive and provide helpful insights into the process of analysis and writing which are rarely found in methods texts. However, their work could be characterized under Van Maanen's heading of 'confessional tales'. Indeed it is interesting that in both cases the authors describe work that they were doing as graduate students. This adds an additional dynamic to their accounts. Their reflexive, confessional tales contribute to a narrative about their own research careers. By reflecting on their past selves as neophyte researchers they are able to create a distance between their current identities as established researchers and the 'mistakes' they may have made in the past.[6] In addition, however, as Van Maanen has argued, these confessional accounts do not fundamentally undermine the results obtained in the original research.

If the aim is therefore to avoid producing confessional accounts as apologia for earlier realist tales, and instead to construct the 'impressionist tales' and 'collective stories' advocated by authors such as Van Maanen and Richardson, this raises questions about whether this type of writing is *only* possible within the qualitative paradigm or whether quantitative research, such as the results of event history analyses, can also be represented in this way. As yet there are no authors that I know of who have published quantitative research findings that experiment with such new literary forms. There is clearly the danger that others, working with quantitative data, would reject such a research account as being too playful or post-modern, and as undermining the authority that is usually afforded those using complex statistical techniques. Indeed, given the process of peer review, impressionist accounts of quantitative research would be unlikely to get published. At the same time, those more familiar with qualitative methodologies are often reluctant to engage with accounts which include statistics of any kind, professing that they are 'no good with numbers', or simply dismissing any work that includes a table of coefficients as being 'positivist' and therefore beyond redemption. Although receptive to innovative approaches to reflexivity in social research, they would therefore be unlikely to champion its cause in quantitative, statistically based studies. This points to the need for greater interchange of ideas between those adopting a primarily quantitative or a primarily quantitative approach to research. The benefits and difficulties of trying to bridge the gap that has become established between the two approaches forms the basis for the final chapter.

It is beyond the scope of this chapter to specify precisely what an impressionist tale would look like within quantitative research. Indeed, new approaches to representing research are unlikely to be successful if prescribed by a single author. Rather, what is needed is an evolution of practice or a paradigm shift involving a critical mass of researchers who share a commitment to producing more reflexive accounts of quantitative research and analysis. As has been discussed above, however, the elements that might contribute to a more impressionist account of quantitative research include:

1   Detailed discussion of how data were collected and constructed.
2   A focus on the historical and geographical context which frames the quantitative data.
3   An explicit discussion of the start and end points of any longitudinal analysis and the impact this is likely to have on the findings.

Summary

This chapter has argued that the growing interest in narrative among qualitative researchers has fostered a greater awareness of the importance of reflexivity with respect to the collection, analysis, and presentation of research evidence. In particular, those adopting qualitative approaches to research are increasingly advocating reflexive practices as a possible solution to the 'crisis of representation'. However, this chapter has also suggested that reflexivity should not be understood as solely the preserve of those working with qualitative data or conducting qualitative analyses. It has been argued that one of the advantages of becoming more aware of the narrative properties of the results of quantitative analysis, and particularly event history models, is that it opens up the possibility of considering the ways in which different methods of research, including different quantitative methods, shape particular representations of individuals' lives. In the final section of the chapter the process of writing up research, and the narrative quality of both qualitative and quantitative research accounts, were discussed. Using Van Maanen's terminology it was suggested that quantitative researchers as well as qualitative researchers might attempt to move away from producing realist and confessional accounts towards writing impressionist tales that invite the reader to participate more fully in the interpretive process of research.

Further reading

Aldridge, J. (1993) 'The textual disembodiment of knowledge in research account writing', *Sociology*, 27 (1): 53–66.

Alvesson, M. and Skoldberg, K. (2000) *Reflexive methodology*. London: Sage.

Mauthner, N. and Doucet, A. (1998) 'Reflections on a voice-centred relational method: analysing maternal and domestic voices', in J. Ribbens and R. Edwards (eds), *Feminist Dilemmas in Qualitative Research: Public Knowledge and Private Lives*, London: Sage. pp. 119–46

McCormack, C. (2004) 'Storying stories: a narrative approach to in depth interview conversations', *International Journal of Social Research Methodology*, 7: 219–36.

Richardson, L. (1990) *Writing Strategies: Reaching Diverse Audiences*. Thousand Oaks, CA: Sage.

Stanley, L. (1993) 'The knowing because experiencing subject: narratives, lives, and auto-biography', *Women's Studies International Forum*, 16 (3): 205–15.

Exercise

Find two short chapters or articles that report on some empirical research that interests you, one that uses qualitative methods and one that uses quantitative methods.

1 How does the author refer to him-or herself in each piece of writing – does the author mainly use the first person or the third person?
2 How much information does the author give about the process of research and the decisions made during the project?
3 How would you classify each piece of writing – as a 'realist tale', a 'confessional tale', or an 'impressionist tale'?
4 What type of identity does the author construct in each piece of writing – do you get a sense of the author's intellectual auto/biography?

Notes

1 Paul Atkinson (1990) makes the point that in ethnographic research writing has two distinct phases. The first consists of 'writing down' field notes of observations and conversations and the process of writing is understood as little more than making a record of what was seen and heard. In the second phase of 'writing up', these field notes are used as data and there is greater acknowledgement that the resulting text is *constructed* by the author.
2 Alvesson and Skoldberg use the terms reflective and reflexive interchangeably in the opening sections of their book.
3 Note that there are interesting echoes here of Singer et al.'s approach to analysing quantitative longitudinal research.
4 The event history techniques used and the results of this study have previously been discussed in Chapter 5.
5 As was discussed in Chapter 3, it is striking that in many research studies using in-depth interviews, the researcher's questions are not provided for the reader, only extracts from what the interviewee has said.
6 Linde (1993: 147–9) provides a useful discussion of how narrative can be used to distance the self as narrator from the self as character constituted within the text of an autobiographical account.

Telling better stories? Combining qualitative and quantitative research

There is already a substantial literature on the advantages and potential difficulties of combining qualitative and quantitative methods in a single research project (Brannen, 1992; Bryman, 1988; 1992; 1998; Morgan, 1998; Pearce, 2002; Thompson, 2004). The aim in this chapter is therefore not to rehearse in detail the existing debate about whether it is possible to integrate approaches that emphasize individuals' subjective beliefs and experiences with approaches that provide a numerical description of the social world. Rather the focus will be on the ways in which an interest in narrative might inform attempts to integrate qualitative and quantitative evidence. In particular, drawing on material discussed in the previous four chapters, the aim is to explore three main themes. First, the potential of combining qualitative and quantitative techniques for reaching a better understanding of causal processes and for allowing a prominent place for the role of human agency in sociological explanations. Second, the implications of understanding identity in narrative terms for attempting to amalgamate qualitative and quantitative material. Third, the role of narrative in encouraging researchers to be more reflexive about the way they write up their research, whether they are presenting primarily qualitative or quantitative evidence.

However, before turning to a detailed examination and discussion of each of these topics, it is necessary to say something about the issue of whether qualitative and quantitative approaches represent different clusters of technical methods or whether they should be understood as different paradigms built on contrasting epistemological assumptions (Bryman, 1984; 1992; 1998). This question is central because it underpins the debate as to whether it is possible to reconcile the two approaches within a single research study. If the use of a structured survey is evidence of a commitment to positivist assumptions while a preference for qualitative methods indicates anti-positivist or hermeneutic approaches to knowing the social world, then the argument is that both quantitative and qualitative research are based on such different foundational assumptions that they cannot be successfully integrated. Conversely if the differences in the two approaches are no more than technical or practical then it is argued that there should be no problem in combining them and indeed research that uses mixed methods can potentially capitalize on the strengths of each approach.

As was discussed in Chapter 1, the distinction between qualitative and quantitative approaches is certainly a useful one at a practical level. Methods of collecting qualitative data (e.g. interviewing, observing, and conducting focus groups) are readily distinguishable from techniques for collecting quantitative data (e.g. structured interviews and self-completion questionnaires). In addition, it is usual for standardized quantitative data to be analysed and summarized using statistics, while textual qualitative material is generally subject to the interpretations of the researcher and then presented in a more discursive form. This means that for the majority of researchers the terms qualitative and quantitative provide useful shorthand descriptions of distinct approaches to both collecting and analysing research evidence. As Bryman (1998) has highlighted, these terms are also routinely used in job advertisements and by editors of social science journals and therefore the qualitative/quantitative distinction has a wide currency among social scientists.

However, as has been shown by examples of research discussed in Chapters 3 and 5, it is not *necessarily* the case that qualitative material will be interpreted and presented in a textual form and conversely that quantitative material will be analysed solely using statistical techniques (Baerger and McAdams, 1999; Franzosi, 1998b; 2003; Singer et al., 1998). This means that there is already some blurring at the boundaries between the two clusters of techniques. Moreover, although it is important to acknowledge that there are different epistemological assumptions that can underpin social research, these do not map onto the qualitative/quantitative distinction in any straightforward way. Discussions about the philosophy of the social sciences frequently make a contrast between positivism and hermeneutics, and it is then a short step to equate positivism with survey research and quantitative forms of analysis and to suggest that qualitative approaches are appropriate where research questions are more hermeneutic in nature. In practice, researchers rarely make explicit the philosophy that lies behind the methods they choose and this is particularly true of those who adopt a quantitative approach. Rather, decisions about the techniques that will be adopted to answer a particular research question are more likely to be a product of the researcher's own expertise and a notion of the appropriate way of gaining relevant evidence or data about a particular substantive question.[1]

In addition, as was discussed in Chapter 2, there are also a number of distinctions that can be drawn *within* those adopting qualitative approaches to research. In particular, the naturalist and constructivist approaches can be contrasted. While those adopting a naturalist approach to qualitative research proceed on the basis that the use of in-depth interviews and observation can provide direct evidence of individuals' experiences together with the meanings they make of those experiences, constructivists question the ability of research to provide an unproblematic window onto the social world. For constructivists the research encounter itself becomes part of the analytic process and the focus is as much on *how* individuals provide accounts as on *what* those accounts consist of. These differences among those using qualitative techniques in the course of their research mean that it is no longer possible simply to ask whether qualitative and quantitative research can be combined, rather we need to focus on what type of qualitative approach is being adopted and whether it is compatible with quantitative techniques.

The recent interest in the notion of narrative identity adds an additional dimension to this debate. As was discussed in Chapter 7, one of the key differences between qualitative and quantitative research is that while *some* qualitative approaches allow for a conception of the self as being socially constructed and constantly revised and negotiated, quantitative methods assume a more fixed and immutable identity with less room for ambiguity and change. Even longitudinal data and methods of analysis, which go some way to allowing researchers to focus on individuals' life trajectories, rather than just patterns of aggregate change, still rely on a modernist notion of an underlying essential self with fixed traits and characteristics. This suggests that the differences in the philosophical underpinnings of qualitative and quantitative research may be ontological as much as epistemological. The implications of this for the ways in which qualitative and quantitative research may be combined will be discussed in more detail below. First, however, it is helpful to start by considering the question of causality. In particular, to focus on how qualitative and quantitative approaches may be used in tandem to provide explanations of social phenomena which might be thought of as causal in that they not only describe regularities in the way that one variable behaves in relation to another, but also provide a possible mechanism underlying that relationship. This is what Franzosi has termed 'narrative causality' (2003).

Extensive and intensive evidence and causality in social research

As has been discussed in previous chapters, the use of longitudinal data and, in particular, event history analysis can take us a great deal further than standard *cross-sectional* multivariate techniques in understanding processes, temporal dependencies, and the changing significance of variables over time. However, explicit attention to the narrative properties of this type of analysis has also revealed the limitations of this approach. As was discussed in Chapter 5, although the analysis of longitudinal data shares some of the features of narratives in that it allows us to incorporate an explicitly temporal dimension into our analyses, the approaches that are used most frequently might still be thought of as 'variable centred' rather than 'case centred'. In common with other modelling techniques the analysis of longitudinal data focuses on the regularities in relations between variables. This means that, even if the problems of 'model uncertainty' are put aside, an event history model that describes the statistically significant associations between variables could be argued to fall short of a satisfactory *causal* explanation. This is because it omits to provide an account of *how* the prior variables affect the subsequent event.

This shortcoming of event history analysis and quantitative research more generally is suggestive of an approach to methodological triangulation that fits with the conception of quantitative research as providing 'extensive' evidence, in contrast to qualitative research that provides more 'intensive' evidence, about the social world (Duncan and Edwards, 1999; Halford et al., 1997; Sayer, 1992). As Sayer explains:

> In intensive research the primary questions concern how some causal process works out in a particular case or limited number of cases. Extensive research, which is more common, is concerned with discovering some of the common properties and general patterns of a population as a whole. Typical methods of extensive research are descriptive and inferential statistics and numerical analysis (e.g. cross-tabulations) and the large scale formal questionnaire of a population or 'representative sample' thereof. Intensive research uses mainly qualitative methods such as structural and causal analysis, participant observation and/or informal and interactive interviews. (1992: 243–4)

As was discussed in Chapter 6, while clues to the nature of the mechanisms underlying observed regularities among variables may be provided by existing theory, qualitative evidence can also be central to understanding the processes that are at work. For example, in his research on the levels and determinants of fertility rates for women on welfare in the United States, Rank (1989) uses quantitative data as a source of 'extensive' evidence, and qualitative data as 'intensive' evidence, about women's fertility behaviour. While the longitudinal analysis of administrative data on women in receipt of welfare benefits (such as Aid to Families with Dependent Children) demonstrates that women in receipt of benefit have lower rates of fertility than those not on benefits, Rank uses in-depth interviews to 'provide insight into the process of and attitudes towards childbearing' (1989: 298). In other words, he uses the qualitative evidence to complement his quantitative analysis and to address the question of *why* the rate of fertility among women on welfare is relatively low. Rank reports that women receiving public assistance described strong feelings about not wanting to have any more children. They perceived themselves as struggling to survive on the low rates of welfare benefits and said that having any more children would make it even more difficult to get by. Having additional children was also perceived as reducing opportunities to get a job and to escape welfare. Those women who did get pregnant while in receipt of benefits reported that it was accidental rather than part of a planned choice to have more children. As Rank states:

> Although far from conclusive, the qualitative data are suited to exploring the potential reasons behind the overall demographic and statistical patterns.... The interviews enabled women on welfare to construct their experiences and

attitudes regarding pregnancy and childbirth. These experiences and attitudes shed considerable light on why fertility behavior appears to be suppressed. (1989: 302)

There are clearly benefits to be gained from combining intensive and extensive evidence within a research study. However, it is rare to find individual researchers who have sufficient skills and experience to use both qualitative and quantitative techniques effectively (Morgan, 1998). The resource implications of combining sophisticated and well-designed qualitative and quantitative research methods, coupled with the fact that many researchers have expertise in either one approach or the other rather than both, mean that it is still relatively unusual to find examples of research projects where qualitative and quantitative methods have been given equal weight. An alternative is not to expect methods to be combined in a single project but rather to 'pursue the integration of qualitative and quantitative research across a field of studies. In that case, experts in each method would concentrate on their own technical expertise, but they would use the knowledge produced by other methods as inputs to their own work' (Morgan, 1998: 373). A good example of this is provided by Maume's (1999) paper 'Glass ceilings and glass escalators', which examines whether the occupational attainment of men and women is influenced by whether they are working in occupations dominated by men or women.

In the introduction to his paper, Maume uses the qualitative research carried out by Williams (1992) to suggest the processes by which men may succeed and rise to managerial positions in occupations traditionally done by women. However, as he emphasizes: 'Although Williams' argument is provocative, it is based on interviews with 76 men and 23 women in four semi-professions' (Maume, 1999: 488). In contrast, Maume's research involves the multivariate analysis of quantitative data from the Panel Study of Income Dynamics to test whether there is evidence for the outcomes of the organizational and interpersonal dynamics, described by Williams, in a large, representative national sample of the workforce. In particular, Maume demonstrates that the processes identified by Williams do result in men moving into managerial positions more quickly in occupations where they form the minority of workers.

There are therefore a number of examples of research where quantitative and qualitative approaches have been combined effectively. The quantitative methods have proved useful in establishing robust relationships between variables that are generalizable to a population beyond the sample in the research itself, while the qualitative methods have provided evidence about the possible mechanisms that lie behind the relationships detected using quantitative research. Where these mechanisms rely on individual motivations and perceptions, qualitative research can be particularly useful in understanding what lies behind people's choices and behaviour and the meaning they attribute to their experiences.

Combining qualitative and quantitative methods: life course research

As was discussed in Chapter 4, in the United States a strand of work has developed within sociology that stresses the need to understand individuals' lives and experiences as arising out of the interplay between individual agency and historical context. This conceptual framework has become known as the life course approach and has provided the foundations for a wide range of research, including work on the impact of the Second World War on the lives of a group of gifted men (Elder, 1987; Elder et al., 1994); the factors that result in some women pursuing innovative paths combining family and career (Giele, 1995; 1998); the consequences of the Great Depression for individuals' lives (Clausen, 1993); and the impact of the closure of a textile plant on a local community (Haraven, 1982). The central tenets of the life course approach, namely that people's lived experience is shaped by historical and geographical location, relations or social ties to others, variations in the timing of biographical events, and individual agency or personal control, make its proponents particularly amenable to combining qualitative and quantitative methods. As Giele (1998) has described, the approach involves using quantitative evidence to make comparisons across different cohorts in order to understand the impact of changing historical contexts on individuals' lives. However, it also requires that researchers make comparisons within cohorts and examine the different life patterns of individuals to ascertain what particular constellation of factors result in individuals following different pathways. Elder et al. (1994) also stress the need to construct case studies in order to understand the processes that result in different outcomes for individuals who have had similar experiences of historical events.

It is important to note, however, that the type of qualitative research advocated by those adopting the life course approach is closer to the naturalist or humanist approach than the constructivist approach described in Chapters 2 and 3. The emphasis on individual differences and individual agency within life course research does not therefore extend to an interest in the reflexive individual or the concept of the narrative constitution of identity discussed in Chapter 7. Indeed, little attention is paid to post-modern deconstructions of the concept of the self or identity and instead the emphasis is on the individual as a cluster of relatively stable goals and dispositions.

Sampson and Laub's research on criminal careers provides a good practical example of how those adopting the life course approach have integrated quantitative and qualitative evidence. Their research has already been discussed in Chapters 4 and 7 and will not be described in detail here. However, they argue that the strategy of combining qualitative and quantitative research methods has two distinct benefits. First, the quantitative findings are enhanced by the qualitative data, which are able to illuminate the processes that result in persistence or desistance within criminal careers. Second, the examination of 'residual cases' that do not fit with the mainstream quantitative results encourages an expansion and enrichment of the analytic model and can generate new hypotheses about factors which may be important for predicting outcomes. In describing their particular approach to triangulation, Laub and Sampson state that they 'merge quantitative and qualitative analyses to provide a more complete portrait of criminal offending over the life course' (1998: 221).

One of the key challenges or dilemmas for the life course approach, and for other research which places an emphasis on understanding the role of human agency, is that there is a risk that a focus on individual capacities and choices within explanatory models may result in accounts that appear overly voluntaristic and that differences between people may be understood in terms of variations in their innate capacities rather than drawing attention to their structural locations. However, at its best qualitative research, such as the analysis of in-depth biographical interviews, can reveal the tensions and ambiguities in individuals' attitudes and orientations and can also potentially show how elements of people's identities may not be stable over time. For example, Proctor and Padfield's (1999) analysis of qualitative biographical interviews with a small sample of young women demonstrated how difficult it was to categorize or classify these women in terms of their orientations to work or family life. By re-interviewing the women two years later they also showed how women's orientations were not immutable but rather were largely shaped by their circumstances. This qualitative study therefore provides evidence that challenges Hakim's 'Preference theory', which has largely been derived through analysis of quantitative data (Hakim, 2000). Whereas Hakim characterizes women as a heterogeneous group who nonetheless individually have relatively enduring preferences for a career or for family, Proctor and Padfield (1999) suggest that women are frequently ambivalent about their role as both mother or worker and that the centrality of employment or motherhood to a woman's sense of identity changes over time.

There are, therefore, perhaps two related contributions that can be made by qualitative material when it is used in conjunction with quantitative data to understand causal processes and mechanisms. First, qualitative evidence can, in some cases, simply provide more detailed information about the processes that are suggested by the multivariate analysis of quantitative data. Second, as was suggested above, qualitative evidence can provide an insight into the *meanings* attached to individuals' behaviour and experiences. In this way, qualitative evidence can help us to form an understanding of the values and motivations that lie behind people's actions and decision making. This could be understood as a more hermeneutic approach to qualitative material. In simple terms, it represents an attempt to understand the social world and people's behaviour within that world from the perspective of those being studied. As was discussed in Chapters 2 and 3, it is the spontaneously occurring narratives within qualitative interview material that can be particularly helpful in uncovering the cultural assumptions that underlie what is said. Careful analysis of personal narratives can reveal what is taken for granted, what is treated as an adequate causal link, what is seen as needing no explanation, and conversely what is in need of justification – what behaviour should be accounted for. It is therefore to these first-order narratives that we must turn if we are to understand the dominant cultural assumptions that help shape individuals' decisions and behaviour.

Narrative and identity in qualitative and quantitative research

As was suggested above, the recent interest in the conception of 'narrative identity' raises additional questions about the possibility and desirability of combining qualitative and quantitative approaches to research. In Chapter 7 it was demonstrated that longitudinal quantitative research allows for analysis which foregrounds individual trajectories and demonstrates how aggregate or societal change may be lived out at an individual level. However, it was also shown that quantitative methods rely on a modernist understanding of identity. That is, individuals are assumed to have a fixed set of characteristics or traits that contribute to shaping their behaviour and experiences. Although, as was discussed in Chapter 5, modelling of discretized quantitative life history data does allow for the incorporation of time-varying covariates, there is still an assumption that the individual him- or herself does not change over time. Indeed the more sophisticated random effects and fixed effects models, which allow the researcher to explore duration dependencies and temporal processes more thoroughly, rest on an assumption that there are differences between individuals that are unmeasured or unmeasurable, but which are relatively stable. Quantitative research is therefore based on the conception of an individual who acts in the social world but who is not reflexively responsible for constructing and maintaining his or her own individual identity. Putting it in the strongest terms, it could be argued that quantitative methods, such as event history analysis, represent a fundamental denial of the active reflexivity of the subject. One of the main problems with 'variable-centred approaches' to social research is therefore that they deny agency to cases (Abbott, 1992b). However, it is important to be clear about what is meant by individual agency here. As was stressed at the end of Chapter 5, event history models can potentially provide relatively good descriptions of *active* cases, getting married or cohabiting, deciding to have children, and leaving and re-entering employment. That is, they allow for individual agency understood as the 'centred source of action'. What they can never reveal, however, is the individual's active role in maintaining or challenging concepts such as gender, social class, or race, which by structuring an individual's understandings of his or her own identity also have an important impact on decisions and behaviour. It is this shortcoming of quantitative techniques that contrasts most starkly with the potential of qualitative biographical material to contribute to an understanding of the reflexive nature of identity. The strength of a more qualitative narrative approach to research is therefore not just that it gives a voice to those with marginalized identities (as was discussed in Chapter 8), but that it allows for a specific focus on the construction and maintenance of those identities. This is what Somers is arguing when she suggests that:

> The concept of a narrative identity dovetails with the move of identity politics to reintroduce previously excluded subjects and suppressed subjectivities into theories of action. At the same time however, the narrative identity approach firmly rejects the tendencies of identity theories to normalize new

categories that are themselves fixed and as removed from history as their classical predecessors. (1994: 621)

However, despite this potential for qualitative research to allow for the reflexive maintenance of identity, there are still relatively few empirical studies that fully embrace the concept of the narrative construction of identity. As yet there is a great deal more *theoretical* work in this area than research that puts these ideas into practice. There is even less research that has attempted to combine qualitative and quantitative methods and that has used the qualitative aspects of the research to investigate the way individuals understand and work on their own identities. As Lucius-Hoene and Deppermann have argued:

> Whereas a good deal of systematic work has been done on the philosophical, epistemological and psychological aspects of narrative identity leading to an elaborate concept of the storied character of human experience and personal identity (Bruner, 1990; McAdams, 1993, 1996; Polkinghorne, 1988, 1998; Randall, 1995; Ricoeur, 1990; Thoma, 1998), the empirical substrate of narrative identity remains to be clearly specified. (2000: 200)

An interesting example of the way in which qualitative and quantitative methods can be combined, which *has* incorporated the notion of narrative identity, is provided by a recent study of the careers of managers based in large companies (Wajcman and Martin, 2002). The research was carried out in six Australian-based companies, each of which employed between 1200 and 6000 people at the time of the study. Two types of data were collected in each company. A self-completion questionnaire about career issues was returned by a random sample of 470 managers and in-depth interviews were conducted with a smaller sample of 136 individuals – between 18 and 26 managers in each company. Approximately one-fifth of both the survey respondents and the interviewees were women. Like the questionnaires, the interviews focused on managers' careers and also covered issues such as the reasons behind job changes, domestic arrangements, and barriers to success. In contrast to the questionnaires, the interviews were very loosely structured so that as the researchers state: 'Questions and probes (in the interviews) were framed to avoid dictating the narratives that interviewees would use in answering them' (Wajcman and Martin, 2002: 989).

Analysis of the quantitative survey data revealed very few differences between the careers of male and female managers. Gender did not appear to have any impact on the number of companies a manager had worked in, the length of tenure in the current company, or the likelihood that the manager had worked overseas. Gender also had no impact on the proportion of managers who stated that they see work as 'a central part of who I am'. However, there were some gender differences uncovered by the survey in that women were found to earn considerably less than men ($75,986 vs. $96,308) and were over twice as likely as the male managers in the sample to say that 'men and women do not have equal chances of promotion in current company' (50.4% vs. 22.1%). Overall, however, the quantitative survey data suggested that the career experiences and work orientations of men and women in the sample hardly differed.

What makes this research particularly relevant for the current discussion is that the in-depth interviews, which accompanied the structured questionnaire, concentrated on 'the identities managers give themselves in their narratives of career and private life' (Wajcman and Martin, 2002: 991). The researchers therefore describe their analysis as focusing on 'the kinds of narratives managers use and the ways they position themselves in these stories' (p. 992). Using this approach, the interviewees are described as telling their career stories in the form of a 'market narrative'. In contrast to the traditional 'bureaucratic narrative' based around long-term commitment to a single organization, the market narrative is described as more individualized and stresses choice and action within the labour market. In these accounts interviewees presented themselves as consumers of jobs so that decisions to take particular jobs were understood as active choices based on the challenges, stimulation, and interest that would be offered by a particular job or employer. The managers interviewed were therefore described as representing themselves as 'largely autonomous agents, unconstrained by authoritative norms and life patterns'. The researchers describe these market narratives used by managers as 'having no overt gender content' and as being used equally by both men and women in the research; however, they do highlight some important gender differences in the way that men and women relate their career narratives to their private or domestic lives. Although the male managers in the sample did occasionally refer to the difficulties of maintaining an appropriate balance between work and family life, they found it relatively straightforward to accommodate their family responsibilities within their career narrative. In contrast, the women managers found it much more complicated to reconcile their career narrative with their private or family story and described deep conflict between the demands of a career and the demands of family life. As the researchers state: 'Few of the women in our study are able to integrate their public gender-neutral career narratives with a feminine identity that includes being mother and wife' (Wajcman and Martin, 2002: 999).

What is particularly interesting about this research study is that it has not only combined quantitative survey research with in-depth biographical interviews, but also explicitly focused on the narrative identities constructed or produced within those interviews. By contrasting the 'market career narratives' produced by interviewees with more traditional bureaucratic or organizational narratives it suggests that the meaning of a career as a manager is changing, and relates this to the theoretical work on reflexive modernization by authors such as Giddens and Beck. This is suggestive of the fact that qualitative research allows identities to be less coherent and fixed than quantitative work. Indeed Wajcman and Martin explicitly state that their approach 'neither accepts nor rejects the unity of identity' so that one focus of their analysis is 'on the different narrative identities managers adopt; whether they mesh successfully and whether these patterns differ between men and women'. However, in this example, what underpins and links both the qualitative and the quantitative analysis is the comparison between men and women.

While the similarity between the career narratives used by male and female managers goes some way to breaking down a dichotomous view of gender difference, this binary divide is re-established once the researchers examine the way that interviewees integrate their private stories with accounts about their careers. In other words, the researchers do not treat gender as a resource that interviewees may use to make sense of their lives and to structure the biographical narratives produced within the research interviews. Rather, by comparing the narratives of male and female managers, even in the qualitative analysis, gender is treated as a fixed attribute or variable and operates as an axis of comparison in the same way that it does within the quantitative analysis.

Gender may be a relatively durable social dimension, but it should also be understood as having the potential for change, as a concept that is negotiated and worked on by reflexive individuals. As was discussed in relation to the research of Ronai and Cross, at the end of Chapter 7, individuals may use gender or other widely recognized elements of identity to structure their narratives and place themselves in comparison with others. In addition, gender can be used to make sense of decisions and behaviour in narratives about careers. Within qualitative approaches to research it is possible to investigate the ways that individuals use a concept like gender in practice. Through their narratives they have the ability not only to reinforce but subtly to renegotiate the meaning of variables that are permanent markers of identity within survey research. It is this aspect of variables, such as gender, as resources for individuals to use, that is lost in quantitative event history analysis and means that we run the risk or reifying such concepts and thus providing an overly static description of the social world.

Writing up qualitative and quantitative research: narrative and reflexivity

In the previous chapter it was argued that quantitative researchers should attempt to be more reflexive in the way that they write up and present the results of their research. Whereas there is now a substantial literature on reflexivity within qualitative approaches to research, there are almost no discussions of how a more reflexive approach to *quantitative* research might be accomplished (although, as discussed in Chapter 9, Aldridge (1993), Pugh (1990), and Farran (1990) do give 'confessional' accounts of their experiences of presenting quantitative results). The writing of accounts about the process of research is therefore another area in which an increased exchange of ideas between those adopting qualitative and quantitative approaches to describing the social world could be productive. In particular, it could result in research accounts that, while they make use of statistics, are more compelling and more accessible for a lay or policy audience (Bertaux, 1981). As was briefly mentioned in Chapter 7, there are a few examples of researchers using predominantly statistical analysis of large samples who have included brief 'pen portraits' of individuals as part of their research accounts in order to illustrate the implications of the statistical results presented (Bynner et al., 1997).

181

In addition to using individual case histories, or narratives about individuals to bring to life the results of research that are mainly concerned with large aggregations, more detailed and qualitative descriptions of the *context* in which quantitative research has taken place can also be useful in locating the results in time and place. This avoids the implication that the statistical relationships reported exist outside the very material conditions of a specific societal context. One of Blumer's criticisms of the dominance of 'variable sociology' in the United States in the 1950s was that it attempted to produce law–like statements with the capacity to transcend local, social, conditions (Blumer, 1956). This is echoed in Hinchman and Hinchman's suggestion (highlighted in Chapter 6) that whereas causal theories attempt to 'capture and elaborate some timeless essential reality "behind" the world of human events…narratives organize and render meaningful the experiences of the narrator in that world' (1997: ix). A narrative approach to presenting the results of quantitative research would therefore make more explicit the specific context in which the data were collected and the scope of the findings reported.

As was briefly discussed in Chapter 4, longitudinal research based on data such as those collected by the British cohort studies has the greatest potential for framing the results of quantitative research within a specific historical and cultural context. In particular, when cross–cohort comparisons are made, there is potential for examining how changes in society might shape the way that individuals experience particular events or difficulties in their lives and, in addition, may reduce or increase the impact of those events on individual outcomes. For example, a number of authors have suggested that the negative impact of parental divorce on children may be reduced as divorce becomes more common in society. It would be expected that as the incidence of divorce increases, the stigma attached to having divorced parents will decrease, and, in addition, there will be more services available to help parents and children through the process of divorce. The impact of parental divorce on children in more recent decades is therefore likely to be tempered by the fact that they share this experience with many of their contemporaries. Research by Ely et al., which examines the association between having divorced parents and educational outcomes for three cohorts of British children born in 1946, 1958, and 1970, is able directly to test this 'reduced effect hypothesis' (Ely et al., 1999). By contrasting the effect sizes for the association between parental divorce and subsequent educational outcomes for children in the three different cohorts, Ely et al. demonstrate that in fact there is little evidence that the impact of divorce has diminished for more recent cohorts of children. However, what is particularly interesting about this research within the current discussion is that it includes an explicit discussion of social changes in Britain during the post-war period focusing on changes in family life and the expansion of educational opportunities. Although this piece of research is not described as 'narrative', it might be thought of as sharing some of the key elements of narrative in that it is firmly oriented in time and place and is also able to trace the impact of an event in childhood on subsequent academic outcomes. In other words, the research both analyses data that have something of a narrative form and then presents the results in the context of a narrative about the changing British family. There are also clear parallels between the theoretical background to this paper and the life course approach described above. This therefore provides an example of how those using quantitative methods can situate their analyses in historical and societal contexts.[2]

Conversely, those using qualitative methods could often go further in providing a backdrop for their interpretations based on a descriptive analysis of census and surveys. The increased availability of large datasets such as those described in the Appendix means that it is relatively straightforward for any academic researcher to gain access to high-quality statistical information. In addition, the rapid advances in computing and the widespread availability of menu-based software packages for statistical analysis (such as SPSS) facilitate at least basic analysis of large datasets. Duncan and Edwards' research on employment and lone mothers, which was described briefly in Chapter 7, provides an excellent example of research that is predominantly qualitative in nature but which uses data from the British Census both to inform the sampling of individuals for interview and to contextualize the findings (Duncan and Edwards, 1999). They interview a relatively small sample of lone mothers in two very different local contexts. First, Lambeth and Southwark, an area of high unemployment and with high concentrations of people on income support and of black ethnic groups in inner city London. Second, Brighton and Hove, a more 'average' area on the south coast of Britain, with moderate levels of unemployment, a low proportion of black ethnic groups, and most housing in owner occupation. Without access to census data, Duncan and Edwards' contextual description of the neighbourhoods in which their sample was based would be much more impressionistic. The use of descriptive statistics about the type of housing in an area, the proportion of families headed by a lone parent, car-ownership and employment rates provides a valuable orientation for the individual narratives that emerge from the qualitative interviews in the study.

As was discussed in Chapter 2, those adopting more hermeneutic approaches to the analysis of evidence frequently do not aim to make the same claims about generalizability as those using statistical methods; however, descriptive statistics from large-scale surveys could clearly be used more often to contextualize the small samples interviewed in qualitative studies. This would not be to devalue the narratives produced by research about individuals' lives and experiences, but would rather situate these accounts within a broader description of society. Indeed, where longitudinal data (from the cohort studies or the longitudinal study of the British Census, for example) are used to provide the context for qualitative enquiry a kind of nesting of narratives within narratives may be achieved. As was discussed in relation to Walby's research in Chapter 7, this can be productive in showing whether and how aggregate change, in labour market behaviour for example, is experienced at an individual level. Mills' often quoted edict that 'The sociological imagination enables us to grasp history and biography and the relations between the two within society' (Mills, 1959: 12) would also point to the fact that good sociology requires stronger links to be made between qualitative research that reveals something about the individual and quantitative research which shows how the aggregation of individual's behaviour results in particular patterns or outcomes for society as a whole.

Qualitative and quantitative research as different genres

Bryman (1988; 1998) has emphasized that in thinking about the differences between qualitative and quantitative approaches and the potential for combining them in a research study, it is also important to consider the 'rhetorics of persuasion' or modes of discourse used to present qualitative and quantitative results. As he argued in 1988:

> To a very large extent, these two research traditions [i.e. qualitative and quantitative approaches] can be thought of as divergent *genres*, especially in regard to their modes of presenting research findings and programmatic statements....The employment of a scientistic rhetoric – experiment, variables, control etc. – in quantitative research, imposes expectations on the reader about the sort of framework that is about to be encountered....By contrast the self-conscious endorsement by many qualitative researchers of styles of presentation and literary devices which entail a rejection of a scientific rhetoric can be seen as a countervailing genre. (Bryman, 1988: 5)

Following these introductory remarks, Bryman's text on qualitative and quantitative methods does not say much more about the way that qualitative and quantitative writers present their findings and the techniques they use to convince their readers of the validity of their research. However, in a chapter published a decade later he provides a more detailed examination of the distinct modes of presentation used by authors adopting a qualitative or quantitative approach (Bryman, 1998). In summary, Bryman argues that one of the main distinguishing features of reports of quantitative data is that a 'management metaphor' is employed to highlight the researcher's ingenuity and competence, so that articles based on quantitative research talk about the 'design of research', 'controlling variables', 'managing data', and 'generating tables'. In contrast, reports of qualitative research make greater use of a 'naturalistic metaphor'. The emphasis is on presenting the perspective of those being interviewed and to demonstrate that the authenticity of the research setting has been preserved. An alternative way to conceptualize this difference would be to suggest that while quantitative researchers have to demonstrate that they have *done something* to their data, qualitative researchers are more often concerned to allow their evidence to speak for itself. It is this lack of discussion of how textual data have been 'analysed' in the majority of qualitative reports that leads to the frustrations of authors such as Mauthner and Doucet (discussed in the previous chapter) who argue that there are 'few detailed presentations of the step-by-step processes of how transcripts are analysed' (1998: 120).

This distinction between the style of qualitative and quantitative research reports raises questions about how those using mixed methods might write about their research. As Bryman (1998) points out, however, it is still very rare indeed to find research that gives equal weight to qualitative and quantitative evidence. Researchers tend to prioritize one or other method and this is likely to result in a research report that mirrors the rhetoric associated with one particular approach. For example, what is interesting about the book produced by Duncan and Edwards as a result of their research on lone mothers, discussed above, is that although it combines results from the more qualitative and quantitative aspects of their research, these are still largely compartmentalized into separate chapters. This means that in the writing process qualitative and quantitative results are not integrated as fully as they might be. In addition, it is noteworthy that where qualitative and quantitative results are discussed side by side (in Chapter 5, for example) Duncan and Edwards stick to a naturalistic metaphor. The statistics that they present are relatively straightforward consisting of cross-tabulations demonstrating the relation between two variables at a time rather than modelling multivariate associations. This means that percentages and sample sizes are presented in the text and there are no complex models, which would require rather more explanation. The data manipulation and analysis that has taken place is minimized and the authors do not employ the management metaphor to describe their handling of the census data. Arguably, therefore, it is the simplicity of the quantitative analyses presented that allows the authors to preserve a naturalistic metaphor throughout their research account. Indeed in contrast to the majority of studies based on statistical analysis there is no explicit 'methods section' accompanying Duncan and Edwards' presentation of data from the census. Their broad approach to combining intensive and extensive research is discussed in the introduction, but the rest of the book is almost exclusively focused on the *results* of research rather than on the processes by which these results were obtained. As Bryman (1998) has noted of much research that combines qualitative and quantitative methods, what is most striking about Duncan and Edwards' work is its strongly realist tone. The findings are imbued with a 'fixed "out there" quality…and the reader is left with the sense of a definitive account of an external reality' (Bryman, 1998: 153).

As was discussed at the end of the last chapter, a major challenge for quantitative researchers is how to engage with some of the discussions about reflexivity which are going on within the community of qualitative researchers. It might be hoped that those combining qualitative and quantitative approaches would be more likely to be reflexive about the way they present their research and avoid the straightforward 'realist tales' which have characterized much of social science writing in the past. However, it would seem from Bryman's analysis, and from the example given above, that a strong element of realism is to be found even in accounts that have engaged with both qualitative and quantitative material. This points to the fact that it is not qualitative methods per se that encourage a radically different approach to questions of epistemology and ontology, but rather that the analysis of qualitative material offers greater *potential* for engaging with recent debates about the nature of identity and for paying greater attention to the production of research evidence. Moreover, the interpretive and literary skills associated with much analysis of qualitative material provide the foundations for more experimental or impressionist representations of research findings. Given the increased interest in narratives, and narrative form, among qualitative researchers over the past two decades it would be expected that greater attention will be paid to the construction of research accounts in future.

Some conclusions

By focusing on narrative and the temporal qualities of social experience, this book has aimed to discuss both qualitative and quantitative approaches to research and to explore some of the more innovative techniques and methodological approaches that have been adopted by social researchers over the past two decades. Those working with quantitative data and estimating multivariate models may be pursuing rather different research questions from those analysing transcripts of in-depth biographical interviews. However, it is hoped that a common interest in social change, in social processes, and in understanding the factors that shape individuals' life trajectories may encourage those working on either side of the qualitative/quantitative divide to engage with each other's work. The increased availability of quantitative longitudinal data and the development of statistical techniques, which enable researchers more fully to exploit the temporal properties of this type of evidence, mean that quantitative research can no longer be criticized for presenting an overly static or simplistic understanding of the social world. At the same time, there is a growing awareness among many quantitative researchers that statistical models cannot provide definitive answers about the relationships between variables and that it is important to take account of human agency and cultural influences on behaviour. This means that researchers who are conducting 'extensive' research increasingly recognize the value of 'intensive' research for illuminating the processes that underlie the statistical associations they have discovered. As was discussed in Chapter 9, greater exchange between qualitative and quantitative researchers could also be productive if it encouraged a more reflexive approach to the presentation of research findings by quantitative researchers. In addition, as discussed above, qualitative research could more often be contextualized using descriptive statistical information about the population within which research subjects are situated.

From the discussion above and in Chapter 7, it should be clear that alongside the sophisticated descriptions of individuals' trajectories provided by event history models it is important to pay attention to the insights gained through qualitative narrative approaches to the analysis of biographical interviews. It is only by focusing on individuals' narrative constructions of their lives and experiences that we can come close to understanding more about the way that they reflexively construct and maintain their social identities. This is not to suggest that these different approaches can always be straightforwardly integrated or that this form of methodological triangulation leads to a more accurate, complete, and analytically satisfying representation of the social world. Rather, the concept of narrative provides a kind of reflexive bridge between the traditions of quantitative and qualitative methods. That is, by attending to the narrative properties of data, by using narrative to inform our analysis, and, most importantly, by recognizing our-selves as the narrators of sociological accounts, we are forced to examine our own role in the construction and maintenance of the social world. While it may not be possible thoroughly to integrate the alternative conceptions of variables such as race, class, and gender provided by qualitative and quantitative methods, it is important to learn to tolerate the tensions and ambiguities that they create in our research narratives. These tensions may indeed be productive if they begin to challenge and disrupt the hegemony that currently preserves the dichotomy of qualitative and quantitative methodologies.

Summary

This chapter has examined the potential of narrative for bridging the divide that has become established between qualitative and quantitative methods. It has been argued that on one level, if the focus is on causality, an attention to narrative provides a sound basis for combining quantitative and qualitative methods in order to capitalize on the relative strengths and weaknesses of the different approaches. However, on another level, the concept of the narrative constitution of identity discussed in Chapter 7 disrupts any straightforward attempt to integrate qualitative and quantitative representations of individual's lives. If research is based within a critical or political agenda so that the aim of the research is, at least in part, emancipatory, there is a tension between adopting the more conventional 'variable-based' or quantitative approaches which are invaluable for documenting and measuring the extent and patterning of inequalities and disadvantage and turning to a qualitative approach which avoids reifying the variables that, in some senses, fix individuals into disadvantaged positions. Finally this chapter has extended the discussion of the role of narrative in encouraging a more reflexive approach to writing up and presenting the results of research that was begun in Chapter 9.

Further reading

Bryman, A. (1998) 'Quantitative and qualitative research strategies in knowing the social world', in T. May and M. Williams (eds), *Knowing the Social World*. Buckingham: Open University Press. pp. 138–56.

Laub, J.H. and Sampson, R.J. (1998) 'Integrating quantitative and qualitative data', in J.Z. Giele and G.H. Elder (eds), *Methods of Life Course Research: Qualitative and Quantitative Approaches*. Thousand Oaks, CA: Sage. pp. 213–30.

Pearce, L.D. (2002) 'Integrating survey and ethnographic methods for systematic anomalous case analysis', *Sociological Methodology*, 32: 103–32.

Wajcman, J. and Martin, B. (2002) 'Narratives of identity in modern management: the corrosion of gender difference?', *Sociology*, 36: 985–1002.

Readings for discussion

Morgan, D.L. (1998) 'Practical strategies for combining qualitative and quantitative methods: applications to health research', *Qualitative Health Research*, 8: 362–76.

Thompson, P. (2004) 'Researching family and social mobility with two eyes: some experiences of the interaction between qualitative and quantitative data', *International Journal of Social Research Methodology*, 7: 237–57.

1 *How might you classify Thompson's research on step-families in terms of the priority–sequence model outlined by Morgan?*
2 *Does Thompson suggest that the retrospective accounts collected in his qualitative research are more or less accurate than the more structured quantitative data collected as part of the National Child Development Study? How might you account for the differences in the information provided by the two approaches?*
3 *Is Morgan correct to suggest that few researchers possess the skills and experience to conduct both qualitative and quantitative research? Why might this be and how could this problem be overcome?*
4 *Identify a research study in your own field of interest that uses both qualitative and quantitative research methods. Can you locate it within Morgan's priority sequence model?*

Notes

1 Research on 'sensitive' topics, e.g. on health or sexuality, often uses qualitative methods while research on more mundane issues, e.g. job satisfaction and employment experiences, more frequently employs structured surveys.
2 Ferri et al.'s (2003) 'Changing Britain, changing lives' provides a further example of how cross-cohort comparisons can be presented together with a description of changes in British society to achieve a more narrative presentation of quantitative results.

Appendix: Details of some major longitudinal quantitative datasets

The aim of this appendix is to provide some basic information about a selection of major quantitative longitudinal studies from Britain, Europe, and the United States that are available to researchers who wish to conduct secondary analysis. It should be stressed that the datasets outlined below represent only a tiny proportion of the longitudinal studies that have been conducted and archived. For example, there are over 200 longitudinal studies from the United States included in the Inventory of Longitudinal Studies (Young et al., 1991). The final section of this appendix therefore gives a selection of institutions and web addresses from which more information about longitudinal data can be obtained. Studies in the appendix are listed in order of when they first started.

The MRC National Study of Health and Development

Start date: 1946
Research design: Prospective/catch-up study
Initial sample size: 16,500
Nature of sample: Cohort of men and women born in a single week of 1946
Website: http://www.nshd.mrc.ac.uk/

The NSHD is one of the longest-running large-scale studies of human development in the world. Its aim is to map biological and social pathways to health and disease, from early life to ageing. Following concern over falling birth rates, a national maternity survey was designed after the Second World War to investigate the cost of childbirth and the quality of associated health care. The initial study took as its subjects all 16,500 births that occurred in England, Wales, and Scotland during one week of 1946. A follow-up survey was designed to examine the health and development of a representative sample (5,362) of this population, which has now been studied twenty-one times, most recently at age 53 years. In addition to its wide range of scientific publications, the study has contributed to health care, education, and social policy in Britain during the past fifty years. The NSHD has been continuously funded by the Medical Research Council since 1962, and has been supported by additional research grants from a range of sources. In contrast to the other three British cohort studies, data from the NSHD are not available from the ESRC data archive. Those wishing to analyse the data must do so in collaboration with the researchers responsible for the study based at University College London.

The Wisconsin Longitudinal Study

Start date: 1957
Research design: Prospective/catch-up study
Initial sample size: 10,317
Nature of sample: Cohort of men and women graduating from high school in 1957
Website: http://dpls.dacc.wisc.edu

The Wisconsin Longitudinal Study was originally formulated as a survey of educational and occupational aspirations and attainments over the life course. Data have subsequently been collected on respondents' family background, academic abilities, social support, the timing and sequencing of adult educational and occupational achievements, events related to employment and to the family, physical and mental health. To date there have been a total of three waves of data collection in 1957, 1975, and 1992/3. In 1975, over 97% of the original respondents were traced despite being geographically dispersed (Clarridge et al., 1978). In 1992/3 telephone interviews were carried out with 8493 (90%) of the living respondents and 6877 postal questionnaires were completed. The dataset therefore provides longitudinal data on a large sample of American men and women who were in their mid-fifties when the final wave of data collection took place at the beginning of the 1990s.

The National Child Development Study

Start date: 1958
Research design: Prospective/catch-up study
Initial sample size: 17,000
Nature of sample: British cohort born in 1958
Website: http://www.cls.ioe.ac.uk/

The National Child Development Study (NCDS) is the second of four British cohort studies. It has followed all those born in the first week of March 1958 so that data have been collected from the same individuals at intervals through childhood and into adult life. The survey started as the Perinatal Mortality Survey (PMS), it was funded by the National Birthday Trust Fund, and its original aim was to examine the administration of maternity services in Britain and investigate the causes of perinatal mortality (Davie et al., 1972). The initial sample size was 17,414 and was estimated to include 98% of all births in Great Britain born in the week of 3 to 9 March. To date, six subsequent sweeps of the cohort have been carried out. In 1965 when the cohort members were aged 7, and then again in 1969 (age 11); 1974 (age 16); 1981 (age 23); 1991 (age 33); and 2000 (age 42). The questions included in each sweep have been modified to reflect the life stage of the cohort and the agendas of the various agencies that have provided funding for the continuation of the study. The aims of the study as a whole have been to investigate social and economic change together with human development. The information gathered from the cohort over the years has covered health, social, and economic circumstances, as well as material and psychological well-being. The 1991 sweep also included a retrospective self-completion, detailed, life history questionnaire which collected information on the dates of cohabitation, marriage, separation and divorce, dates of birth of any children, episodes of employment, unemployment and education, and dates of moving house.

In 1999/2000, for the first time, BCS70 undertook a survey jointly with NCDS to interview cohort members on a wide range of topics. Both the NCDS and BCS70 now receive core funding from the ESRC and it is planned to survey both cohorts every four years, alternating between a full face-to-face interview study and a shorter telephone survey.

The Panel Study of Income Dynamics

Start date: 1968
Research design: Prospective panel study
Initial sample size: 4802 households, approximately 16,000 individuals
Nature of sample: Sample of households
Website: http://psidonline.isr.umich.edu/

The Panel Study of Income Dynamics was set up in 1968 with the aim of gathering information on individuals and families related to poverty and changes in economic well-being. The study is therefore mainly economic in focus and very little attitudinal or psychological data are included. The annual interviews collect information on income, education, labour force participation, occupation, work hours, commuting, housing, housework, child care, family composition, changing jobs, and moving house. Other topics have been covered in specific years of the study. For example in the thirteenth year of the study respondents were asked about emergency help in the form of time or money that they would expect to give or receive from friends or relatives.

Initially, in 1968, the sample was 70% white and 30% African–American. However, an additional 2000 Latino families were added to the sample in 1990 so that the race/ethnicity of the sample became 55.6% white; 22.2% African–American; and 22.2% Hispanic.

The PSID was originally funded by the Department of Health, Education, and Welfare and is currently principally funded by the National Science Foundation. Interviews are carried out annually with all (co-resident) members of the families in the sample. Using a similar methodology to the BHPS (described below), the PSID follows individuals who leave their family of origin to form new households. This means that as children from the original sample of families grow up and leave home to form their own families, they continue to be included in the sample and their spouse or cohabiting partner is added to the sample. This means that the PSID sample continues to grow year by year and information has now been collected on over 37,000 people. The longevity of the PSID means that extensive intergenerational information is now available. The yearly response rate to the PSID is high and ranges between 97% and 98%; however, cumulatively this still results in considerable panel attrition.

The British Cohort Study 1970

Start date: 1970
Research design: Prospective/catch-up study
Initial sample size: Approximately 17,000
Nature of sample: British cohort born in one week of 1970
Website: http://www.cls.ioe.ac.uk/

The British Cohort Study 1970 (BCS70) is a continuing, multi-disciplinary longitudinal study which takes as its subjects all those living in Great Britain who were born in a particular week in 1970.

Following the initial birth survey in 1970 – the British Births Survey (BBS) – there have been, to date, five attempts to gather information from the full cohort. In addition there have been a number of studies of subsamples of the cohort, and more recently a sample of the cohort members' children has also been included in the study.

With each successive attempt, the scope of enquiry has broadened from a strictly medical focus at birth to encompass physical and educational development at the age of 5 (Child and Health Education Study (CHES)), physical, educational, and social development at the ages of 10 (CHES) and 16 (Youthscan), and physical, educational, social, and economic development at 26 years. In 1999/2000, for the first time, BCS70 undertook a survey jointly with NCDS to interview cohort members on a wide range of topics. Both the NCDS and BCS70 now receive core funding from the ESRC and it is planned to survey both cohorts every four years, alternating between a full face-to-face interview study and a shorter telephone survey.

The ONS Longitudinal Study

Start date: 1971
Research design: Linked panel (sample from the British census)
Initial sample size: 500,000
Nature of sample: Individuals born on one of four dates, i.e. approximately 1% sample
Website: http://www.celsius.lshtm.ac.uk/what.html

The ONS Longitudinal Study (LS) contains data on approximately 1% of the population of England and Wales, linking their census records from 1971, 1981, 1991, and 2001 together with data for events such as deaths, births, cancer registrations, and emigrations. It therefore represents a way of linking the cross-sectional data collected at each decennial census to create a longitudinal dataset. Census information is also included for all people living in the same household as the LS member. However, the LS is different from household panel surveys such as the GSOEP or the BHPS in that it is primarily a sample of individuals and therefore does not follow all household members from census to census. The LS includes data on basic demographic and economic variables such as age, sex, marital status, fertility, housing type, employment status, occupation, and educational qualifications. There are also some limited data on health from the 1991 and 2001 censuses. The major strengths of the LS are its size and representative coverage. The fact that it is based on the census means that response rates are much higher than for standard longitudinal surveys. For research on minority groups such us those from ethnic minorities the LS is the only British longitudinal study big enough to give adequate sample sizes. The main limitation of the LS is that it is restricted to the relatively small number of variables included in the British Census. The LS is restricted to England and Wales although a Scottish LS is being developed.

In order to ensure that the confidentiality of the sample members is preserved, the LS can only be analysed on the ONS computer and only statistical abstracts and tables can be released to researchers. The ESRC funds the Centre for Longitudinal Study Information and User Support

(CeLCIUS) at the London School of Hygiene and Tropical Medicine to facilitate the use of the LS by academics.

The National Longitudinal Survey of Youth 1979 (NLSY79)

Start date: 1979
Research design: Cohort panel study interviewed regularly
Initial sample size: 12,686
Nature of sample: Young men and women in the United States aged 14–22 in 1979
Website: http://www.bls.gov/nls/home.htm

The National Longitudinal Survey of Youth is one of a set of surveys in the United States that were designed to gather information at multiple points in time on the labour market activities and other significant life events of several groups of men and women. Details of the other surveys can be found on the website given above.

The National Longitudinal Survey of Youth (1979) comprises a national probability sample of young men and women living in the United States and born between 1 January 1957 and 31 December 1964. The sample was designed to over-represent blacks, Hispanics, and economically disadvantaged non-blacks and non-Hispanics. An additional sample from the military was also selected for interviewing. Individuals from the NLSY79 were initially interviewed annually, but since 1994 have been interviewed every two years. The main purpose of the NLSY79 is the collection of information about each respondent's labour force experiences together with their investments in education and training. However, the content of the NLSY79 has covered a broad range of issues over the years. There has been some attrition of the sample so that by 1998 the total sample had reduced from 12,868 to 8399 individuals.

In 1986 an additional survey of all the children born to female respondents of the NLSY79 was set up. This is funded by the National Institute of Child Health and Human Development and includes assessments of each child as well as additional demographic and development information collected from either the mother or child. The number of children born to interviewed mothers was 5255 in 1986 and has increased to more than 8105 in 1996.

Since 1986, the NLSY79 has been administered by the Bureau of Labor Statistics (BLS), which is an agency of the US Department of Labor. The data collection for the NLSY79 and the children of the NLSY sample is subcontracted to the National Opinion Research Center at the University of Chicago. Almost all of the NLSY79 data are available to the public on

CD-ROM at a small charge. The data consist of a cumulative longitudinal record of each respondent from 1979 to the most recent interview date.

Although it covers a rather broader cohort, there is obviously scope for comparative research using the NLSY79 in the United States and the NCDS in Great Britain.

The German Socio-Economic Panel Study

Start date: 1984
Research design: Prospective panel study
Initial sample size: 5921 households, 12,290 adults (GSOEP West)
Nature of sample: Sample of households
Website: www.diw.de/english/sop/index.html

The German Socio-Economic Panel Study (GSOEP) is similar to the British Household Panel Study and the Panel Study of Income Dynamics, in that it is a representative longitudinal survey of private households that covers a wide range of issues. In particular it focuses on household change, employment and professional mobility, and occupational and family biographies. When the GSOEP was launched in 1984 it was solely a sample of the West German population (although approximately a quarter of households sampled were headed by non-German immigrants). In June 1990 the sample was extended to include the territory of the former East Germany: 2179 households containing 4453 adults were surveyed as the 'GSOEP East' sample. Members of the sample of households are interviewed each year. Those who move continue to be included in the survey as long as they are still living within Germany. Retention of the original sample is reasonably good. In 2002, the GSOEP West sample consisted of 3889 households with 7175 adults and the GSOEP East sample comprised 1818 households with 3466 people. In 2000 a major extension to the GSOEP took place to enable the possibility of analysis of minority groups. A new sample of 6052 households containing 10,890 individuals was drawn to supplement the original sample.

An English-language public use version of the GSOEP is available to researchers and is free of charge to universities and research centres.

The British Household Panel Survey

Start date: 1991
Research design: Prospective panel study
Initial sample size: 5500 households, 9900 adults
Nature of sample: Cluster sample of households
Website: www.iser.essex.ac.uk/bhps/

The British Household Panel Survey (BHPS) is an annual survey of a panel of British households. The first data collection took place in 1991 and the aim was to collect a wide range of information about work, family life, leisure activities, household finances, and health. Every adult member of the original sample of 5500 households was interviewed and became 'panel members'. They have subsequently been interviewed each year. In addition, each of the panel member's children are enrolled in the panel as soon as they reach 16. The focus of the survey is on households and on the relations between people in households. This means that if a new person joins one of the original sample of households, or if a panel member leaves a household to form a new one, any members of the new household are interviewed. In the second wave of the survey, in 1992, marriage and cohabitation histories were collected for all those over the age of 16. In the following wave, in 1993, employment histories were collected. These retrospective life histories complement the data collected each year on changes in marital status and changes in employment.

From 1994 onwards the BHPS incorporated a new questionnaire for all youth in the sample of households aged between 11 and 15. This covers issues such as relationships with parents, leisure activities, drinking, smoking, and drug taking. The youth questionnaire is administered using a tape-recorder and a self-completion questionnaire.

Attrition is a potential problem with all panel surveys. In wave 7 of the BHPS (in 1997), 76% of the original sample was still included and, of this sample, 90% had been interviewed in each of the seven waves to date.

The European Community Household Panel (ECHP)

Start date: 1994
Research design: Annual household panel
Initial sample size: 61,000 households comprising 130,000 adults
Nature of sample: Households from the European member states
Website: www-rcade.dur.ac.uk/echp/

The aim of the European Community Household Panel is to provide the European Commission with regional-level statistical information on the standard of living in member states. It includes micro-level data on living conditions, income, housing, health, and employment in the European Union. The longitudinal panel design of the ECHP makes it very similar to the GSOEP and the BHPS. Members of the initial sample are interviewed each year together with any new household members. The study is based on a probability sample of households drawn from each of the EU member states. There are funds available from the EU for researchers to visit the ISER in Essex and CEPS/INSTEAD in Luxembourg to use the data.

The Millennium Cohort Study

Start date: 2001
Research design: Prospective/catch-up study
Initial sample size: Approximately 19,000
Nature of sample: Births in the twelve months from June 2001, selected from a random sample of electoral wards, disproportionately stratified to ensure adequate representation of all four British countries, deprived areas, and areas with high concentrations of black and Asian families
Website: http://www.cls.ioe.ac.uk/

The survey for the first sweep of the Millennium Cohort Study began in June 2001 and gathered information from the parents of 18,819 babies born in Britain. The aim is to understand more about the social conditions surrounding birth and early childhood. In contrast to the three earlier British cohort studies, the sample is not based on the births in a single week. Instead birth dates are spread over a twelve-month period and living in selected British wards at age 9 months. The second sweep of the Millennium Cohort Study took place when the sample members were aged 3 and further sweeps are planned for ages 5 and 7.

The survey is managed and administered by the Centre for Longitudinal Studies, which is also responsible for the National Child Development Study and the British Cohort Study 1970. The Millennium Cohort Study is funded by the Economic and Social Research Council and a consortium of government departments.

Useful websites with information about longitudinal studies

Keeping Track website

http://www.iser.essex.ac.uk/ulsc/projects/ldr4ss/index.php

Aims to provide an up-to-date guide to major longitudinal sources of data and allows users to search for relevant longitudinal datasets using research topics of interest.

ESDS Longitudinal

http://www.esds.ac.uk/longitudinal/introduction.asp

Provides a web-based download service and support for the national Child Development Study, the British Cohort Study 1970, the Millennium Cohort Study, and the British Household Panel Study.

UK Data Archive Search catalogue

http://www.data-archive.ac.uk/Search/searchStart.asp

Longitudinal Data Analysis Research Unit

http://www.cas.1ancs.ac.uk/alcd/#ldaru

Based at the University of Lancaster, the general aim of the Longitudinal Data Analysis Research Unit is to research and disseminate good statistical practice in the analysis of panel and other micro-level longitudinal data in the social sciences.

Murray Research Center

http://www.radcliffe.edu/murray/index.php

The Murray Center's data holdings include studies with both female and male subjects from a wide range of ages and racial, ethnic, and socio-economic class groups. These data were collected using a variety of methods, but there are a large number of longitudinal studies included in the archive, many of which are relatively small scale and on specific topics. In keeping with the center's interest in qualitative records, the archive also includes some videotaped and/or audiotaped data.

Glossary

Attrition   The decrease in sample size over time in longitudinal prospective panel studies resulting from respondent refusal, failure to trace all respondents for repeated data collection, emigration, and death.

Boolean algebra   A system of symbolic logic used in computing algorithms and devised by the logician George Boole. It uses the two truth functions true and false and the functions AND, OR, NOT. It can therefore be used systematically to examine and represent the relations between a number of dichotomous variables.

Censored cases   Those cases in an event history analysis which do not experience the event of interest during the time they are observed. For example, in analysis of the age at first motherhood, those women who remained childless would be censored cases. Right censoring occurs when the event of interest happens after the period of observation and left censoring occurs when the event of interest happens before the period of observation begins.

Chicago tradition/the Chicago school   The Chicago tradition refers to a particular approach to sociology that was particularly successful and dominant at the University of Chicago from around the 1920s until the late 1950s. The Chicago school consisted of two main areas of interconnected research. First, there was the work of Park and Burgess that focused on the social organization of the city, migration patterns, and the sociology of urban life. Second, there was work associated with Hughes and Whyte which focused on deviants and on people in low-prestige occupations. The work of the Chicago school is characterized by its attention to detail and its concern to provide rich descriptions of urban life.

Chronicle   A historical account of events or facts presented in the order in which they occurred. White (1987) makes a distinction between a chronicle and a narrative so that a chronicle does not achieve the conclusion, resolution, or closure expected of a narrative. It is closer to a list of events than a fully formed story.

Cohort study   A cohort study is a longitudinal research study that follows a group of individuals, who share a common starting point, over time. Examples in Britain include the 1946, 1958, 1970 birth cohort studies and the Millennium Cohort Study. Each focuses on the health, well-being, development, and ageing of individuals born in the same year.

Constructivism   Constructivism recognizes that all knowledge about ourselves and the social world is 'constructed'. Knowledge does not straightforwardly reflect an external reality, but is contingent on convention, human perception, and social experience.

Conversation analysis   Conversation analysis developed out of Garfinkel's ethnomethodological approach to sociology and is associated with the work of Harvey Sacks. It aims to provide a detailed description of how individuals manage the process of turn taking in verbal communication with each other. In common with ethnomethodology more generally, its focus is on how individuals in society routinely accomplish something which is taken for granted and which therefore requires tacit rather than explicit knowledge.

Cox proportional hazards model   A popular method for modelling continuous event history data in the social sciences which allows an assessment of the relative impact of a number of independent variables on the likelihood of a specific event occurring. It makes it possible to estimate the relative effects of explanatory variables without making any assumptions about the baseline probability distribution of the durations.

Cross-sectional data   Information about the circumstances of a set of research cases at a single point in time.

Dependent variable   An outcome variable that is thought to depend on a number of other variables. For example, in an analysis of the effect of smoking on lung function, the measure of lung function would be the dependent variable. Dependent variables are sometimes also referred to as 'exogenous' variables.

Empathy   Within the hermeneutic approach to the social sciences, the word empathy is employed in a slightly different way from its common usage. Empathy is the recreation in the mind of the researcher of the feelings and motivations of the objects of study. It is the means by which we understand that a man swinging an axe is chopping wood, or that a group of people standing in a line in the street are probably waiting for a bus. Empathy is a basic process of social observation where what is observed are purposive actions rather than raw physical objects and behaviour from which action is inferred. According to Winch (1958) empathic understanding is not a feeling, rather it is an ability to participate in a form of life.

Epistemology   Epistemology is concerned with evaluating claims about the ways in which we can know about the world. It is an enquiry into the conditions of the possibility of knowledge.

Ethnography   Richly descriptive writing about particular groups of people and their culture. The word is a composite of the terms 'ethno', meaning folk or people, and 'graph', which derives from 'writing'.

Event history data   Data recorded concerning the exact timing of events, usually relating to an individual's life. For example, the timing of job changes, moving house, getting married, and the births of any children.

Extensive research   Extensive research aims to produce descriptions of the common properties of and patterns in a population as a whole. It relies on large-scale surveys of representative samples and uses statistics to make inferences to the population. The aim is to provide generalizable descriptions rather than accounts with explanatory power. The term was coined by Harré (1979) who contrasts intensive designs with extensive designs.

Hazard rate/hazard function (also known as the failure rate)   A measure of the probability that an event will occur at a particular point in time given that the individual case is still at risk at that time. In more formal terms, a measure of the probability that an event occurs at time t, conditional on it not having occurred before t.

Hermeneutics/hermeneutic tradition   An approach to the analysis of textual material, such as interview transcripts, diaries, auto/biographies, that emphasizes the importance of understanding the meaning of the material from the perspective of the individual who produced it. In other words, the social world must be understood from within, not explained from without. The term hermeneutics derives from the Greek word *hermeneus*, an interpreter, and was originally used to describe an approach to the interpretation of passages from the Christian Bible that sought to understand the historical and cultural context in which they were written.

Ideographic   A description pertaining to the individual case. Qualitative research may be described as ideographic in that it attempts to understand the individual case.

Independent variables/covariates   Independent variables are the explanatory variables that are included in analysis to determine whether they have an association with or effect upon the outcome variable of interest. For example, in an analysis to ascertain the factors which impact on an individual's income at age 40 variables such as gender, level of education, type of industry would all be included in the analysis as independent variables. These are also sometimes referred to as endogenous variables.

Inferential statistics   In contrast to descriptive statistics, which aim to provide a numerical summary of a set of data (e.g. the mean and standard deviation), inferential statistics aim to test the relation between observed data in a sample and the broader population from which that data have been collected. For example, the chi-square statistic is an example of an inferential statistic because it tests whether an association observed between two categorical variables is statistically significant. That is, whether the relationship observed in the sample is likely to apply in the population as a whole.

Intensive research   Intensive research aims to produce causal explanations and focuses on a particular case or a small number of cases to understand what produces a particular outcome in a specific context. The term was coined by Harré (1979) who contrasts intensive designs with extensive designs.

Life course research   An approach to research in sociology that stresses the interconnection of social change, social structure, and individual action. It emphasizes the need to understand the importance of the timing of events in individual lives and also the historical and cultural context of those lives. Elder's book *The Children of the Great Depression* (1974) is one of the most frequently cited examples of research that adopts the life course approach.

Logistic regression   A method of analysis that investigates the relation between a number of continuous and categorical explanatory or 'independent' variables and a single dichotomous or binary outcome.

Longitudinal data   Information concerning what has happened to a set of research cases over a series of points in time.

Methodology   Refers to decisions made by researchers about sampling, data collection, and analysis.

Methods   Specific research techniques either for collecting or analysing data, such as a telephone survey or a focus group or a particular statistical procedure.

Model uncertainty   In recent years, advances in statistical methodology and computing have made powerful modelling tools more widely available. The unstated assumption behind the reporting of a model is that it adequately approximates the underlying process of interest. If the model successfully approximates the underlying process, inferences and forecasts based on it should be reasonably good. However, analysts never know the 'true' underlying process and there are potentially hundreds of different models that could be estimated and shown statistically to fit the observed data adequately. Most analyses ignore the uncertainty associated with the selection of a particular model and simply state that the factors included in the model have a statistically significant association with the outcome of interest. However, over the past decade there has been greater attention paid to the problem of 'model uncertainty' across a number of disciplines (McKim, 1997).

Multivariate modelling   A generic term describing forms of analysis that aim to investigate the links between a number of explanatory or independent variables and a single outcome or dependent variable.

Narrative   A narrative is a discourse or text that connects events in a clear sequential order and gives meaning to those events in relation to a specific resolution or conclusion. Further discussion of the definition of narrative is given in Chapter 1.

Narrative positivism   Andrew Abbott's term for an approach to the quantitative analysis of sequence data which attempts to identify and describe common patterns within sequences (corresponding to patterns of jobs within careers, for example) rather than focusing on the factors which cause particular patterns to occur.

Naturalism   A model of research which attempts as much as possible to understand subjects' experiences in their own terms.

Nomothetic   Involving the identification of abstract universal principles or laws. Often used to characterize quantitative research which uses large-scale survey or census data to look for robust relationships between variables that can be generalized to the whole population of interest.

Ontology   Ontology is that branch of philosophy that enquires as to what kind of things really exist in the world. Ontological questions are therefore questions about existence and identity.

Ordinary least squares regression analysis   This is a method of analysis that investigates the relation between a number of continuous explanatory or 'independent' variables and a single continuous outcome.

Positivism   The term positivism is difficult to define as it is used in a number of different ways within social science and philosophy. Broadly speaking, it refers to the belief that a scientific method can be applied to studying society. In other words, that objective, value-free enquiry is both possible and desirable. Underlying positivism therefore is the belief that science is the study of an objective reality that exists outside and separate from the scientific endeavour. Positivism is often contrasted with hermeneutics or interpretive social science. Whereas the goal of positivism is seen as being able to provide causal *explanations* or covering laws, the goal of a hermeneutic social science is to achieve a better *understanding* of society.

Prospective research   Research which follows a sample of cases over time and collects data successively by a series of current reports on present circumstances.

Realism   In philosophy realism is contrasted with 'nominalism' and constructivism. It is the belief that the social world exists independently of our beliefs and conceptions.

Reliability   Reliability is generally defined as the replicability or stability of research findings over a short space of time.

Retrospective research   Research which collects information about the past relying on individuals' present recollections of their life histories.

Risk set   In an event history analysis, the group of individuals who are considered to be at risk of an event occurring. This will reduce in number over time as more individuals experience the event of interest and therefore leave the risk set.

Time-varying covariates   Variables that may change their value over a period of time and also change their value within an analysis. For example, age of the youngest child in the household.

Triangulation   Involves using different kinds of data (e.g. quantitative and qualitative) to answer a specific research question.

Validity   Validity refers to the ability of research to reflect an external reality or to measure the concepts of interest. Questions in a survey are said to have high validity if they measure what the researcher intends them to measure. A distinction is usually made between internal and external validity, where internal validity refers to the ability to produce results that are not simply an artefact of the research design, and external validity is a measure of how far the findings relating to a particular sample can be generalized to apply to a broader population.

References

Abbott, A. (1988) *The System of Professions: An essay on the division of expert labor*. Chicago: University of Chicago Press.

Abbott, A. (1990) 'Conceptions of time and events in social science methods', *Historical Methods*, 23 (4): 140–50.

Abbott, A. (1992a) 'From causes to events: notes on narrative positivism', *Sociological Methods and Research*, 20 (4): 428–55.

Abbott, A. (1992b) 'What do cases do?', in C. Ragin and H.S. Becker (eds), *What is a Case?*. Cambridge: Cambridge University Press. pp. 53–82.

Abbott, A. (1997) 'Of time and space: the contemporary relevance of the Chicago School', *Social Forces*, 75 (4): 1149–82.

Abbott, A. (1998) 'The causal devolution', *Sociological Methods and Research*, 27 (2): 148–81.

Abbott, A. and DeViney, S. (1992) 'The welfare state as transnational event', *Social Science History*, 16: 245–74.

Abbott, A. and Forrest, J. (1986) 'Optimal matching methods for historical data', *Journal of Interdisciplinary History*, 16: 473–96.

Abbott, A. and Hrycak, A. (1990) 'Measuring resemblance in sequence data: an optimal matching analysis of musicians' careers', *American Journal of Sociology*, 96 (1): 144–85.

Abbott, A. and Tsay, A. (2000) 'Sequence analysis and optimal matching techniques in sociology', *Sociological Methods and Research*, 29 (1): 3–33.

Adam, B. (1990) *Time and Social Theory*. Oxford: Polity Press.

Adam, B. (1995) *Timewatch: the social analysis of time*. Cambridge: Polity Press.

Agar, M. and Hobbs, J.R. (1982) 'Interpreting discourse: coherence and the analysis of ethnographic interviews', *Discourse Processes*, 5: 1–32.

Agronick, G. and Helson, R. (1996) 'Who benefits from an examined life? Participation in a longitudinal study', in R. Josselson (ed.), *Ethics and Process in the Narrative Study of Lives*. Thousand Oaks, CA: Sage.

Aldridge, J. (1993) 'The textual disembodiment of knowledge in research account writing', *Sociology*, 27 (1): 53–66.

Allison, P.D. (1984) *Event History Analysis: regression for longitudinal event data*. Beverly Hills, CA: Sage.

Alvesson, M. and Skoldberg, K. (2000) *Reflexive Methodology*. London: Sage.

American Psychological Association (2003) 'Ethical principles of psychologists and code of conduct'. Available online: http://www.apa.org/ethics/code2002.html.

Anderson, J. and Poole, M. (1994) *Thesis and Assignment Writing*. Brisbane: Wiley.

Annandale, E. and Clark, J. (1996) 'What is gender? Feminist theory and the sociology of human reproduction', *Sociology of Health and Illness*, 18 (1): 17–44.

Arksey, H. and Knight, P. (1999) *Interviewing for Social Scientists*. London: Sage.

Atkinson, J.M. and Herritage, J. (1984) *Structures of Social Action*. Cambridge: Cambridge University Press.

Atkinson, P. (1990) *The Ethnographic Imagination: textual constructions of reality*. London: Routledge.

Atkinson, P. (1997) 'Narrative turn or blind alley?', *Qualitative Health Research*, 7: 325–44.

Baerger, D. and McAdams, D.P. (1999) 'Life story coherence and its relation to psychological well-being', *Narrative Inquiry*, 9: 69–96.

Bakan, D. (1996) 'Some reflections about narrative research and hurt and harm', in R. Josselson (ed.), *Ethics and Process in the Narrative Study of Lives*. Thousand Oaks, CA: Sage.

Balnaves, M. and Caputi, P. (2001) *Introduction to Quantitative Research Methods: an investigative approach*. London: Sage.

Barry, J., Francis, B. and Davies, R. (1990) 'SABRE: Software for the Analysis of Binary Recurrent Events – a guide for users', Department of Applied Statistics, University of Lancaster.

Bartley, M. (1991) 'Health and labour force participation: stress, selection and the reproduction costs of labour power', *Journal of Social Policy*, 20: 327–64.

Baumeister, R.F. and Newman, L.S. (1994) 'How stories make sense of personal experiences: motives that shape autobiographical narratives', *Personality and Social Psychology Bulletin*, 20: 676–90.

Baumer, E. (1997) 'Levels and predictors of recidivism: the Malta experience', *Criminology*, 35: 601–28.

Bearman, P., Faris, R. and Moody, J. (1999) 'Blocking the future: new solutions for old problems in historical social science', *Social Science History*, 23 (4): 501–33.

Beck, U. (1992) *Risk Society: towards a new modernity*. London: Sage.

Beck, U. (1994) 'The Reinvention of politics: towards a theory of reflexive modernization', in U. Beck, A. Giddens and S. Lash (eds), *Reflexive Modernization: politics, tradition and aesthetics in the modern social order*. Cambridge: Polity Press.

Beck, U. and Beck-Gernshein, E. (2002) *Individualization*. London: Sage.

Becker, H.S. (1996) 'The epistemology of social research', in R. Jessor, A. Colby, and R.A. Shweder (eds), *Ethnography and Human Development: Context and Meaning in Social Inquiry*. Chicago: University of Chicago Press. pp. 53–72.

Benney, M. and Hughes, E.C. (1956) 'Of sociology and the interview', *American Journal of Sociology*, 62: 137–42.

Berger, P. and Kellner, H. (1964) 'Marriage and the construction of reality', *Diogenes*, 46: 1–25.

Berk, R.A. (1983) 'An introduction to sample selection bias in sociological data', *American Sociological Review*, 48: 386–98.

Bernstein, C. (1997) 'Labov and Waletzky in context', *Journal of Narrative and Life History*, 7 (1–4): 45–51.

Bertaux, D. (1981) 'From the life-history approach to the transformation of sociological practice', in D. Bertaux (ed.), *Biography and Society: the life history approach in the social sciences*. Beverly Hills, CA: Sage. pp. 29–46.

Bertaux, D. and Bertaux-Wiame, I. (1981) 'Life stories and the baker's trade', in D. Bertaux (ed.), *Biography and Society: the life history approach in the social sciences*. Beverly Hills, CA: Sage. pp. 169–90.

Beynon, H. (1973) *Working for Ford*. London: Allen Lane.

Blair-Loy, M. (1999) 'Career patterns of executive women in finance', *American Journal of Sociology*, 104: 1346–97.

Blane, D., Smith, G.D. and Bartley, M. (1993) 'Social selection: what does it contribute to social class differences in health', *Sociology of Health and Illness*, 15: 1–15.

Blossfeld, H.-P. and Rohwer, G. (1995) *Techniques of Event History Modeling: new approaches to causal analysis*. Mahwah, NJ: Lawrence Erlbaum.

Blossfeld, H.-P. and Rohwer, G. (1997) 'Causal inference, time and observation plans in the social sciences', *Quality and Quantity*, 999: 361–83.

Blumer, H. (1956) 'Sociological analysis and the variable', *American Sociological Review*, 21: 683–90.

Boje, D.M. (1991) 'The storytelling organisation', *Administrative Science Quarterly*, 36: 106–26.

Borland, K. (1991) '"That's not what I said": Interpretive conflict in oral narrative research', in S.B. Gluck and D. Patai (eds), *Women's Words*. London: Routledge. pp. 63–6.

Boudon, R. (1974) *Education, Opportunity and Social Inequality*. New York: Wiley.

Brannen, J. (1992) 'Combining qualitative and quantitative approaches: an overview', in J. Brannen (ed.), *Mixing Methods: qualitative and quantitative research*. Aldershot: Avebury. pp. 3–38.

Brenner, B. (1985) 'Intensive interviewing', in M. Brenner, J. Brown and D. Canter (eds), *The Research Interview: uses and approaches*. London: Academic press. pp. 147–61.

British Sociological Association (2002) 'Statement of ethical practice for the British Sociological Association'. Available online: http://www.britsoc.co.uk/Library/Ethicsguidelines2002.doc.

Brown, G. (1995) *Speakers, Listeners and Communication*. Cambridge: Cambridge University Press.

Bruner, J. (1986) *Actual Minds, Possible Worlds*. Cambridge, MA: Harvard University Press.

Bruner, J. (1987) 'Life as narrative', *Social Research*, 54 (1): 11–32.

Bruner, J. (1990) *Acts of Meaning*. Cambridge, MA: Harvard University Press.

Bryman, A. (1984) 'The debate about quantitative and qualitative research: a question of method or epistemology?', *British Journal of Sociology*, 35: 75–92.

Bryman, A. (1988) *Quantity and Quality in Social Research*. London: Routledge.

Bryman, A. (1992) 'Quantitative and qualitative research: further reflections of their integration', in J. Brannen (ed.), *Mixing Methods: qualitative and quantitative research*. Aldershot: Avebury. pp. 57–80.

Bryman, A. (1998) 'Quantitative and qualitative research strategies in knowing the social world', in T. May and M. Williams (eds), *Knowing the Social World*. Buckingham: Open University Press. pp. 138–56.

Butler, J. (1990) *Gender Trouble: feminism and the subversion of identity*. London: Routledge.

Bynner, J. and Fogelman, K. (1993) 'Making the grade: education and training experiences', in E. Ferri (ed.), *Life at 33: The fifth follow-up of the National Child Development Study*. London: National Children's Bureau. pp. 36–59.

Bynner, J., Ferri, E. and Smith, B.H. (1997) 'Getting somewhere, getting nowhere in the 1990s', in J. Bynner, E. Ferri and P. Shepherd (eds), *Twenty-something in the 1990s: getting on, getting by, getting nowhere*. Aldershot: Ashgate.

Carr, D. (1997) 'Narrative and the real world: an argument for continuity', in L.P. Hinchman and S.K. Hinchman (eds), *Memory, Identity, Community: the idea of narrative in the human sciences*. New York: State University of New York. pp. 7–25.

Chamberlayne, P. and Rustin, M. (1999) 'From biography to social policy: final report of the SOSTRIS project', Centre for Biography in Social Policy, University of East London, London.

Chamberlayne, P., Bornat, J. and Wengraf, T. (2000) *The Turn to Biographical Methods in Social Science*. London: Routledge.

Chan, T.-W. (1995) 'Optimal matching analysis', *Work and Occupations*, 22: 467–90.

Charmaz, K. (1991) *Good Days, Bad Days: the self in chronic illness and time*. New Brunswick, NJ: Rutgers University Press.

Chase, S.E. (1995a) 'Taking narrative seriously: consequences for method and theory in interview studies', in R. Josselson and A. Lieblich (eds), *Interpreting Experience: The Narrative Study of Lives*, vol. 3. Thousand Oaks, CA: Sage. pp. 1–26.

Chase, S.E. (1995b) *Ambiguous Empowerment: the work narratives of women school superintendents*. Amherst, MA: University of Massachusetts Press.

Chase, S.E. (1996) 'Personal vulnerability and interpretive authority in narrative research', in R. Josselson (ed.), *Ethics and Process in the Narrative Study of Lives*. Thousand Oaks, CA: Sage. pp. 45–59.

Chatfield, C. (1995) 'Model uncertainty, data mining and statistical inference', *Journal of the Royal Statistical Society, Series A*, 158 (3): 419–66.

Chatman, S. (1978) *Story and Discourse: narrative structure in fiction and film*. Ithaca, NY: Cornell University Press.

Clandinin, D.J. and Connelly, F.M. (2000) *Narrative Inquiry: experience and story in qualitative research*. San Francisco: Jossey-Bass.

Clarridge, B.R., Sheehy, L.L. and Hauser, T.S. (1978) 'Tracing members of a panel: a 17-year follow-up', *Sociological Methodology*, 10: 185–203.

Clausen, J.A. (1993) *American Lives: looking back at children of the Great Depression*. New York: Free Press.

Clifford, J. (1986) 'Introduction: partial truths', in J. Clifford and G.E. Marcus (eds), *Writing Culture: The Poetics and Politics of Ethnography*. Berkeley, CA: University of California Press. pp. 1–26.

Clogg, C.C. and Haritou, A. (1997) 'The regression method of causal inference and a dilemma confronting this method', in V.R. McKim and S.P. Turner (eds), *Causality in Crisis? Statistical Methods and the Search for Causal Knowledge in the Social Sciences*. Notre Dame, IN: University of Notre Dame Press. pp. 83–112.

Coates, J. (1996) *Women Talk*. Oxford: Blackwell.

Coffey, A. and Atkinson, P. (1996) *Making Sense of Qualitative Data*. Thousand Oaks, CA: Sage.

Cohan, M. (1997) 'Political identities and political landscapes', *The Sociological Quarterly*, 38 (2): 303–19.

Collins, P. (1998) 'Negotiating selves: reflections on unstructured interviewing', *Sociological Research Online*, 3 (3): 1–19.

Connelly, F.M. and Clandinin, D.J. (1999) *Shaping a Professional Identity: stories of educational practice*. New York: Teachers' College Press.

Cortazzi, M. (1991) *Primary Teaching: how it is – a narrative account*. London: David Fulton.

Cox, D.R. (1972) 'Regression models and life tables', *Journal of the Royal Statistical Society, Series B*, 34: 187–202.

Cox, D.R. (1992) 'Causality: some statistical aspects', *Journal of the Royal Statistical Society, Series A*, 155 (2): 291–302.

Cox, S.M. (2003) 'Stories in decisions: how at-risk individuals decide to request predictive testing for Huntingdon Disease', *Qualitative Sociology*, 26: 257–80.

Crossley, M.L. (1999) 'Making sense of HIV infection: discourse and adaptation to life with a long-term HIV positive diagnosis', *Health*, 3 (1): 95–119.

Dale, A. and Davies, R. (1994) *Analyzing Social and Political Change: a casebook of methods*. London: Sage.

Davie, R., Butler, N. and Goldstein, H. (1972) *From Birth to Seven: a report of the National Child Development Study*. London: Longman.

Davies, R.B. (1994) 'From cross-sectional to longitudinal analysis', in A. Dale and R.B. Davies (eds), *Analyzing Social and Political Change: a casebook of methods*. London: Sage. pp. 20–40.

Day-Sclater, S. (1998a) 'Nina's story: an exploration into the construction and transformation of subjectivities in narrative accounting', *Auto/Biography*, VI: 67–77.

Day-Sclater, S. (1998b) 'Creating the self: stories as transitional phenomena', *Auto/Biography*, VI: 85–92.

Dempster-McClain, D. and Moen, P. (1998) 'Finding respondents in a follow-up study', in J.Z. Giele and G.H. Elder (eds), *Methods of Life Course Research: qualitative and quantitative approaches*. Thousand Oaks, CA: Sage. pp. 128–51.

Denzin, N.K. (1983) 'Interpretive interactionism', in G. Morgan (ed.), *Beyond Method: strategies for social research*. Beverly Hills, CA: Sage.

Denzin, N.K. (1989) *Interpretive Biography*. New York: Sage.

Dex, S. (1991) 'The reliability of recall data: a literature review', Working Papers of the ESRC Research Centre on Micro-social Change, Paper 11, University of Essex.

Dex, S. (1995) 'The reliability of recall data: a literature review', *Bulletin de Methodologie Sociologique*, 49: 58–80.

Dex, S. and McCulloch, A. (1998) 'The reliability of retrospective unemployment history data', *Work Employment and Society*, 12: 497–509.

Dex, S., Joshi, H., Macran, S. and McCulloch, A. (1998) 'Women's employment transitions around child bearing', *Oxford Bulletin of Economics and Statistics*, 60: 79–97.

Drew, D. and Herritage, J. (1992) *Talk at Work*. Cambridge: Cambridge University Press.

Duncan, S.S. and Edwards, R. (1999) *Lone Mothers' Paid Work and Gendered Moral Rationalities*. Houndmills: Macmillan.

Edwards, R. and Ribbens, J. (1998) 'Living on the edges: public knowledge, private lives, personal experience', in J. Ribbens and R. Edwards (eds), *Feminist Dilemmas in Qualitative Research*. London: Sage. pp. 1–23.

Elder, G.H. (1974) *The Children of the Great Depression: social change in life experience*. Chicago: University of Chicago Press.

Elder, G.H. (1987) 'War mobilization and the life course: a cohort of World War II veterans', *Sociological Forum*, 2: 449–72.

Elder, G.H. (1992) 'Life course', in B.E.F. and M.L. Borgatta (eds), *Encyclopedia of Sociology*, vol. 3. New York: Macmillan. pp. 1120–30.

Elder, G.H., Shanahan, M.J. and Clipp, E.C. (1994) 'When war comes to men's lives: life-course patterns in family, work and health', *Psychology and Aging*, 9: 5–16.

Elliott, B.J. (2001) 'Success stories? Narrative representations of women's lives', PhD thesis, University of Manchester.

Elliott, J. (1999) 'Models are stories are not real life', in D. Dorling and S. Simpson (eds), *Statistics in Society: the arithmetic of politics*. London: Arnold. pp. 95–102.

Elliott, J. (2002a) 'The value of event history techniques for understanding social processes: modelling women's employment behaviour after motherhood', *International Journal of Social Research Methodology*, 5: 107–32.

Elliott, J. (2002b) 'Longitudinal analysis and the constitution of the concept of gender', in E. Ruspini and A. Dale (eds), *The Gender Dimension of Social Change*. Bristol: Policy Press. pp. 229–60.

Ely, M., Richards, M.P.M., Wadsworth, M.E.J. and Elliott, B.J. (1999) 'Secular changes in the association of parental divorce and children's educational attainment – evidence from three British birth cohorts', *Journal of Social Policy*, 28 (3): 437–55.

Esser, H. (1996) 'What is wrong with "Variable Sociology"?', *European Sociological Review*, 12: 159–66.

Ewick, P. and Silbey, S.S. (1995) 'Subversive stories and hegemonic tales: toward a sociology of narrative', *Law and Society Review*, 29 (2): 197–226.

Ezzy, D. (1997) 'Subjectivity and the labour process: conceptualising "good work"', *Sociology*, 31 (3): 427–44.

Faircloth, C.A. (1999) 'Revisiting thematisation in the narrative study of epilepsy', *Sociology of Health and Illness*, 21 (2): 209–27.

Farran, D. (1990) 'Seeking Susan: producing statistical information on young people's leisure', in L. Stanley (ed.), *Feminist Praxis*. London: Routledge. pp. 91–102.

Featherman, D.L. (1980) 'Retrospective longitudinal research: methodological considerations', *Journal of Economics and Business*, 32: 152–69.

Feinstein, L., Duckworth, K. and Sabates, R. (2004) 'A model of the inter-generational trans-mission of educational success', The Centre for the Wider Benefits of Learning, London.

Ferber, A.L. (2000) 'A comment on Aguirre: taking narrative seriously', *Sociological Perspectives*, 43 (2): 341–9.

Ferri, E., Bynner, J. and Wadsworth, M.E.J. (2003) *Changing Britain, Changing Lives: three generations at the turn of the century*. London: Institute of Education.

Finch, J. (1984) '"It's great to have someone to talk to": the ethics and politics of interviewing women', in C. Bell and H. Roberts (eds), *Social Researching*. London: Routledge & Kegan Paul. pp. 70–87.

Finn, M.A. and Muirhead-Steves, S. (2002) 'The effectiveness of electronic monitoring with violent male parolees', *Justice Quarterly*, 19: 293–312.

Finnegan, R. (1992) *Oral Traditions and the Verbal Arts: a guide to research practice*. London: Routledge.

Forster, E.M. (1963) [1927] *Aspects of the Novel*. Harmondsworth: Penguin.

Foucault, M. (1990) *The History of Sexuality, vol. 1, an Introduction*, trans R. Hurley. London: Penguin.

Franzosi, R. (1994) 'From words to numbers – a set-theory framework for the collection, organization, and analysis of narrative data', *Sociological Methodology*, 24: 105–36.

Franzosi, R. (1998a) 'Narrative analysis – or why (and how) sociologists should be interested in narrative', *Annual Review of Sociology*, 24: 517–54.

Franzosi, R. (1998b) 'Narrative as data: linguistic and statistical tools for the quantitative study of historical events', *International Review of Social History*, 43: 81–104.

Franzosi, R. (2003) *From Words to Numbers: a journey in science*. Cambridge: Cambridge University Press.

Gainey, R.R., Payne, B.K. and O'Toole, M. (2000) 'The relationship between time in jail, time on electronic monitoring, and recidivism: an event history analysis of a jail-based program', *Justice Quarterly*, 17: 733–52.

Garfinkel, H. (1967) *Studies in Ethnomethodology*. Englewood Cliffs, NJ: Prentice Hall.

Gayle, V., Berridge, D. and Davies, R.B. (2000) 'Young people's routes to higher education: exploring social processes with longitudinal data', *Higher Education Review*, 33: 47–64.

Gayle, V., Berridge, D. and Davies, R.B. (2002) 'Young people's entry into higher education: quantifying influential factors', *Oxford Review of Education*, 28: 5–20.

Gee, J.P. (1986) 'Units in the production of narrative discourse', *Discourse Processes*, 9: 391–422.

Geertz, C. (1988) *Works and Lives: the anthropologist as author*. Stanford, CA: Stanford University Press.

Gergen, K. and Gergen, M. (1988) 'Narrative and the self as relationship', in L. Berkowitz (ed.), *Advances in Experimental Social Psychology*. San Diego, CA: Academic Press. pp. 17–56.

Gergen, K.J. and Gergen, M.M. (1983) 'Narratives of the self', in T.R. Sarbin and K.E. Sceibe (eds), *Studies in Social Identity*. New York: Praeger. pp. 254–73.

Gergen, M.M. (1992) 'Life stories: pieces of a dream', in G.C. Rosenwald and R.L. Ochberg (eds), *Storied Lives: the cultural politics of self understanding*. New Haven, CT: Yale University Press. pp. 127–44.

Gershuny, J., Rose, D., Scott, J. and Buck, N. (1994) 'Introducing household panels', in N. Buck, J. Gershuny, D. Rose and J. Scott (eds), *Changing Households: the BHPS 1990–1992*. Colchester: ESRC Centre on Micro-Social Change.

Giddens, A. (1991) *Modernity and Self Identity: self and society in the late modern age*. Cambridge: Polity Press.

Giddens, A. (1994) 'Living in a post-traditional society', in U. Beck, A. Giddens and S. Lash (eds), *Reflexive Modernization: politics, tradition and aesthetics in the modern social order*. Cambridge: Polity Press.

Giele, J.Z. (1995) *Two paths to women's equality: temperance, suffrage and the origins of modern feminism*. New York: Twayne.

Giele, J.Z. (1998) 'Innovation in the typical life course', in J.Z. Giele and G.H. Elder (eds), *Methods of Life Course Research: Qualitative and Quantitative Approaches*. London: Sage. pp. 231–63.

Giele, J.Z. and Elder, G.H. (1998) *Methods of Life Course Research: qualitative and quantitative approaches*. Thousand Oaks, CA: Sage.

Gill, R. (1998) 'Dialogues and Differences: Writing, Reflexivity and the Crisis of Representation', in K. Henwood, L.J. Griffin and A. Phoenix (eds), *Standpoints and Differences: Essays in the Practice of Feminist Psychology, Gender and Psychology*. London: Sage. pp. 18–44.

Glueck, S.S. and Glueck, E. (1930) *Five Hundred Criminal Careers*. New York: Knopf.

Goldthorpe, J.H. (1996) 'Class analysis and the reorientation of class theory: the case of persisting differentials in educational attainment', *British Journal of Sociology*, 47: 481–505.

Goldthorpe, J.H. (2001) 'Causation, statistics, and sociology', *European Sociological Review*, 17: 1–20.

Goodwin, J. and Horowitz, R. (2002) 'Introduction: the methodological strengths and dilemmas of qualitative sociology', *Qualitative Sociology*, 25: 33–47.

Goodwin, M.H. (1997) 'Towards families of stories in context', *Journal of Narrative and Life History*, 7 (1–4): 107–12.

Gorard, S. (2003) *Quantitative Methods in Social Science*. London: Continuum.

Graham, H. (1984) 'Surveying through stories', in C. Bell and H. Roberts (eds), *Social Researching*. London: Routledge & Kegan Paul. pp. 104–24.

Graham, H. (1990) 'Behaving well: women's health behaviour in context', in H. Roberts (ed.), London: Routledge.

Green, J.M., Coupland, V.A. and Kitzinger, J.V. (1988) 'Great Expectations: a prospective study of women's expectations and experiences of childbirth', Child Care and Development Group, University of Cambridge, Cambridge.

Gubrium, J.F. and Holstein, J.A. (1995) 'Individual agency, the ordinary, and postmodern life', *Sociological Quarterly*, 36 (3): 555–70.

Gubrium, J.F. and Holstein, J.A. (1997) *The New Language of Qualitative Method*. Oxford: Oxford University Press.

Gubrium, J.F. and Holstein, J.A. (1998) 'Narrative practice and the coherence of personal stories', *Sociological Quarterly*, 39 (1): 163–87.

Gubrium, J.F., Holstein, J.A. and Buckholdt, D.R. (1994) *Constructing the Lifecourse*. Dix Hills, NY: General Hall.

Hakim, C. (2000) *Work-lifestyle Choices in the 21st Century*. Oxford: Oxford University Press.

Hakim, C. (2002) 'Lifestyle preferences as determinants of women's differentiated labor market careers', *Work and Occupations*, 29: 428–59.

Halford, S., Savage, M. and Witz, A. (1997) *Gender, Careers and Organisations: current developments in banking, nursing, and local government*. Basingstoke: Macmillan.

Halliday, M. (1973) *Explorations in the Function of Language*. London: Edward Arnold.

Halpin, B. and Chan, T.W. (1998) 'Class careers as sequences: an optimal matching analysis of work-life histories', *European Sociological Review*, 14 (2): 111–30.

Hammersley, M. (2003) 'Recent radical criticism of interview studies: any implications for the sociology of education', *British Journal of Sociology*, 24: 119–26.

Han, S.-K. and Moen, P. (1999) 'Clocking out', *American Journal of Sociology*, 105: 191–236.

Haraven, T.K. (1982) *Family Time and industrial time: the relationship between family and work in a New England industrial community*. Cambridge: Cambridge University Press.

Harding, S. (1992) *Whose Science? Whose knowledge?*. Milton Keynes: Open University Press.

Harré, R. (1970) *The Principles of Scientific Thinking*. London: Macmillan.

Harré, R. (1979) *Social Being*. Oxford: Blackwell.

Harris, S.R. (2003) 'Studying equality/inequality: naturalist and constructionist approaches to equality in marriage', *Journal of Contemporary Ethnography*, 32: 200–32.

Hartsock, N.C.M. (1997) *The Feminist Standpoint Revisited*. New York: Basic Books.

Heaton, T.B. and Call, V.R.A. (1995) 'Modeling family dynamics with event history techniques', *Journal of Marriage and the Family*, 57: 1078–90.

Hedstrom, P. and Swedberg, R. (1998) 'Social mechanisms: an introductory essay', in P. Hedstrom and R. Swedberg (eds), *Social Mechanisms*. Cambridge: Cambridge University Press. pp. 1–32.

Helson, R. (1993) 'The Mills classes of 1958 and 1960: college in the 50s; young adulthood in the 1960s', in K.D. Hulbert and D.T. Schuster (eds), *Women's Lives Through Time*. San Francisco: Jossey-Bass. pp. 190–210.

Hermanowicz, J.C. (2002) 'The great interview: 25 strategies for studying people in bed', *Qualitative Sociology*, 25: 479–99.

Hester, S. and Francis, D. (1994) 'Doing data: the local organization of a sociological interview', *British Journal of Sociology*, 45: 675–95.

Hinchman, L.P. and Hinchman, S.K. (1997) 'Introduction', in L.P. Hinchman and S.K. Hinchman (eds), *Memory, Identity, Community: the idea of narrative in the human sciences*. New York: State University of New York. pp. xiii–xxxii.

Hollway, W. and Jefferson, T. (1998) '"A kiss is just a kiss": date rape, gender and contradictory subjectivities', *Sexualities*, 1: 405–24.

Hollway, W. and Jefferson, T. (2000) *Doing Qualitative Research Differently: free association, narrative and the interview method*. London: Sage.

Holmes, J. (1997) 'Struggling beyond Labov and Waletzky', *Journal of Narrative and Life History*, 7 (1–4): 91–6.

Holstein, J. and Gubrium, J. (1995) *The Active Interview*. Thousand Oaks, CA: Sage.

Holstein, J. and Gubrium, J. (2000) *The Self We Live By: narrative identity in a postmodern world*. New York: Oxford University Press.

Hughes, J. and Sharrock, W. (1997) *The Philosophy of Social Research*. Harlow: Longman.

Hutchison, D. (1988) 'Event history and survival analysis in the social sciences', *Quality and Quantity*, 22: 203–19.

Jacobs, S.C. (2002) 'Reliability and recall of unemployment events using retrospective data', *Work, Employment and Society*, 16: 537–48.

James, William (1952) *The Varieties of Religious Experience*. London: Longmans.

Johnstone, B. (1997) 'Social characteristics and self-expression in narrative', *Journal of Narrative and Life History*, 7 (1–4): 315–20.

Joshi, H. and Hinde, P.R.A. (1993) 'Employment after childbearing in post-war Britain: cohort study evidence on contrasts within and across generations', *European Sociological Review*, 9 (3): 203–27.

Josselson, R. (1996) 'On writing other people's lives: self-analytic reflections of a narrative researcher, in R. Josselson (ed.), *Ethics and Process in the Narrative Study of Lives*. Thousand Oaks, CA: Sage.

Josselson, R. and Lieblich, A. (1993) *The Narrative Study of Lives*. Newbury Park, CA: Sage.

Kelly, M.P. and Dickinson, H. (1997) 'The narrative self in autobiographical accounts of illness', *Sociological Review*, 45 (2): 254–78.

Kerlinger, F.N. (1973) *Foundations of Behavioural Research*. New York: Holt, Rinehart and Winston.

Kleinman, A. (1988) *The Illness Narratives: suffering, healing and the human condition*. New York: Basic Books.

Korteweg, A.C. (2001) 'It won't change a thing: the meanings of marriage in the Netherlands', *Qualitative Sociology*, 24: 507–25.

Krieger, S. (1983) *The Mirror Dance: identity in a women's community*. Philadelphia: Temple University Press.

Kvale, S. (1989) 'To validate is to question', in S. Kvale (ed.), *Issues of Validity in Qualitative Research*. Lund: Studentlitteratur. pp. 73–92.

Kvale, S. (1996) *InterViews: an introduction to qualitative research interviewing*. Thousand Oaks, CA: Sage.

Labov, W. (1972) 'The transformation of experience in narrative syntax', in W. Labov (ed.), *Language in the Inner City: studies in the black English vernacular*. Philadelphia: University of Pennsylvania Press. pp. 354–96.

Labov, W. and Waletzky, J. (1967) 'Narrative analysis: oral versions of personal experience', in J. Helm (ed.), *Essays on the Verbal and Visual Arts*. Seattle: University of Washington Press. pp. 12–44.

Labov, W. and Waletzky, J. (1997) 'Narrative analysis: oral versions of personal experience' (Reprinted from 'Essays on the Verbal and Visual Arts, Proceedings of the 1996 annual spring meeting of the American Ethnological Society', pp. 12–44, 1967), *Journal of Narrative and Life History*, 7 (1–4): 3–38.

Lancaster, T. (1990) *The Econometric Analysis of Transition Data*. Cambridge: Cambridge University Press.

Laub, J.H. and Sampson, R.J. (1998) 'Integrating quantitative and qualitative data', in J.Z. Giele and G.H. Elder (eds), *Methods of Life Course Research: Qualitative and Quantitative Approaches*. Thousand Oaks, CA: Sage. pp. 213–30.

Leitch, T.M. (1986) *What Stories Are: Narrative Theory and Interpretation*. University Park, PA: Pennsylvania State University Press.

Lieberson, S. (1985) *Making it Count: The Improvement of Social Research and Theory*. Berkeley/Los Angeles: University of California Press.

Lieberson, S. and Silverman, A.R. (1965) 'The precipitants and underlying conditions of race riots', *American Sociological Review*, 30: 887–98.

Lieblich, A. (1996) 'Some unforeseen outcomes of conducting narrative research with people of one's own culture', in R. Josselson (ed.), *Ethics and Process in the Narrative Study of Lives*. Thousand Oaks, CA: Sage. pp. 172–86.

Lieblich, A., Tuval-Maschiach, R. and Zilber, T. (1998) *Narrative Research: reading, analysis, and interpretation*. Thousand Oaks, CA: Sage.

Linde, C. (1993) *Life Stories: The Creation of Coherence*. Oxford: Oxford University Press.

Link, B.G. and Phelan, J. (1995) 'Social conditions as fundamental causes of diseases', *Journal of Health and Social Behavior*, Extra Issue: 80–94.

Lloyd, G. (1993) *Being in Time: selves and narrators in philosophy and literature*. London: Routledge.

Lucius-Hoene, G. and Deppermann, A. (2000) 'Narrative identity empiricized: a dialogical and positioning approach to autobiographical research interviews', *Narrative Inquiry*, 10: 199–222.

Lynch, G. (1997) 'The role of community and narrative in the work of the therapist: a post-modern theory of the therapist's engagement in the therapeutic process', *Counselling Psychology Quarterly*, 10 (4): 353–63.

MacIntyre, A. (1981) *The Virtues, the Unity of a Human Life, and the Concept of a Tradition*. Notre Dame, IN: University of Notre Dame Press.

Marsh, C. (1982) *The Survey Method*. London: Allen and Unwin.

Martin, W. (1986) *Recent Theories of Narrative*. Ithaca, NY: Cornell University Press.

Maume, D. (1999) 'Glass ceilings and glass escalators', *Work and Occupations*, 26: 483–509.

Mauthner, N. and Doucet, A. (1998) 'Reflections on a voice-centred relational method: analysing maternal and domestic voices', in J. Ribbens and R. Edwards (eds), *Feminist Dilemmas in Qualitative Research: public knowledge and private lives*. London: Sage. pp. 119–46.

Mayer, K.U. and Bruckner, E. (1989) 'Lebensverlaufe und Wohlfahrtsentwicklung. Konzeption, Design und Methodik der Erhebung von lebensverlaufen der Gerburtsjahrgange 1929–1931, 1939–1941, 1949–1951', Materialien aus der Bildungsforschung, no. 35, Max-Planck-Institut fur Bildungsforschung, Berlin.

Maynard, M. (1994) 'Methods, practice and epistemology: the debate about feminism and research', in M. Maynard and J. Purvis (eds), *Researching Women's Lives from a Feminist Perspective.* London: Taylor & Francis. pp. 10–26.

McCormack, C. (2004) 'Storying stories: a narrative approach to in-depth interview conversations', *International Journal of Social Research Methodology,* 7: 219–36.

McKim, V.R. (1997) 'Introduction', in V.R. McKim and S.P. Turner (eds), *Causality in Crisis? Statistical Methods and the Search for Causal Knowledge in the Social Sciences.* Notre Dame, IN: University of Notre Dame Press. pp. 1–20.

Mills, C.W. (1959) *The Sociological Imagination.* Harmondsworth: Penguin.

Mishler, E.G. (1984) *The Discourse of Medicine.* Norwood, NJ: Ablex.

Mishler, E.G. (1986) *Research Interviewing: context and narrative.* Cambridge, MA: Harvard University Press.

Mishler, E.G. (1995) 'Models of narrative analysis: a typology', *Journal of Narrative and Life History,* 5 (2): 87–123.

Mishler, E.G. (1997) 'A matter of time: when, since, after Labov and Waletzky', *Journal of Narrative and Life History,* 7 (1–4): 69–73.

Mishler, E.G. (1999) *Storylines: Craft Artists' Narratives of Identity.* Cambridge, MA: Harvard University Press.

Moffat, B.M. and Johnson, J.L. (2001) 'Through the haze of cigarettes: teenage girls' stories about cigarette addiction', *Qualitative Health Research,* 11: 668–81.

Morgan, D.L. (1998) 'Practical strategies for combining qualitative and quantitative methods: applications to health research', *Qualitative Health Research,* 8: 362–76.

Morgan, S.L. and Teachman, J. (1988) 'Logistic regression: description, examples and comparisons', *Journal of Marriage and the Family,* 50: 929–36.

Mott, H. and Condor, S. (1997) 'Sexual harassment and the working lives of secretaries', in W.I. Thomas and C. Kitzinger (eds), *Sexual Harassment.* Buckingham: Open University Press.

Murray, K. (1989) 'The construction of identity in the narratives of romance and comedy', in J. Shotter and K. Gergen (eds), *Texts of Identity.* London: Sage. pp. 176–205.

National Longitudinal Surveys Handbook (2003) US Department of Labor and Bureau of Labor Statistics. Available online: http://www.bls.gov/nls/handbook/nlshndbk.htm.

Ni Bhrolchain, M. (2001) '"Divorce Effects" and causality in the social sciences', *European Sociological Review,* 17: 33–57.

Norusis, M.J. (1994) *SPSS Advanced Statistics 6.1.* Chicago: SPSS Inc.

Oakley, A. (1981) 'Interviewing women: a contradiction in terms', in H. Roberts (ed.), *Doing Feminist Research.* London: Routledge. pp. 30–61.

Ochberg, R.L. (1996) 'Interpreting life stories', in R. Josselson (ed.), *Ethics and Process in the Narrative Study of Lives.* Thousand Oaks, CA: Sage.

Ochs, E. and Taylor, C. (1995) 'The "Father knows best" dynamic in dinnertime narratives', in K. Hall and M. Bucholz (eds), *Gender Articulated: language and the socially constructed self.* New York: Routledge. pp. 97–120.

Okley, J. (1992) 'Anthropology and autobiography: participatory experience and embodied knowledge', in J. Okley and H. Callaway (eds), *Anthropology and Autobiography.* London: Routledge. pp. 1–28.

Outhwaite, W. (1985) 'Hans-Georg Gadamer', in S. Quentin (ed.), *The Return of Grand Theory in the Human Sciences.* Cambridge: Cambridge University Press. pp. 21–40.

Parr, J. (1998) 'Theoretical voices and women's own voices: the stories of mature women students', in J. Ribbens and R. Edwards (eds), *Feminist Dilemmas in Qualitative Research.* London: Sage. pp. 87–102.

Pearce, L.D. (2002) 'Integrating survey and ethnographic methods for systematic anomalous case analysis', *Sociological Methodology,* 32: 103–32.

Plummer, K. (1983) *Documents of Life.* London: Allen and Unwin.

Plummer, K. (1995) *Telling Sexual Stories: power, change, and social worlds.* London: Routledge.

Poland, B.D. (1995) 'Transcription quality as an aspect of rigor in qualitative research', *Qualitative Inquiry,* 1: 290–310.

Polanyi, L. (1985) 'Conversational storytelling', in T.A. Van Dijk (ed.), *Handbook of Discourse Analysis: discourse and dialogue*, vol. 3. London: Academic Press. pp. 183–202.

Polkinghorne, D. (1988) *Narrative Knowing and the Human Sciences*. Albany, NY: State University of New York Press.

Polkinghorne, D.E. (1995) 'Narrative configuration in qualitative analysis', in J.A. Hatch and R. Wisniewski (eds), *Life History and Narrative*. London: Falmer Press. pp. 5–17.

Portelli, A. (1991) *The Death of Luigi Trastulli and Other Stories: form and meaning in oral history*. Albany, NY: State University of New York Press.

Potter, J. and Mulkay, M. (1985) 'Scientists' interview talk: interviews as a technique for revealing participants' interpretative practices', in M. Brenner, J. Brown, and D. Canter (eds), *The Research Interview: uses and approaches*. London: Academic Press.

Proctor, I. and Padfield, M. (1998) 'The effect of the interview on the interviewee', *International Journal of Social Research Methodology*, 1: 123–36.

Proctor, I. and Padfield, M. (1999) 'Work orientations and women's work: a critique of Hakim's theory of the heterogeneity of women', *Gender, Work and Organization*, 6 (3): 152–62.

Pugh, A. (1990) 'My statistics and feminism – a true story', in L. Stanley (ed.), *Feminist Praxis*. London: Routledge. pp. 91–102.

Ragin, C.C. (1987) *The Comparative Method: moving beyond qualitative and quantitative strategies*. Berkeley, CA: University of California Press.

Rank, M.R. (1989) 'Fertility among women on welfare: incidence and determinants', *American Sociological Review*, 54: 296–304.

Reinharz, S. (1979) *On Becoming a Social Scientist: from survey research and participant observation to Experimental Analysis*. New York: Jossey-Bass.

Reskin, B. (1988) 'Bringing the men back in: sex differentiation and the devaluation of women's work', *Gender and Society*, 2: 58–81.

Ribbens, J. and Edwards, R. (1998) *Feminist Dilemmas in Social Research: public knowledge and private lives*. London: Sage.

Richardson, L. (1990) *Writing Strategies: reaching diverse audiences*. Thousand Oaks, CA: Sage.

Richardson, L.W. (1985) *The New Other Woman: contemporary single women in affairs with married men*. New York: Macmillan.

Ricoeur, P. (1981) *Hermeneutics and the Human Sciences*. Cambridge: Cambridge University Press.

Ricoeur, P. (1984) *Time and Narrative*, vol. 1, trans. K. McLaughlin and D. Pellauer. Chicago: University of Chicago Press.

Ricoeur, P. (1988) *Time and Narrative*, vol. 3. Chicago: University of Chicago Press.

Ricoeur, P. (1991) 'Life in quest of narrative', in D. Wood (ed.), *On Paul Ricoeur*. London and New York: Routledge.

Ricoeur, P. (1992) *Oneself as Another*. Chicago: University of Chicago Press.

Riessman, C.K. (1989) 'Life events, meaning and narrative: the case of infidelity and divorce', *Social Science and Medicine*, 29 (6): 743–51.

Riessman, C.K. (1990) *Divorce Talk*. New Brunswick, NJ: Rutgers University Press.

Riessman, C.K. (1991) 'Beyond reductionism: narrative genres in divorce accounts', *Journal of Narrative and Life History*, 1: 41–68.

Riessman, C.K. (1993) *Narrative Analysis*. Thousand Oaks, CA: Sage.

Rimmon-Kenan, S. (1983) *Narrative Fiction: contemporary poetics*. London and New York: Methuen.

Ronai, C.R. and Cross, R. (1998) 'Dancing with identity: narrative resistance strategies of male and female stripteasers', *Deviant Behavior*, 19: 99–119.

Rose, N. (1989) *Governing the Soul*. London: Routledge.

Rosenthal, L. (1991) 'Unemployment incidence following redundancy: the value of longitudinal approaches', in S. Dex (ed.), *Life and Work History Analyses*. London: Routledge. pp. 187–213.

Ruspini, E. (2002) *Introduction to Longitudinal Research*, ed. M. Bulmer. London: Routledge.

Ryder, N.B. (1965) 'The cohort as a concept in the study of social change', *American Sociological Review*, 30: 843–61.

Sacks, H. (1974) 'On the analysability of stories by children', in R. Turner (ed.), *Ethnomethodology*. Harmondsworth: Penguin.

Sacks, H. (1992) *Lectures on Conversation*. London: Blackwell.

Sampson, R.J. and Laub, J.H. (1993) *Crime in the Making: pathways and turning points through life*. Cambridge, MA: Harvard University Press.

Savage, M. and Egerton, M. (1997) 'Social mobility, individual ability and the inheritance of class inequality', *Sociology*, 31 (4): 645–72.

Sayer, A. (1992) *Method in Social Science*. London: Routledge.

Scott, J. and Alwin, D. (1998) 'Retrospective versus prospective measurement of life histories in longitudinal research', in J.Z. Giele and G.H. Elder (eds), *Methods of Life Course Research: qualitative and quantitative approaches*. Thousand Oaks, CA: Sage. pp. 98–127.

Seale, C. (1998) 'Qualitative interviewing', in C. Seale (ed.), *Researching Society and Culture*. London: Sage. pp. 202–16.

Seidman, S. (1994) 'Introduction', in S. Seidman (ed.), *The Postmodern Turn: new perspectives on social theory*. Cambridge: Cambridge University Press. pp. 1–23.

Seidman, I. (1998) *Interviewing as Qualitative Research*. New York: Teacher's College Press.

Shadish, W.R., Cook, T.D. and Campbell. D.T. (2002) 'Experiments and generalized causal inference', in W.R. Shadish, T.D. Cook, and D.T. Campbell (eds), *Experimental and Quasi-Experimental Designs for Generalised Causal Inference*. Boston: Houghton Mifflin.

Shaw, C.R. (1931) *The Natural History of a Delinquent Career*. Chicago: City of Chicago Press.

Shaw, C.R. (1966) *The Jack-Roller: a delinquent boy's own story*. Chicago: University of Chicago Press.

Shaw, C.R. and McKay, H.D. (1938) *Brothers in Crime*. Chicago: University of Chicago Press.

Silverman, D. (1993) *Interpreting Qualitative Data: methods for analysing talk, text and interaction*. London: Sage.

Singer, B., Ryff, C.D., Carr, D. and Magee, W.J. (1998) 'Linking life histories and mental health: a person centered strategy', *Sociological Methodology*, 28: 1–51.

Smith, D.E. (1987) *The Everyday World as Problematic: a feminist sociology*. Boston: Northeastern University Press.

Smith, J.A. (1994) 'Reconstructing selves: an analysis of discrepancies between women's contemporaneous and retrospective accounts of the transition to motherhood', *British Journal of Psychology*, 85: 371–92.

Smith, S. (1996) 'Uncovering key aspect of experience: the use of in-depth interviews in a study of women returners to education', in E.S. Lyon and J. Busfield (eds), *Methodological Imaginations*. Houndmills: Macmillan. pp. 58–74.

Smythe, W.E. and Murray, M.J. (2000) 'Owning the story: ethical considerations in narrative research', *Ethics and Behaviour*, 10: 311–36.

Somers, M.R. (1994) 'The narrative construction of identity: a relational and network approach', *Theory and Society*, 22: 605–49.

Somers, M.R. and Gibson, G.D. (1994) 'Reclaiming the epistemological "Other": narrative and the social constitution of identity', in C. Calhoun (ed.), *Social Theory and the Politics of Identity*. Cambridge, MA: Blackwells. pp. 37–99.

Sorensen, A.B. (1998) 'Theoretical mechanisms and the empirical study of social processes', in P. Hedstrom and R. Swedberg (eds), *Social Mechanisms*. Cambridge: Cambridge University Press. pp. 238–66.

Squire, C. (1999) '"Neighbours who might become friends": selves, genres and citizenship in narratives of HIV', *Sociological Quarterly*, 40 (1): 109–37.

Standing, K. (1998) 'Writing the voices of the less powerful: research on lone mothers', in J. Ribbens and R. Edwards (eds), *Feminist Dilemmas in Qualitative Research: public knowledge and private lives*. London: Sage.

Stanley, L. (1990) *Feminist Praxis: Research Theory and Epistemology in Feminist Sociology*. London: Routledge.

Stanley, L. (1992) *The auto/biographical I*. Manchester: Manchester University Press.

Stanley, L. and Wise, S. (1983) *Breaking Out: feminist consciousness and feminist research*. London: Routledge & Kegan Paul.

Stanley, L. and Wise, S. (1993) *Breaking Out Again*. London: Routledge.

Stovel, K., Savage, M. and Bearman, P. (1996) 'Ascription into achievement: models of career systems at Lloyds Bank, 1890–1970', *American Journal of Sociology*, 102 (2): 358–99.

Tagg, S.K. (1985) 'Life story interviews and their interpretation', in M. Brenner, J. Brown and D. Canter (eds), *The Research Interview: uses and approaches*. London: Academic Press. pp. 162–200.

Tannen, D. (1980) 'A comparative analysis of oral narrative strategies: Athenian Greek and American English', in W.L. Chafe (ed.), *The Pear Stories*. Norwood, NJ: Ablex. pp. 51–87.

Taris, T.W. (2000) *A Primer in Longitudinal Data Analysis*. London: Sage.

Taylor, C. (1987) 'Interpretation and the sciences of man', in P. Rabinow and W.M. Sullivan (eds), *The Interpretive Turn: a second look*. Berkeley/Los Angeles: University of California Press. pp. 33–81.

Thomas, W.I. and Znaniecki, F. (1958) [1918] *The Polish Peasant in Europe and America*. New York: Dover.

Thompson, P. (1978) *The Voice of the Past: oral history*. Oxford: Oxford University Press.

Thompson, P. (2004) 'Researching family and social mobility with two eyes: some experiences of the interaction between qualitative and quantitative data', *International Journal of Social Research Methodology*, 7: 237–57.

Todorov, T. (1990) [1978] *Genres in Discourse*. Cambridge: Cambridge University Press.

Tuma, N.B. and Hannan, M.T. (1979) 'Dynamic analysis of event histories', *American Journal of Sociology*, 84 (4): 820–54.

Van Maanen, J. (1988) *Tales of the Field: on writing ethnography*. Chicago: University of Chicago Press.

Wajcman, J. and Martin, B. (2002) 'Narratives of identity in modern management: the corrosion of gender difference?', *Sociology*, 36: 985–1002.

Walby, S. (1991) 'Labour markets and industrial structures in women's working lives', in S. Dex (ed.), *Life and Work History Analyses*. London: Routledge. pp. 167–86.

Walker, H.A. and Cohen, B.P. (1985) 'Scope statements: imperatives for evaluating theory', *American Sociological Review*, 50: 288–301.

Ward-Schofield, J. (1993) 'Increasing the generalizability of quantitative research', in M. Hammersley (ed.), *Social Research, Philosophy, Politics and Practice*. London: Sage.

Watson, I. (1993) 'Life history meets economic theory: the experience of three working-class women in a local labour market', *Work, Employment and Society*, 7 (3): 411–35.

Weiss, R.S. (1994) *Learning from Strangers*. New York: Free Press.

Wengraf, T. (2001) *Qualitative Research Interviewing: biographic narrative and semi-structured methods*. London: Sage.

White, H. (1987) *The Content of the Form*. Baltimore, MD: Johns Hopkins University Press.

Williams, C.L. (1992) 'The glass escalator: hidden advantages for men in the "female" professions', *Social Problems*, 39: 253–67.

Williams, G. (1997) 'The genesis of chronic illness: narrative reconstruction', in L.P. Hinchman and S.K. Hinchman (eds), *Memory, Identity, Community: the idea of narrative in the human sciences*. Albany, NY: State University of New York Press. pp. 185–212.

Williams, M. (1998) 'The social world as knowable', in T. May and M. Williams (eds), *Knowing the Social World*. Buckingham: Open University Press. pp. 5–21.

Williamson, J. (1989) 'Every virus tells a story', in E. Carter and S. Watney (eds), *Taking Liberties*. London: Serpent's Tail. pp. 69–80.

Winch, P. (1958) *The Idea of a Social Science and its Relation to Philosophy*. London: Routledge & Kegan Paul.

Workman, T.A. (2001) 'Finding the meanings of college drinking: an analysis of fraternity drinking stories', *Health Communication*, 13: 427–47.

Wu, L.L. (2000) 'Some comments on "Sequence analysis and optimal matching methods in sociology: review and prospect"', *Sociological Methods and Research*, 29 (1): 41–64.

Yamaguchi, K. (1991) *Event History Analysis*. Newbury Park, CA: Sage.

Young, C., Savola, K.L. and Phelps, E. (1991) *Inventory of Longitudinal Studies on the Social Sciences*. Newbury Park, CA: Sage.

Zukier, H. (1986) 'The paradigmatic and narrative modes in goal guided inference', in R. Sorrentino and E. Higgins (eds), *Handbook of Motivation and Cognition*, vol. 1. New York: Guildford. pp. 465–502.

Index